MIDDLE AND HIGH SCHOOL ENGLISH LEARNERS AND THE COMMON CORE STANDARDS

Equitable Instruction in Content Area Classrooms

MIDDLE AND HIGH SCHOOL ENGLISH LEARNERS AND THE COMMON CORE STANDARDS

Equitable Instruction in Content Area Classrooms

Annette M. Daoud
California State University San Marcos

PEARSON

Boston Columbus Indianapolis New York San Francisco Upper Saddle River Amsterdam
Cape Town Dubai London Madrid Milan Munich Paris Montréal Toronto
Delhi Mexico City São Paulo Sydney Hong Kong Seoul Singapore Taipei Tokyo

Vice President and Editorial Director: Jeffery Johnston
Senior Acquisitions Editor: Julie Peters
Editorial Assistant: Andrea Hall
Executive Field Marketing Manager: Krista Clark
Senior Product Marketing Manager: Christopher Barry
Program Manager: Laura Messerly
Project Manager: Barbara Strickland
Editorial Production Service: S4Carlisle Publishing Services
Manufacturing Buyer: Linda Sager
Electronic Composition: S4Carlisle Publishing Services
Interior Design: S4Carlisle Publishing Services
Photo Researcher: Jorgensen Fernandez
Cover Designer: Central Covers
Text Font: 11/13 Meridien

Credits and acknowledgments borrowed from other sources and reproduced, with permission, in this textbook appear on the appropriate page within text.

Cover Image Credit: © Shutterstock/Rido

Library of Congress Cataloging-in-Publication Data

Daoud, Annette M.
Middle and high school English learners and the common core standards: equitable instruction in content area classrooms/Annette M. Daoud, California State University San Marcos.—First edition.
pages cm
ISBN-13: 978-0-13-309051-2
ISBN-10: 0-13-309051-5
1. English language—Study and teaching (Secondary)—Foreign speakers. 2. Language arts (Secondary)—Standards—United States. I. Title.
PE1128.A2D344 2014
428.0071′2—dc23

2013044315

10 9 8 7 6 5 4 3 2 1

PEARSON

ISBN-13: 978-0-13-309051-2
ISBN-10: 0-13-309051-5

brief contents

contents

Appendices

preface

I have been using the lesson planning process described in *Middle and High School English Learners and the Common Core Standards: Equitable Instruction in Content Area Classrooms* to train teachers and teacher candidates on how to teach language and content to their English learner students for more than 15 years in both secondary teacher credential programs and through professional development workshops for middle and high school teachers. The following aspects of this book make it distinctive from other textbooks or professional development resources:

- *Focus on English learners enrolled in secondary content area classrooms.* This book is designed for middle and high school teachers. Language development is a process that looks different in middle and high school content area classrooms from how it looks in an elementary school classroom. Middle and high school content area teachers need to teach English language development and content to the English learner students in their classes, and differentiate their instruction based on those English learners' English proficiency levels. This presents unique challenges for middle and high school content area teachers who have not been trained to teach English language development. Teaching strategies and student activities are presented in each content area chapter (English Language Arts, Mathematics, Science, and Social Studies) that address the unique challenges English learners might have with your content.
- *A step-by-step lesson planning process that can be used across all content area classrooms.* A four-step lesson planning process is outlined in this book that can be used in any content area class. Each step is clearly defined with examples that walk teachers and teacher candidates through the step so that they can apply the information directly to their own classroom. The four steps to the lesson planning process are:

  Step 1: Know your English learners

  Step 2: Choose standards for your lessons

  Step 3: Design differentiated assessments and student-centered activities

  Step 4: Select culturally relevant/multicultural materials and resources

  Teachers and teacher candidates can use this process to design lessons covering any content in their classes. The lesson planning process can also be used to enhance lessons that teachers may already be using. Teachers do not need to completely re-invent what they are currently doing. Rather, they should take a lesson they are currently teaching and adapt it to include the four-step lesson planning process.
- *The lesson planning process is aligned to the Common Core State Standards and state-adopted ELD/ELP standards.* The book outlines how

the lesson planning process is aligned to the Common Core State Standards as well as to the English language development (ELD)/ English language proficiency (ELP) standards adopted by any state. Examples are provided in each content chapter that describe how teachers and teacher candidates can choose Common Core State Standards and ELD/ELP standards for their lessons.

- *Concrete examples of lessons and rubrics, including tools for identifying English learners' proficiency levels.* Examples of lessons at the middle and high school levels are provided in each content area chapter. These lessons were designed by teachers and/or teacher candidates and then modified by the author to include all steps in the lesson planning process. To accompany each lesson, rubrics are provided to illustrate how to differentiate assessments based on English learners' proficiency levels so that teachers and teacher candidates are accurately assessing their language development and content area knowledge. Similarly, concrete examples are provided that walk teachers through the process of identifying their English learners' proficiency levels in all four language areas: listening, speaking, reading, and writing.

acknowledgments

I would like to acknowledge the dedication of the middle and high school teachers and teacher candidates with whom I have had the pleasure of working throughout my career. It can be challenging to teach secondary English learners content and English language development in math, science, social studies, or English classes, particularly for teachers who specialize in their content and not in teaching English. I have found over the years that teachers continually meet this challenge when they are given resources to do so. It is my hope that this book will serve as a resource for teachers and teacher candidates who want to differentiate their instruction for English learner students, but just don't know where to begin.

I would also like to thank my colleagues in the Secondary Credential Program at California State University San Marcos. I have had the honor of working collaboratively with them to continually reflect upon and improve our practice. The lesson planning process presented in this book is a direct result of that collaboration and the commitment to educational equity for English learners that we all share. I would also like to extend my gratitude to peer reviewers who provided constructive comments on drafts of chapters: Tammy B.H. Brown, Marywood University; Diana L. Carr, Elgin Junior High School (Green Camp, OH); Kay Elaster, Wayne RESA; Amy J. Heineke, Loyola University Chicago; Tawnya L. Lubbes, Eastern Oregon University; Emily Morgan, Fairmont Junior High School (Boise, ID); Bency M. Manglicmot, Chaparral High School & Nevada State College (Las Vegas, NV); Roberta Murata, Robert F. Kennedy Charter HS (Albuquerque NM); and Barbara Noel, George Mason University. Finally, I would also like to thank my family for all their support and encouragement throughout my career.

part 1

Introduction and Conceptual Frameworks

Ian Wedgewood/Pearson Education

The two chapters in this section outline the purpose and intended use of the book. Chapter 1 introduces a four-step lesson planning process that teachers can use to design lesson plans for middle and high school English learners across all content area classes: English language arts, mathematics, science, and social studies. The lesson planning process incorporates content, English language development, and literacy standards based on the Common Core State Standards. Chapter 2 highlights the conceptual frameworks that form the basis of the lesson planning process. Together, the chapters provide readers with an understanding of how using the lesson planning process creates equitable instruction for middle and high school English learners.

chapter 1

Introduction

Learning Outcomes

- Discuss reasons why it is important to design lessons that incorporate content, literacy, and language development for English learners.
- Describe how to provide equitable instruction for English learners by using the four-step lesson planning process.
- Describe the key aspects of each step in the lesson planning process.

Rationale for the Book

It is becoming increasingly common for middle and high school teachers to teach mixed classes of English learners and native-English speakers across the content areas of English language arts, mathematics, science, and social studies. Under No Child Left Behind (NCLB), English learners' test scores are included in a school's Annual Yearly Progress (AYP), increasing pressure on teachers to understand how to effectively teach language and content to the English learners in their classrooms. Schools with an English learner subgroup risk falling into program improvement if they cannot effectively teach English learners (Crawford, 2007). English learners are defined as students who lack clearly defined language skills in the areas of listening, speaking, reading, and writing necessary to succeed in a school's regular instructional programs (California Department of Education, 2012a). Teachers of English language development (ELD) or sheltered classes are trained in strategies on how to effectively teach the English learner students in their classes; however, until recently their colleagues in content areas may have had few English learners in their classes. With the introduction of the Common Core State Standards (CCSS), middle and high school teachers are required to teach content, literacy skills, and English language development in their classes that enroll English learner students. While this may seem like a daunting task, middle and high school English learners can become proficient in English, learn content knowledge, and develop their literacy skills when teachers combine language, literacy, and content instruction in their classes; when they have opportunities to interact with their native-English-speaking peers; and when the curriculum is culturally and socially relevant to their lives.

Research on second language acquisition shows that it takes four to seven years to develop academic literacy skills (Collier, 1995; Thomas & Collier, 2002); thus, at the secondary level English learners need English language development across all content classes in order to excel in school. Research also indicates that issues such as limited time in school, tracking, and high-stakes testing are more consequential to English learners (ELs) at the secondary level and contribute to inequitable opportunities for them both in and beyond high school (Callahan, 2005; Rumberger & Gandara, 2004). Additionally, high school English learners often take multiple English as Second Language (ESL) classes, thus limiting their access to "mainstream" content classes (Barron & Sanchez, 2007; Rumberger & Gandara, 2004). This also limits interactions between English learners and middle and high school content teachers.

To help English learners overcome these challenges, teachers must understand who these students are by learning about their language proficiency level, knowledge base in the content area, and interests and learning styles. Teachers also need to learn how to incorporate literacy and language development into their content classes. The CCSS require middle and high school teachers to incorporate literacy skills in the language domains of reading and writing into their classes in the areas of history/social studies, science, and other technical subjects. The skills required of these CCSS literacy standards are challenging for many middle and high school students, particularly so for English learners who may not be proficient enough in the language to successfully engage in activities, assignments, and assessments on the CCSS literacy standards. It is equally challenging for teachers, who may require targeted professional development to learn how to teach English language development to their English learner students and literacy skills to all students in their classes.

Goals of the Book

This book is intended to be used as a professional development tool and/or as a textbook in a course in a secondary teacher credential program. This text has two goals. First, it is designed to provide middle and high school teachers (grades 6–12) across all subjects with the necessary information and tools to be effective teachers of English learners at various proficiency levels. The book outlines the skills English learners have at various proficiency levels from *entering* to *bridging* and provides strategies for teachers to use in their classrooms to differentiate instruction and teach English learner students at each level. Teachers will learn how to use ELD standards for middle school (grades 6–8) or high school (grades 9–12). An additional focus is on the content areas of English language arts, mathematics, science, and social studies; sample lesson plans are provided with assessments, teaching strategies, and student activities to effectively teach English learners in each content area. The CCSS for Literacy in History/Social Studies, Science, and Technical Subjects classes outline literacy skills students need to master in the content areas. Therefore, the chapters on social studies and science content outline a lesson planning process that includes language, literacy, and content objectives derived from ELD standards (language objectives), CCSS (literacy objectives) and state content standards (content objectives), as well as the students' English language proficiency levels.

The CCSS for Mathematics are literacy-based and will be difficult for English learners to master without additional language development support. The CCSS for English Language Arts and literacy in other core subjects are literacy and language-based and still require scaffolded language development for English learners. The content area chapters on mathematics and English language arts outline the process to include language objectives derived from ELD standards alongside the respective CCSS for each content area. As content standards, the CCSS in English Language Arts and Mathematics can generally be viewed as the "what" of any lesson, the core content students will master at the end of this lesson. The CCSS for Literacy in History/Social Studies, Science, and Technical Subjects can also be viewed as addressing lesson content, but they represent core literacy content that is taught in conjunction with each area's content standards. If the CCSS are the "what," then the ELD standards can be viewed as the "how," outlining skills English learners need to master to attain the necessary proficiency to learn lesson content. The steps to teach English learners the "what" and the "how" in every lesson teachers design are presented in each content area chapter. These chapters also include effective teaching strategies and differentiated assessments that are aligned to the objectives identified in the lesson.

The second goal of this book is to provide teachers of English learners with strategies, activities, and resources to design curriculum in their content area that is rooted in principles of educational equity. Within the framework of this book, educational equity for English learners is defined as providing them access to the following: the core curriculum, native-English-speaking peers, and curriculum that is relevant to students' lives and the world in which they live. Understanding and implementing the process described in this text on how to differentiate instruction for English learners will help students access the core curriculum across the content areas as well as the skills outlined in the CCSS. Explicitly using teaching techniques and strategies that focus on both language development and content knowledge gives English learners the opportunity to fully understand the concepts and vocabulary embedded within each content area. Designing group activities where English learners interact with their native-English-speaking peers helps English learners practice their language development and gives them access to their peers' knowledge of the social and cultural capital of the school and the U.S. educational system. Finally, incorporating resources into lessons that are relevant to the students' lives and the world they live in helps them connect the content knowledge they are learning to a broader context both in and beyond the classroom. For the purposes of this book, these resources are referred to as culturally relevant/multicultural resources. The resources can range from a local news story that connects to the content you are teaching to using references on gender, socioeconomic status, race, ethnicity, religion, sexual orientation, and (dis)ability into your lessons. The resources can be a central part of the lesson or used as an opener or closer activity. Analyzing and using supplemental resources are skills students must acquire to meet the Common Core State Standards. Therefore, using culturally relevant/multicultural resources to help students acquire these skills can easily become part of your lesson planning process.

Combined, the two goals of this text present teachers with a holistic teaching approach to providing equitable educational opportunities for English learners in their content area classrooms. Freire (1990) stresses the importance of teaching students, including English learners, how to read the word and the world. In classes with a mix of English learners and native-English speakers, students have the opportunity to learn from one another and together learn about the world they live in from multiple perspectives. We can thus cultivate global citizens who can apply the knowledge they learn in the classroom to their lives both in and beyond high school (Banks, 2003). Giving English learners this opportunity to excel in content area classes brings us one step closer to educational equity for all students.

How to Provide Equitable Instruction for English Learners in Content Area Classes

The lesson planning process described in this book is presented as a professional development model that allows teacher candidates and teachers to provide equitable instruction for English learners by designing lessons in their content area classes that support students' English language development and content area knowledge mastery. The process is the same for middle or high school teachers who have English learners in their content area classes. The lesson planning process is rooted in research on effective practices for teaching English learners and offers teacher candidates and teachers a step-by-step process to learn how to use content standards, ELD standards, and the CCSS to develop lessons for content classes that include English learner students. The process also is based in the tenets of social justice and educational equity for English learners in that teacher candidates and teachers who include language and content objectives in their lessons, as well as differentiate assessments based on students' English language proficiency levels, are providing equitable educational opportunities for them. The lesson planning process has been designed for teachers and teacher candidates in a structured and accessible format and consists of four scaffolded steps: know your English learners, choose standards for your lesson, design differentiated assessments and student-centered activities, and select culturally relevant/multicultural materials and resources.

Step 1: Know Your English Learners

The first step in the process is for teachers to know and fully understand who their English learner students are and how they learn. Teachers should learn about their English learners' knowledge base—their language ability as well as their content knowledge. Teachers should also learn about their students' backgrounds in order to "match" content with students' cultures and interests to make the curriculum relevant to them. Surveying students to learn about their interests, learning styles, content knowledge, and language abilities and reviewing students' data profiles are two methods teachers can use to gather information on their English learner students that can be used in the lesson planning process. The more teachers understand about who their English learner students are and how they learn, the more prepared they are to accurately plan lessons that are engaging for them.

It is also important for teachers to identify their English learners' language proficiency levels in each of the language domains of listening, speaking, reading, and writing. Teachers can identify their English learners' language proficiency level through standardized test scores, language proficiency test scores, discussions with the ELD coordinator at the school, or a combination of any of these methods. Depending on which ELD standards your state uses, English learners' language skills are divided into three, five, or six proficiency levels in the four language domains of listening, speaking, reading, and writing. ELD standards that are divided into five proficiency levels generally represent the following levels: entering, emerging, developing, expanding, and bridging. Most ELD standards that are divided into three proficiency levels generally represent the emerging, expanding, and bridging levels.[1] Identifying English learners' proficiency levels allows teachers to differentiate their instruction based on the identified proficiency levels.

Step 2: Choose Standards for Your Lessons

For each lesson, teachers should choose standards appropriate for the lesson. In content area middle and high school classrooms, these standards include ELD, state content, and CCSS. When an English learner's language proficiency level is determined, it should be noted that she or he can perform each skill listed in ELD standards independently and automatically at that level. In lesson planning, teachers should choose the language skill that is one level above the English learner's current proficiency level (i+1). English learners will use their current proficiency skills as a base to build on through this type of scaffolded instruction. For example, a teacher has a group of English learners at the exit stage of the *expanding* level in her science class. The teacher will target her instruction at the *bridging* level by scaffolding her instruction through strategies and activities that make the content accessible to her *expanding*-level English learners.

[1]ELD standards are being revised by states and a few consortia of states to align with the CCSS and the assessments being developed to measure the standards.

As ELD standards are developmental and focus on the four language domains (listening, speaking, reading, and writing), teachers should revisit specific standards throughout the year so that their English learners can practice language skills needed to become proficient. Continually revisiting standards also helps English learners develop the oral and written communication skills necessary to accomplish tasks outlined in the CCSS. A focus on developing vocabulary through varied language skills within the context of the content being taught will help English learners attain a level of academic language necessary for success in all middle and high school classes.

Teachers should choose an ELD standard that complements the CCSS and content standards addressed in the lesson. While it does not hold as a constant rule, as stated previously, the CCSS serves as the "what" while the ELD standards often serve as the "how" of the lesson. For example, if the CCSS calls for students to develop claims and/or counterclaims in their writing, then teachers can choose a complementary ELD standard such as *writing—summaries* that outlines specific skills students will develop on text organization and structure in their summaries. Once standards are chosen, teachers then write language, literacy, and content objectives for the lesson that outline how students will demonstrate they have met the standard. It is important for English learners to have as much practice as possible with the English language in order to become proficient. Teachers can choose activities that incorporate several language skills to include in their lessons to help English learners practice and communicate in English. However, it is recommended that each lesson focus on one or two ELD standards. As assessment is aligned to standards, this allows the assessment to specifically focus on the language skill covered in the standard chosen, allowing teachers to accurately assess if English learners have mastered that skill.

Step 3: Design Differentiated Assessments and Student-Centered Activities

As noted previously, at each proficiency level English learners can perform a language skill independently and automatically. Targeting instruction one proficiency level above their current level helps English learners attain overall language proficiency. Following this tenet, an accurate assessment for English learners should be targeted at one level above their current proficiency level as well. Using ELD standards with three proficiency levels as an example, English learners at the *entering* level should be assessed on the standards at the *emerging* level. Designing assessments at proficiency levels above the *emerging* level (for this example, at the *bridging* level) may require language skills and knowledge that go beyond the English learners' current proficiency level and thus will not be an accurate assessment of the student's language development. While English learners may fully understand the content, they may not have adequate English proficiency to communicate their mastery of the content in either oral or written form.

Following backwards mapping principles, assessment should be aligned to the language, CCSS, and content standards and objectives chosen for each lesson. Content area teachers who have both native-English speakers and

English learners in their class should create one assessment plan for their lesson that aligns to the language and content standards and objectives selected for the lesson. While the language objectives are specifically designed for the English learners in the class, the skills covered in the language standards may also be beneficial for the native-English speakers in the class (e.g., presenting, analyzing language choices, and writing—literary and informational texts). For English learners, the assessment is equitable in that it accurately assesses them based on the language proficiency level that is one level above their current level.

Along with equitable assessments, incorporating student-centered activities into lessons can also been viewed as an equitable instructional practice for English learners. Student-centered activities allow English learners an opportunity to practice their English language development while mastering the content knowledge presented. Lessons that include partner or small-group work promote peer interactions that give English learners an opportunity to communicate with their native-English speaking peers. Students can learn lesson content from one another, and English learners have the added benefit of practicing their communication skills in English. As is the case with many students, English learners require additional time to process new concepts learned and understand how these concepts are connected to and/or build on prior concepts learned. Designing activities that are student-centered and promote peer interactions helps English learners have equal access to the same curriculum as their native-English-speaking peers.

Step 4: Select Culturally Relevant/Multicultural Materials and Resources

The final step in the process assists teachers in identifying culturally relevant/multicultural materials and resources to include in their lessons. The information teachers learn about their English learners in Step One can be used to select materials and resources they can use in their lessons. Incorporating culturally relevant/multicultural resources into content area lessons allows students to make connections between the curriculum and their lives or to the world in which they live. These resources also help all students learn about the diversity within their classroom, school, and community based on markers such as culture, language, social class, gender, and sexual orientation. Culturally relevant/multicultural resources can be used in any phase of a lesson, as the basis of the lesson or to introduce, reinforce, or expand on a topic, theme, or issue that was covered in the lesson or unit.

Culturally relevant/multicultural resources can be found on various websites maintained by national organizations such as the National Council for Teachers of Mathematics (NCTM), the Public Broadcasting System (PBS), and Teaching Tolerance. To help students master the CCSS for Literacy in English Language Arts and History/Social Studies, Science, and Technical Subjects, teachers need to identify literacy resources that can be used to present core and supplementary content in their content area classes. This presents an opportunity for teachers to identify culturally relevant/multicultural resources that are aligned to the content area and that reflect issues of diversity, equity, and social justice.

Why I Wrote the Book: My Experiences

I have been using the process described in this book to train teachers and teacher candidates on how to teach language and content to their English learner students for more than fifteen years in both secondary teacher credential programs and through professional development workshops for middle and high school teachers. With the introduction and implementation of the Common Core State Standards, I modified the process to include literacy objectives based on the CCSS in teachers' lesson plans. At the beginning of the course or of the professional development training, teacher candidates and teachers are asked to identify the most challenging question they have to effectively teach their English learner students. Time and again, the most prevalent challenge raised is teaching language and content in an equitable and effective manner for their English learner students. This is understandable given that secondary content area teachers and teacher candidates are "experts" in their content area, not in the area of English language development.

I approach my courses and professional development trainings that focus on teaching middle and high school English learners in content area classes as an issue of educational equity. I am training teachers and teacher candidates to provide socially just and equitable instruction to all their future students and, within this frame, to learn the skills and techniques needed to teach middle and high school English learners in content area classes. Asking teachers to commit to being "change agents" for their English learners students is easy: Most teachers agree that an issue of educational equity exists and should be addressed. However, it has been my experience that moving from talk to action is something teachers cannot do without the assistance of a structured, accessible process. The book is designed to guide middle and high school teachers in differentiating their instruction for English learners in their content area classes by explicitly teaching language skills according to students' proficiency levels and content simultaneously. Few resources are specifically designed to guide secondary teachers through a process to teach English learners in their content area classrooms. It is my hope that the subject matter of this book and the manner in which it is presented will be a useful and accessible resource for middle and high school teachers.

Chapter Preview

This book is divided into four parts. Part 1 consists of this Introduction and Chapter 2, which outlines the conceptual frameworks and foundations that guide the four-step lesson planning process. The process is rooted broadly in the frameworks of multicultural education and the sociocultural aspects of second language acquisition. Within these frameworks, a focus on a social justice approach to teaching secondary English learners is described to highlight aspects of the lesson planning process that promote increased academic achievement and educational equity for a group of students who are often underserved in our middle and high schools. A review of research on the schooling experiences of secondary

English learners, along with surveys and research on teacher perceptions of how to teach English learners, is then presented. Research and survey results reveal that teachers at the secondary level feel they are not prepared or have not been sufficiently trained to teach English learners in their content area classes and that they do not know enough about their English learner students. This area of research sheds light on some of the contributing factors to issues of educational equity and student achievement for secondary English learners. The chapter then describes studies that highlight effective practices for teaching secondary English learners. Bringing all these components together, the chapter ends with a description of a self-study of the lesson planning process that was conducted with teacher candidates in a secondary credential program.

Part 2 presents chapters on differentiation for English learners across the different language domains. Chapter 3 focuses on the language domains of listening and speaking, Chapter 4 on reading, and Chapter 5 on writing. These chapters discuss specific language skills within each language domain that secondary English learners need to comprehend in order to become fully proficient in English. The skills are derived from a compilation of ELD and English language proficiency (ELP) standards from various states and consortia of states with English learner enrollments in their public schools. The language skills are aligned to the literacy skills outlined in the Common Core State Standards for English Language Arts and Literacy in History/Social Studies, Science, and Technical Subjects so teachers understand how they complement one another. The chapters also present a brief profile of English learners at each of five proficiency levels to show what language skills students can perform at each level. Finally, each chapter outlines a process for choosing ELD/ELP standards to include in lessons across all middle and high school content areas classes.

Part 3 details the lesson planning process in the content areas of English language arts (Chapter 6), mathematics (Chapter 7), science (Chapter 8), and social studies (Chapter 9). Each chapter in Part 3 begins with Step One of the lesson planning process—know your English learners—by highlighting difficulties English learners may have with CCSS in the designated content area as well as effective methods to use to help teachers learn about their students. The chapters proceed with Step Two—choose standards for the lesson—which describes how to choose language standards and objectives that complement the content standards selected. Step Three of lesson planning—design differentiated assessments and student-centered activities—is then described in the context of each content area chapter. This section of each chapter outlines how to differentiate assessments for English learners based on their language proficiency levels so that assessments are fair and accurate. It continues with teaching strategies and student activities that are scaffolded to help English learners access the content being taught. The fourth and final step calls on teachers to select culturally relevant/multicultural materials and resources. Each content area chapter presents lesson plan examples at the middle and high school level to demonstrate how each step in the lesson planning process is integrated into a lesson plan. Each of these chapters ends with a detailed discussion of the lessons within the frame of the four-step lesson planning process.

Chapter 10 in Part 4 presents concluding comments on the lesson planning process outlined in the book and is followed by applicable resources. The importance of differentiation for English learners and equitable access to the core curriculum is discussed in the context of the lesson planning process as well as in connections to the literature on teaching English learners. This discussion is followed by an evaluation of the value of incorporating culturally relevant/multicultural resources for all students in content area classes. Chapter 10 ends with a reflection of a high school teacher who has used the lesson planning process in her Algebra II class. Part 4 concludes with a series of resources for teachers to assist them in using the lesson planning process outlined in the book.

Summary

As you reflect on this introductory chapter, keep in mind these main points:

- It is important to remember that middle and high school English learners can become proficient in English, learn content knowledge, and develop their literacy skills when teachers combine language, literacy, and content in their classes; when they have opportunities to interact with their native-English-speaking peers; and when the curriculum is culturally and socially relevant to their lives.
- The lesson planning process presented in this book is designed to be accessible to teacher and teacher candidates who have English learners in their classes and consists of four scaffolded steps: know your English learners, choose standards for your lesson, design differentiated assessments and student-centered activities, and select culturally relevant/multicultural materials and resources.

Applying What You Have Learned

In this chapter, you have learned about the lesson planning process outlined in this book. Demonstrate your understanding of the chapter by responding to the following statements.

- Discuss reasons why it is important to design lessons that incorporate content, literacy, and language development for English learners
- Describe how to provide equitable instruction for English learners by using the four-step lesson planning process
- Describe the key aspects of each step in the lesson planning process
    - Step One: Know your English learners
    - Step Two: Choose standards for your lessons
    - Step Three: Design differentiated assessments and student-centered activities
    - Step Four: Select culturally relevant/multicultural materials and resources

chapter 2

Conceptual Frameworks and Foundations

Learning Outcomes

- Describe what equitable instruction for secondary English learners entails.
- Explain effective strategies for teaching English learners.
- Discuss the lesson planning process in action.

The lesson planning process presented in this book for teaching English learners in content area classes is rooted in the research on effective practices for teaching English learners and tenets of multicultural education. The term *equitable* is used in the book's title to emphasize that the process provides English learners access—to the core curriculum, to their English-speaking peers, and to broader opportunities to succeed in content area classes. At the heart of this definition of equity is the importance of the sociocultural aspects of learning for English learners that can occur in any classroom when teachers explicitly design instructional strategies and student activities that foster it. Collier (1995) identifies a conceptual model of acquiring language in school that encompasses sociocultural, linguistic, academic, and cognitive processes. According to the Collier model, sociocultural processes are central to the analysis of understanding language acquisition in school and interrelate with linguistic, academic, and cognitive processes. Language acquisition is affected by social and cultural processes encompassing a student's past, present, and future, as well as those across the contexts of home, school, community, and the broader society. Building on Collier's framework, English learners' overall academic success in secondary school also includes key factors such as teachers' perceptions of their ability to effectively teach English learners in their content area classes based how well they are able to combine language, literacy, and content in their lessons.

This chapter highlights findings and discussions from research and reports that in combination form the foundation for the four-step lesson planning process outlined in this book. The chapter begins with research on who secondary English learners are and how relationships are formed between content area teachers and their English learner students. It then describes how equitable instruction for English learners is rooted in applying multicultural education tenets and using a social justice approach to teaching. Research on effective strategies for teaching English learners is then described, followed by results and a discussion from a study focused on the lesson planning process outlined in this book.

Research on Secondary English Learners

At the secondary level, the majority of English learners can be characterized as "long-term English learners." While there are variations in the definitions provided by researchers, common characteristics of long-term English learners are that they have been enrolled in U.S. schools for approximately six years or more, they generally have grade point averages of below 2.0, and they have not attained a proficiency level in reading and writing skills needed for academic success in content area classes (Olson, 2010). Long-term English learners perform at much lower academic levels than immigrant students who come to U.S. schools with a range of prior schooling experiences from their home countries (Callahan, 2005). One challenge facing secondary English learners is placement: The classes in which they are placed are often not those required for future attendance in four-year colleges. Secondary English learners often take multiple ESL or ELD classes, thus limiting their access to "mainstream" content classes (Barron & Sanchez, 2007; Callahan, 2005; Rumberger & Gandara, 2004). Unfortunately, it is often the case that the curriculum in ESL or ELD classes is not challenging enough or aligned to college-track classes for long-term English learners to transfer the information learned and be successful in their content area classes.

Additionally, the academic demands for secondary English learners in content area classes are much more complex than those needed for success in elementary schools. At the secondary level, content in textbooks and presented in content area classes reflects an increasingly complex level of academic language, often with specialized vocabulary, grammar, and skills. For secondary English learners, particularly long-term English learners, attaining and practicing a level of academic English is required for any level of success in content area classes. Secondary English learners come to content area classes with a wide range of backgrounds and experiences in school that require a varied level of scaffolding to access the content. To help English learners be academically successful, content area teachers should understand their students' literacy and content knowledge, previous academic experience in U.S. schools, and knowledge of the English language (Dutro & Kinsella, 2010).

Content Area Teachers and Secondary English Learners

"Mainstream" content area teachers at the secondary level may be struggling to know who their English learner students are and how to effectively support them in learning language, literacy, and content. In their study of the school culture at a California high school, Hudley and Daoud (2008) found that how students perceive support by teachers affects their engagement in that particular class and overall in school. Latino students of low socioeconomic (SES) status, predominantly English learners, perceived little support by their "mainstream" teachers and consequently did not engage in those classes to the point of skipping the classes to avoid those teachers. This perceived lack of support may be due to the limited contact that high school content area teachers may have with English learners. In an earlier study at the same California high school, Daoud (2003) found that high school teachers did in fact have limited contact with English learners, and thus some teachers identified these students through the societal lens of negative perceptions of immigrants and their children, Spanish use in school, and Latino boys as troublemakers. These perceptions unfortunately led to English learners becoming invisible to teachers in their classrooms and other students throughout the school; this status and their limited contact with native-English-speaking peers contributed to inequitable opportunities to succeed both in school and beyond (Daoud, 2003).

The relationship between English learners and content area teachers underscores the importance for teacher education programs and professional development trainings to prepare teachers to equitably teach students from culturally and linguistically diverse (CLD) backgrounds. In a survey of California teachers, Gandara, Maxwell-Jolly, and Driscoll (2005) report on challenges that secondary teachers identify in teaching English learners. The most commonly cited challenge for secondary teachers is the language and cultural barriers between themselves and their English learner students. The secondary teachers who participated in the survey stated that the most beneficial professional development trainings are those that focus on understanding the cultural characteristics and learning profiles of English learners they need to effectively teach them. Helfrich and Bosh (2011) note four perceived barriers that beginning and veteran teachers identify when teaching literacy to English learners. Teachers may not understand the importance of literacy development; they may struggle to meet the literacy needs of English learners in their classrooms; they may not fully understand the importance of peer support in teaching English learners; and they may not feel confident using assessment and progress-monitoring tools with English learners.

The more knowledge teachers have about their English learner students, the better able they are to provide equitable educational opportunities to them. It is therefore imperative that secondary teacher credential programs and professional development trainings prepare secondary teachers to provide English learners in their content area classrooms access to the core curriculum in ways that are both comprehensible and academically rigorous. It is also essential that teacher credential and professional development programs explicitly draw from the tenets of multicultural education, social justice, and equity to prepare teachers to provide equitable educational experiences for all their future students.

Equitable Instruction for Secondary English Learners

Creating equitable educational opportunities for English learners is an underlying premise directly connected to two steps in the lesson planning process: know your English learners (Step One) and select culturally relevant/multicultural resources (Step Four). Research in the areas of multicultural education and social justice conceptually frame how these two steps are linked to equitable instruction.

Multicultural Education

Based on the notion that all students learn when the curriculum is meaningful, comprehensible, and relevant to students' lives, the lesson planning process outlined in this book draws from the theoretical foundations of multicultural education and critical pedagogy to provide teachers with the tools needed to motivate English learners, along with all students, to learn. Improving educational experiences through understanding and respect of all students is one of the foundations of the theories and practices of multicultural education (Banks, 2003; Nieto & Bode, 2008; Sleeter, 2005). School achievement improves when instructional practices address students' culture, experiences, and learning styles (Gay, 2010; Ladson-Billings, 2001). It is also clear that the academic and social performance of all students is enhanced when culturally relevant pedagogy is based on academic achievement, cultural competence, and sociopolitical consciousness (Ladson-Billings, 2001, 1994). Culturally responsive (relevant) pedagogy is validating and affirming, comprehensive, multidimensional, empowering, and transformative (Gay, 2010). Curriculum should go beyond simply including snapshots of diversity in certain lessons or units to focusing on big or main ideas that are culturally relevant while still addressing state standards (Sleeter, 2005).

Social Justice Approach

Teacher education programs that are explicitly rooted in tenets of social justice and equity frame teaching as the act of enhancing students' learning and expanding opportunities both in and beyond school (for example, Cochran-Smith et al., 2009; Darling-Hammond, French, & Garcia-Lopez, 2002). Social justice teacher education programs highlight inequities that exist in schools and guide teacher candidates in understanding theories and practices that will help them provide equitable educational opportunities for all their future students. The lesson planning process used in this book approaches social justice from a framework similar to one described by Chubbuck (2010) on conceptualizing and implementing socially just teaching. Teacher candidates reflect on and design their individual socially just and equitable pedagogy to address student learning difficulties using both individual and structural orientations (Chubbuck, 2010). In the lesson planning process, teachers and teacher candidates reflect on who their students are and what supplemental multicultural resources can be chosen for a lesson aligned to state content standards that are covered in their class.

In a study of a teacher education program explicitly centered on social justice and equity, Cochran-Smith and colleagues (2009) found that teacher candidates' definitions of social justice and equity can be grouped into four categories: pupil learning, relationships and respect, teacher as activist, and recognition of inequities. Across the categories, teacher candidates define and enact social justice through their own individual actions rather than through policy change or political actions (Cochran-Smith et al., 2009). In a study of two teacher education programs in California to examine how each implements social justice and equity across its programs, McDonald (2005) found that translating these definitions into actions can be challenging for teacher candidates. Freedman, Bullock, and Duque (2005) also describe challenges when trying to use consciousness-raising activities to guide teacher candidates to transformative actions. Drawing from these studies, one can establish that teacher education programs should present social justice in ways that the candidates are open to learning; teach candidates to define social justice on an individual level; and help candidates translate their definitions into concrete actions in their future classrooms. This lesson planning process provides specific "doable" actions teachers and teacher candidates can integrate into their teaching practices to directly impact the equitable educational opportunities for secondary English learners.

Effective Strategies for Teaching English Learners

Research findings on effective strategies for teaching secondary English learners provide the foundation for Step Two, choose standards for your lessons, and Step Three, design differentiated assessments and student-centered activities, of the lesson planning process.

Teaching methods such as sheltered instruction or Specially Designed Academic Instruction in English (SDAIE) provide secondary teachers with the pedagogy, methodology, and strategies to effectively teach English learners. In sheltered or SDAIE classrooms, language and content objectives are threaded throughout the curriculum so that English learners can learn content while improving English literacy skills (Echevarria, Vogt, & Short, 2010). Sheltered or SDAIE lessons include multiple strategies and methods that help make academically rigorous content accessible to English learners at various language proficiency levels and in multiple contexts, including "mainstream" content classrooms (for example, Chamot & O'Malley, 1994; Diaz-Rico, 2013; Echevarria, Vogt, & Short, 2010).

Research shows that incorporating language and content objectives based on state standards is an effective competency that teachers of secondary English learners use in their lesson planning (Faltis, Arias, & Ramirez-Marin, 2010). Using the standards and objectives as a guide, sheltered or SDAIE lessons include multiple strategies, methods, and assessments that help make academically rigorous content accessible to English learners at various language proficiency levels and in multiple contexts including mainstream content classrooms (i.e., Diaz-Rico, 2008; Echevarria et al., 2010; Faltis et al., 2010).

Supporting academic language development is particularly paramount for secondary English learners who need academic language to be successful across all their content area classes. Effective strategies for supporting English learners' academic language development include explicit teaching of language forms and metacognitive strategies, building background knowledge, and providing opportunities to practice academic language across multiple contexts (Bowers Fitts, Quirk, & Woo, 2010). Additionally, English learners need content presented through explicit scaffolding so they can perform the academic task required (De Jong & Harper, 2005). The amount of scaffolding needed is based on the English learners' language proficiency levels as well as their background knowledge (language, content, and culture). Building on students' background knowledge is an effective strategy to develop language and content mastery as well as to make curriculum culturally and socially relevant to students' lives (De Jong & Harper, 2005; Faltis et al., 2010).

The Lesson Planning Process in Action

In a self-study of the effectiveness of this lesson planning process in a secondary teacher credential program, 99 teacher candidates' lesson plans were analyzed over a two-year period (Daoud, 2011). The teacher candidates completed course assignments that included developing lesson plans for their prospective high school content area classes that enroll both English learners and native-English speakers. The secondary credential program is situated in a public university in southern California, and all of the university's partnership school districts have English learner enrollments. Following the lesson planning process outlined in this book, teacher candidates completed assignments in the program in which they identified who their English learners were, chose appropriate standards for lesson plans designed for their identified students, and then designed assessments based on the chosen standards. Data for this self-study included the lesson plans the teacher candidates designed as well as reflections they wrote based on the professional development model used and the impact of the process on their perceptions of their own abilities to equitably teach their future English learner students. Teacher candidates enrolled in the program individually defined educational equity for English learners based on their own personal beliefs, commitment level, and experiences and designed lesson plans for content area classes accordingly. The lesson plans the teacher candidates designed were the "actions" they developed to demonstrate their commitment to issues of educational equity they had identified and defined. Data presented here focus on two steps of the lesson planning process: choose standards for your lesson and design assessments based on the standards chosen.

Language and Content Objectives

An analysis of the teacher candidates' lessons plans shows that they all incorporated both language and content objectives in their lessons based on ELD standards and content standards chosen for their subject area. In their reflective statements, many of the teacher candidates noted that by doing so, they were providing equitable instruction for their English learners. One physical education teacher candidate designed a lesson on developing motor skills (a state content standard) while allowing her students to deliver oral presentations (a state ELD standard) on their knowledge of the motor skills. In her reflection, she stated that by incorporating ELD standards into her lesson, she was ensuring that her English learners were progressing in their English language learning as well as furthering their understanding of the state content standard. She felt that by doing so, she was providing opportunities for all her English learners and all her students to be successful. A science teacher candidate stated in his reflection that using ELD standards alongside science content standards gave his English learners the opportunity to practice science vocabulary and be confident in using the newly acquired terms in the context of his science class. This process of incorporating ELD standards into high school content area lessons was difficult at first for some teacher candidates, particularly those in the areas of science and mathematics. However, by the end of the semester, they saw the benefit for clearly understanding and assessing their English learners' progress in their content area knowledge acquisition as well as in English language development (Daoud, 2011).

Equitable Outcomes

Along with incorporating language and content objectives based on ELD and state content standards in their lessons, all of the teacher candidates aligned their assessments to the standards they chose and differentiated them based on their English learners' proficiency levels. Of the candidates who wrote about their assessment plans in their reflection assignments, many stated that they had designed their assessments to provide equitable outcomes for their English learner students. One math teacher candidate stated in her reflection that she differentiated her assessments for students to be certain that they are all able to achieve their individual learning goals based on their needs. In her math lesson, she designed a rubric that provided varied levels of mastery based on math content and her English learners' language proficiency levels. Her rubric assessed math content knowledge using varied levels that corresponded to her English learners' language proficiency levels so that all students were accurately assessed. Similarly, a teacher candidate in English language arts wrote in his reflective statement that he felt it was necessary to incorporate numerous informal and formal assessments into his lessons. He felt that by not relying on one type of assessment and then by differentiating all his assessments based on his English learners' proficiency levels, he was providing equitable outcomes for all his students. These students' reflective statements are indicative of those written by their colleagues regarding equitable assessments. Most candidates wrote that they most directly addressed issues of equity regarding the education of their English learner students in their assessments. Throughout their lesson plans, candidates designed varied assessments that were differentiated for students who needed accommodations, including English learners at various English proficiency levels (Daoud, 2011).

As the Common Core State Standards are relatively new, research has not yet been conducted on the impact they have on secondary English learners' overall academic success. The CCSS center on challenging literacy skills that are developmental from kindergarten through the 12th grade. Secondary English learners who enter the U.S. school system as adolescents, in their middle or high school years, will not have the benefit of mastering the less complex versions of these literacy standards in the lower grades, thus eliminating the scaffolded, evolving learning benefits of the CCSS. If they have not had the opportunity to attain the reading and writing skills needed to become proficient in English in the elementary grades, it is very unlikely long-term secondary English learners will be able to master the levels of literacy outlined in the middle and high school CCSS. The four-step lesson planning process outlined in this book addresses many of the academic challenges secondary English learners face. By consistently using the process, secondary content area teachers become the key to an English learner's academic success in middle and high school.

Summary

As you reflect on the conceptual frameworks and foundations that are the basis of the lesson planning process outlined in this book, keep in mind the main points of this chapter:

- It is important to remember that at the secondary level, many students are considered long-term English learners (LTEL) who often perform at lower academic levels than recently arrived immigrant students. Along with educational issues identified for LTEL students, sociocultural, linguistic, academic, and cognitive processes must be considered along with teachers' expectations when examining an English learner's language acquisition at the secondary level. Based on research in the areas of multicultural education and social justice, teachers can use the lesson planning process presented in this book to create equitable educational opportunities for their English learner students.
- Teachers across all content areas can use effective teaching strategies for secondary English, learners, including multiple strategies and methods that help make academically rigorous content accessible to students at various language proficiency levels. Explicitly scaffolding your classroom activities will allow English learners to learn the content you are teaching as well as become more and more proficient in English.

Applying What You Have Learned

In this chapter, you have learned about the conceptual frameworks and foundations for the lesson planning process. Demonstrate your understanding of the chapter by responding to the following statements.

- Describe what equitable instruction for secondary English learners entails
- Explain effective strategies for teaching English learners
- Discuss the lesson planning process in action

part 2

Differentiation for English Learners Across the Language Domains

Annie Pickert Fuller/Pearson Education

Chapters presented in this section outline English language development (ELD) or English language proficiency (ELP) skills in the domains of listening, speaking, reading, and writing. The chapters also present descriptions of how teachers and teacher candidates can incorporate these skills into lessons in their content area classes. Middle and high school students who are identified as English learners need to be proficient in listening, speaking, reading, and writing skills in both academic and social settings. Teachers are introduced to language skills that are derived from a compilation of standards from several states. An explanation of what these skills look like at five proficiency levels is described, along with a step-by-step guide for teachers on differentiating instruction based on students' proficiency levels. On reviewing the information in these chapters, teachers and teacher candidates will understand the listening, speaking, reading, and writing skills English learners need to become proficient in English and to fully comprehend the content presented in their classes. Teachers will also learn how to use ELD standards in lessons they write for their English language arts, mathematics, science, and social studies classes. The goal for English learners is communication. In order to be successful in content area classes, they must acquire the English language skills they need to be effective communicators, both orally and through their writing.

ELD/ELP Standards Vary Across States

Individual states have identified ELD or ELP standards that are aligned to their standards, curriculum, and assessments for English learners. While many states use the ELP standards developed by the World-Class Instructional Design and Assessment (WIDA) Consortium,[1] other states have begun to create their own standards that are aligned to the Common Core State Standards and that can be used across content area classes. The process for equitably teaching English learners in content area classes presented in this book can be used by teachers in any state using any set of ELD or ELP standards. Teachers should use the ELD or ELP standards identified by their state to incorporate language objectives into their lessons so English learner students can learn content while advancing their English proficiency skills.

The language domain chapters presented in this section use the California ELD standards for middle school and high school (grades 6–8 and 9–12) as a foundation upon which standards from other states have been incorporated. The California ELD standards have been chosen as the base because the 2012 revised standards are aligned to the Common Core State Standards and are skills-based. In my experience training teachers and teacher candidates for many years, I have found that by learning how to use skills-based ELD standards, they can understand the specific language skills their English learners need to become proficient in learning the material in their content classrooms. Based on these positive experiences, California's skills-based ELD standards have been chosen as the foundational standards to describe the lesson planning process presented in this book. The California ELD standards are divided into the four language domains that align to standards in other states—listening, speaking, reading, and writing—and then by skills within each language domain. Within each skill, the standards are then divided into proficiency levels. Given that some states divide their standards into five proficiency levels while others use three levels, this book will describe language skills at five proficiency levels with a spotlight on the higher proficiency levels. While English learners at any proficiency level can be placed in secondary content area classes, it is most likely that these classes will enroll students at the higher proficiency levels. The five proficiency levels described in this book are (1) entering, (2) emerging, (3) developing, (4) expanding, and (5) bridging.

[1]The participants in the World-Class Instructional Design and Assessment (WIDA) Consortium are Alabama, Alaska, Delaware, District of Columbia, Georgia, Hawaii, Illinois, Kentucky, Maine, Maryland, Massachusetts, Minnesota, Mississippi, Missouri, Montana, New Hampshire, New Jersey, North Carolina, North Dakota, Oklahoma, Pennsylvania, Rhode Island, South Dakota, Vermont, Virginia, Wisconsin, and Wyoming.

chapter 3

Listening and Speaking Skills

Learning Outcomes

- Discuss the listening and speaking skills English learners need.
- Describe what listening and speaking skills look like at the different proficiency levels.
- Describe how to differentiate instruction based on English learners' listening and speaking proficiency levels.

What Listening and Speaking Skills Do My English Learners Need?

In the language domains of listening and speaking, English learners need to practice and master a variety of listening and speaking skills to become proficient in English and ultimately attain academic success. These skills range from listening to and understanding simple statements and commands to delivering oral presentations on academic topics across content area classes. Using the California ELD standards as a base, the five broad listening and speaking skills are

1. exchanging information and ideas
2. supporting opinions and persuading others
3. adapting language choices
4. listening actively
5. presenting

Many subskills are embedded into these standards, such as "ask and answer questions" and "participate in academic and social classroom discussions," two skills that are specifically listed in ELD or ELP standards from other states. Also of note, the listening and speaking skills outlined in the state standards represent those that are needed to be academically and socially successful in school and classroom contexts. Many subtle nuances of the English language are not covered in standards and/or addressed in classroom settings that English learners attain outside these contexts and that contribute to their overall fluency in English.

How each of these listening and speaking skills is integrated into lessons depends on the content area, the specific lesson taught, and, to a great extent, the vocabulary used in any given content area classroom. Introducing and continually practicing vocabulary words in the context they are used in English, mathematics, science, and social studies classrooms will help English learners become proficient in the listening and speaking skills identified in this chapter. For example, a lesson for an Algebra II class on arithmetic sequences can introduce vocabulary words such as *pattern, sequence,* and *term* within the context of a math class. Continually practicing these vocabulary words through such listening and speaking skills as exchanging information and ideas and presenting allows English learners the opportunity to fully understand the definitions of these words in a mathematical context. It also helps students learn that these vocabulary words have multiple meanings depending on the context in which they are presented. Additionally, placing content area vocabulary into comprehensive and increasingly complex sentences and statements can be difficult for English learners, who may be translating language structures from their native language to English (for example, placing an adjective after a noun as is done in Spanish). These examples underscore the complexity of the English language and highlight why it is so important for English learners to practice vocabulary development through listening and speaking activities in content area classes. The listening and speaking skills presented in this chapter should be incorporated into lessons over the course of the school year repeatedly so English learners have opportunities to develop their overall listening and speaking proficiency. It is not enough to incorporate the skill of supporting opinions and persuading others in one lesson plan at some point during the year. English learners need to practice this skill repeatedly in various contexts in order to fully support opinions and persuade others.

English learners also can develop their vocabulary, learn concepts introduced in content area classes, and engage in the Common Core State Standards (CCSS) for Literacy through progressive and scaffolded use of the listening and speaking skills outlined in this book. For example in an 8th-grade U.S. History class, a teacher begins a unit on constitutional amendments. In the first lesson of the unit, the teacher can introduce the topic and new vocabulary words by incorporating partner work or small-group discussions into the lesson, so that students can begin to negotiate the meaning of the vocabulary and content presented (exchanging information and ideas). In a subsequent lesson on a presentation of a constitutional amendment, the teacher can ask students to respond to comprehension questions while using new vocabulary words and concepts to assess the level of understanding of the topic (listen actively). After the students have learned about the amendment, they can participate in group presentations where they outline the claims of amendment supporters or the counterclaims made by opponents (supporting opinions and persuading others and presenting). These listening and speaking activities can then lead into a written assignment in which students write an argument focused on the claims and counterclaims made by supporters and opponents of the amendment (CCSS Writing standard #1). Incorporating these specific listening and speaking skills into lessons helps English learners progress in their language proficiency and helps build the necessary scaffolds they need to successfully master the skills outlined in the CCSS.

Listening and Speaking Skills and the Common Core State Standards

The CCSS for Literacy in History/Social Studies, Science, and Technical Subjects cover reading and writing skills. However, to become fully proficient in English, listening and speaking skills must also be developed. In the CCSS for English Language Arts, listening and speaking skills are outlined in two areas: (1) comprehension and collaboration and (2) presentation of knowledge and ideas.

Similarly, knowledge of the English language and academic vocabulary specific to content areas needs to be developed for English learners to master the level of academic English needed to be successful. Therefore, content area teachers should incorporate listening and speaking skills into their lessons along with the skills outlined in the CCSS for Literacy in History/Social Studies, Science, and Technical Subjects. In Table 3.1 (middle school, grade 7) and Table 3.2 (high school, grades 9–10), the listening and speaking skills outlined in the CCSS for English Language Arts are used as a foundation to frame the same skills from the ELD/ELP standards. To illustrate this connection, the California ELD standards are presented in the tables as they have been developed to align with the CCSS. For middle school (Table 3.1), the Grade 7 California ELD standards are used, and Grades 9–10 are used for high school (Table 3.2). In these tables, skills outlined for the listening and speaking standards at the two higher proficiency levels of expanding and bridging are presented. These two proficiency levels have been selected because it is likely that English learners at these two levels will be placed in middle and high school content area classes. The tables provide a guide of what listening and speaking skills English learners must attain in content area classes for proficiency in this language domain. While this chapter focuses on listening and speaking skills, the blended skills for all language domains—listening, speaking, reading, and writing—used in this book can be found in Appendix A.

What Do Listening and Speaking Skills Look Like at the Different Proficiency Levels?

As discussed in a previous section, the ELD standards compiled for this book are divided into five proficiency levels. The listening and speaking skills outlined in Tables 3.1 and 3.2 are at the two most prevalent proficiency levels for English learners in content area classes, expanding and

Table 3.1 Listening and Speaking Skills, Middle School (Grade 7)
CCSS Aligned to California ELD Standards at the Expanding and Bridging Levels

	Expanding	Bridging
CCSS—Listening/ Speaking: Comprehension and Collaboration		
ELD Standard/Skill **Exchanging Information/Ideas** (CCSS 1)	Contribute to class, group, and partner discussions by following turn-taking rules, asking relevant questions, affirming others, adding relevant information, and paraphrasing key ideas	Contribute to class, group, and partner discussions by following turn-taking rules, asking relevant questions, affirming others, adding relevant information and evidence, paraphrasing key ideas, building on responses, and providing useful feedback
ELD Standard/Skill **Listening Actively** (CCSS 2) (CCSS 3)	Demonstrate active listening in oral presentation activities by asking and answering detailed questions with occasional prompting and moderate support	Demonstrate active listening in oral presentation activities by asking and answering detailed questions with minimal prompting and support
CCSS—Presentation of Knowledge and Ideas		
ELD Standard/Skill **Supporting Opinions and Persuading Others** (CCSS 4)	Negotiate with or persuade others in conversation using learned phrases and open responses	Negotiate with or persuade others in conversation using an appropriate register, a variety of learned phrases, indirect reported speech, and open responses
ELD Standard/Skill **Adapting Language Choices** (CCSS 6)	Adjust language choices according to purpose(e.g., explaining, persuading), task, and audience	Adjust language choices according purpose (e.g., facilitating a science experiment), task, and audience
ELD Standard/Skill **Presenting** (CCSS 4) (CCSS 5 in all)	Plan and deliver longer oral presentations on a variety of topics using details and evidence to support ideas	Plan and deliver longer oral presentations on a variety of topics in a variety of disciplines, using reasoning and evidence to support ideas, as well as a growing understanding of register

Source: California Department of Education (2012b); Common Core State Standards (2010).

bridging. The specific listening and speaking skill listed under each proficiency level represents the ELD standard for that level. At each level, English learners can independently and automatically perform each language skill identified. Using the listening and speaking skill of presenting as an example, an expanding-level English learner in high school (grades 9–12) can plan and deliver presentations and reports on grade-appropriate topics in content area classes using evidence and facts to support his or her ideas. An expanding-level English learner is proficient enough in English to

Table 3.2 Listening and Speaking Skills, High School (Grades 9–10)
CCSS Aligned to California ELD Standards at the Expanding and Bridging Levels

	Expanding	Bridging
CCSS—Listening/ Speaking: Comprehension and Collaboration		
ELD Standard/Skill **Exchanging Information/Ideas** (CCSS 1)	Contribute to class, group, and partner discussions, sustaining conversations on a variety of grade- and age-appropriate topics by following turn-taking rules; asking and answering relevant, on-topic questions; affirming others; providing additional relevant information; and paraphrasing key ideas	Contribute to class, group, and partner discussions, sustaining conversations on a variety of grade- and age-appropriate topics by following turn-taking rules; asking and answering relevant, on-topic questions; affirming others; and providing coherent and well-articulated comments and additional information
ELD Standard/Skill **Listening Actively** (CCSS 2) (CCSS 3)	Demonstrate comprehension of oral presentations and discussions on a variety of social and academic topics by asking and answering questions that show thoughtful consideration of ideas or arguments with moderate support	Demonstrate comprehension of oral presentations and discussions on a variety of social and academic topics by asking and answering detailed and complex questions that show thoughtful consideration of ideas or arguments with light support
CCSS—Presentation of Knowledge and Ideas		
ELD Standard/Skill **Supporting Opinions and Persuading Others** (CCSS 4)	Negotiate with or persuade others in conversations using a growing number of learned phrases and open responses to express and defend nuanced opinions	Negotiate with or persuade others in conversations in appropriate registers using a variety of learned phrases, indirect reported speech, and open responses to express and defend nuanced opinions
ELD Standard/Skill **Adapting Language Choices** (CCSS 6)	Adjust language choices according to context, purpose, task, and audience	Adjust language choices according to task (e.g., group presentation of a research project), context, purpose, and audience
ELD Standard/Skill **Presenting** (CCSS 4) (CCSS 5 in all)	Plan and deliver a variety of oral presentations and reports on grade-appropriate topics that present evidence and facts to support ideas using growing understanding of register	Plan and deliver a variety of oral presentations and reports on grade-appropriate topics that express complex and abstract ideas, are well supported by evidence and reasoning, and are delivered using an appropriate level of formality and understanding of register

Source: California Department of Education (2012b); Common Core State Standards (2010).

perform this skill independently and automatically, or without assistance from a teacher or peers. In contrast, an English learner at the entering level of English proficiency may only be able to participate in a presentation with peers, contributing to the planning aspect of the presentation but not the delivering portion of the skill. As the complexity of the listening and speaking skills English learners can perform independently and automatically depends on their proficiency levels, teachers should know their students' proficiency levels in each of the language domains.

In ELD or ELP standards for states that outline skills in five proficiency levels, a standard may not be stated for each listening and speaking skill. For example, the skill of adapting language choices may only have standards listed for higher proficiency levels. English learners who are not as proficient—for example, those at the entering level—have not attained the proficiency needed to adapt their language to communicate appropriately for their intended audience, purpose, and subject matter. Adapting language choices is not considered a skill that English learners at the entering proficiency level can do independently and automatically yet. Following are snapshots of what English learners can do independently and automatically in listening and speaking skills at each proficiency level. The snapshots are not meant to be a comprehensive listing of all the listening and speaking skills, but they illustrate the general skills an English learner at each stated level can perform.

Middle School Grades 6–8

Entering At the entering level, English learners can demonstrate that they understand what they are hearing during oral presentations and when instructions are given in English through nonverbal responses such as nodding their head, pointing, and drawing. When speaking, they begin to use single words and simple phrases to ask and answer questions. Entering-level English learners can independently use common social greetings and simple repetitive phrases such as "good morning" and "I am fine, how are you?" with a partner or in a small group.

Emerging At the emerging level, English learners can demonstrate an understanding of oral presentations and activities on familiar topics by asking and answering basic questions with visual support and prompting by the teacher and/or peers. When they speak, emerging-level English learners can adjust their language according to who the listener is (e.g., teacher, peers) and the context in which they are speaking (e.g., classroom, lunch area). They can use phrases such as "I think" or "Could you repeat that, please?" to negotiate with or persuade others in short conversations. With a partner or in a small group, an emerging-English learner can express ideas on familiar topics by asking and answering yes/no and wh- questions (e.g., who, what, when) using simple phrases. An emerging English learner can plan and deliver brief oral presentations on familiar, concrete topics and restate the main idea of information presented in content area classrooms using simple sentences.

Developing English learners at the developing level can listen attentively to information presented in content classes and identify important details and concepts, both verbally and nonverbally. When speaking, developing English learners can make themselves understood but do not follow all grammar rules. They can participate in classroom discussions on topics that are familiar to them by asking and answering questions and soliciting information, and they can work in groups with peers who are native-English speakers. They can respond to messages by asking simple questions to clarify and confirm the accuracy of information presented in class or by briefly restating the message back to the speaker. Developing English learners can summarize information presented to them by restating the main idea along with some supporting details on topics presented in content classes such as familiar literature and texts and key concepts of subject matter content. English learners at the developing level can plan and deliver short oral presentations on ideas, premises, or images from various common sources.

Expanding Expanding-level English learners can demonstrate they understand an oral presentation and activities by asking and answering detailed questions with some prompting by the teacher or peers. At the expanding level, English learners can make themselves understood when speaking by adapting their language appropriately according to the purpose, social setting, and people involved in the discussion. They may make random errors but can use intonation, pitch, and tone correctly when speaking. Expanding-level students can use fixed phrases such as "I agree with X, but . . ." to support their opinions and persuade others in conversations. They can contribute to class, group, and partner discussions on topics that are both familiar and unfamiliar to them. During discussions, expanding English learners can follow turn-taking rules; affirm others; ask and answer relevant, on-topic questions; provide additional information; and paraphrase key ideas on the topic. Expanding-level students can plan and deliver longer oral presentations on a variety of topics using details and evidence to support their ideas.

Bridging English learners at the bridging level can speak clearly and comprehensibly by using standard English and content area vocabulary. They demonstrate active listening during presentations and activities by asking and answering detailed questions with prompting by the teacher or peers. Bridging-level English learners adjust their language choices according to the task (e.g., group presentation, providing peer feedback), purpose, social setting, and audience. In classroom discussions and conversations in which they are supporting opinions or persuading others, students at the bridging-level can use appropriate register along with phrases and indirect reported speech such as, "I heard you say X, but I still think Y because . . ." to express and defend their opinions. They can contribute to class, group, and partner discussions by following turn-taking rules, asking relevant questions, affirming others' responses, and building on them. During discussions, bridging-level students also can paraphrase key ideas, provide useful feedback, and justify their views with evidence. Bridging-level English learners can plan and deliver longer oral presentations on a variety of concrete and abstract topics by using reasoning and evidence to support their ideas.

High School Grades 9–12

Entering At the entering level, English learners can understand some of what is being said to them. They can demonstrate that they understand what they are hearing in English through nonverbal responses such as nodding their head to indicate "yes, I understand." They can speak a few words and phrases and ask and answer questions using simple grammar and verb tenses. With a partner or in a small group, they can orally communicate basic needs using words, gestures, and simple phrases. In a larger class discussion, English learners at the entering level can give simple suggestions, describe events, and express intentions and possibilities. Entering-level English learners can respond to written and oral presentations that summarize the main ideas presented in class with a mixture of gestures, simple words, and phrases when presented with visuals and/or graphic organizer supports.

Emerging At the emerging level, English learners can demonstrate an understanding of discussions and presentations on familiar topics by asking and answering questions with visual support and prompting by the teacher and/or peers. When they speak, emerging-level English learners can adjust their language according to the listener (e.g., teacher, peers) and the context in which they are speaking (e.g., classroom, lunch area). They can use phrases such as "I believe" or "Could you repeat that please?" to negotiate with or persuade others in short conversations. With a partner or in a small group, an emerging English learner can express ideas on familiar topics and current events as well as ask and answer questions with sentences and simple phrases using content area vocabulary. An emerging English learner can prepare and deliver brief oral presentations and reports on familiar topics and restate the main idea of information presented in content area classrooms.

Developing English learners at the developing level can listen attentively to information presented in content classes and identify important details and concepts, both verbally and nonverbally. When speaking, developing English learners can make themselves understood by adapting their language according to audience and purpose while making some grammatical errors. They can participate in discussions with peers on topics that are familiar to them by asking and answering questions, soliciting information, and reporting on situations. Developing English learners can summarize information presented to them by restating the main idea along with some supporting details on topics presented in content classes such as familiar literature and texts and key concepts of subject matter content. English learners at the developing level can plan and deliver short oral presentations on ideas, premises, or images from various common sources.

Expanding Expanding-level English learners can demonstrate they understand an oral presentation or discussion on a variety of social and academic topics by asking and answering questions that are thoughtful and relevant. At the expanding level, English learners can make themselves understood when speaking by adapting their language appropriately according to the context (e.g., classroom, lunch area), purpose, and audience (e.g., teacher, peers). They may make random errors but can use intonation, pitch, and tone correctly when speaking. Expanding-level students can support their opinions and persuade others in classroom discussions and conversations by using fixed phrases such as "You make a valid point, but my view is . . ." to make a claim or counterclaim. They can contribute to class, group, and partner discussions and sustaining conversations on a variety of academic topics that are both familiar and unfamiliar to them. Expanding English learners can follow turn-taking rules, affirm others, and ask and answer relevant, on-topic questions. During discussions, students at the expanding level can provide additional and relevant information and paraphrase key ideas on the topic. These students can prepare and deliver a variety of oral presentations and reports on content area topics that present evidence and facts to support ideas and that follow an organized process.

Bridging English learners at the bridging level can speak clearly and comprehensibly by using standard English and content area vocabulary in complex sentences. When listening to a presentation or discussion on variety of social and academic topics, bridging-level English learners show their comprehension by asking and answering detailed and complex questions. Bridging level English learners consistently adjust their language choices according to the task (e.g., group presentation, individual response), context (e.g., classroom, lunch area), purpose (e.g., to persuade, to provide arguments or counter-arguments), and audience (e.g., teacher, peers, other adults). In classroom discussions and conversations in which they are supporting opinions or persuading others, bridging students can use phrases such as "I've reached a different conclusion on this issue" to express and defend their opinions using appropriate register. They can contribute to class, group, and partner discussions and sustaining conversations on a variety of grade-level academic topics by following turn-taking rules, asking and answering relevant and on-topic questions, and providing coherent and well-articulated comments and additional information. They can initiate complex questions about new information, summarize newly learned content area information, and analyze and critique literary pieces and content area texts. Bridging-level English learners can plan and deliver a variety of oral presentations and reports on grade-level topics in all content area classes. In the presentations, bridging-level students express complex and abstract ideas that are well supported by evidence and reasoning and that are delivered with a level of formality appropriate to the task, purpose, and audience.

How Can I Differentiate My Instruction Based on My English Learners' Listening and Speaking Proficiency Levels?

Teachers can differentiate instruction in the language domain of listening and speaking for their English learners at any proficiency level. Using the four-step lesson planning process outlined in this book, incorporating listening and speaking skills into lessons is covered in the first two steps: know your English learners, and choose standards for your lessons. Each of the steps in the process is described in detail in the Introduction (Chapter 1) as well as in Part 3 of this book (Chapters 6–9) in the context of planning and teaching lessons in content area classes. An expanded description of the first two steps in the lesson planning process follows to help teachers fully understand what they need to know about their English learners' language proficiency levels and how to use that information to accurately chose ELD or ELP standards for their lessons. Following these descriptions is an explanation of how teachers can use listening and speaking skills throughout the year in their lessons.

Step 1: Know Your English Learners

Identifying the language proficiency levels of your English learners is a key element in the process of knowing who your students are. This understanding is necessary as you begin to plan and teach lessons that are equitable for all your students. In the language domain of listening and speaking, equitable planning and teaching starts with learning what skills English learners can do at each proficiency level. You can identify the listening and speaking proficiency levels of the English learners in your class through standardized test scores, language proficiency test scores, discussions with the ELD coordinator at your school, or a combination of these methods. States with a designated percentage of English learners in public schools will have a systematic method for assessing proficiency in the language domains. In California, for example, English learners take a statewide assessment annually, the California English Language Development Test (CELDT), to assess their proficiency level in each language domain. English learners' CELDT scores are determined at the state level, communicated to districts and schools, and then made available to teachers. While this example describes the assessment process in California, it is similar to the processes in other states that have English learner student populations. Depending on the state, English learners' proficiency is divided into multiple levels, usually a range of three to six levels. State departments of education have descriptions of each proficiency level as well as the ELD/ELP standards used in that state available for teachers to view (generally accessible on their websites). Content area teachers can contact their school administrators and/or ELD coordinators at the school or district level for the methods and processes used to identify English learners enrolled in their classes. Once teachers understand the processes used to identify English learners' listening and speaking proficiency levels along with the identified proficiency levels for all English learners in their classes, they can choose appropriate ELD or ELP standards for their lessons.

Step 2: Choose Standards for Your Lessons

After an English learner's listening and speaking proficiency level is determined, the next step in the planning process is to choose a listening and speaking ELD standard for the lesson. As described earlier in this chapter,

English learners can perform each listening and speaking skill outlined in the ELD or ELP standards for their identified proficiency level independently and automatically at that level. Therefore when planning lessons, teachers should choose the listening and speaking skill that is one level above the English learners' current proficiency level (i+1). English learners will use their current proficiency skills as a base to build on to continually develop their English language skills while learning knowledge in content area classes. For example, if English learners are identified at the emerging level in the language domain of listening and speaking, teachers should select the ELD standard at the expanding level for their lesson. Teachers will target their instruction at the expanding level by scaffolding their instruction through strategies and activities that make the content accessible to their emerging English learners (as described in the content chapters in Part 3).

Example #1:

- I have an English learner in my 8th-grade Algebra class who has been identified at the emerging level.
- I will choose the skill listening actively to incorporate into my lesson.
- My emerging-level student can demonstrate active listening by asking and answering basic questions with prompting and visual support independently and automatically.
- I will choose the skill at the expanding level, asking and answering detailed questions with prompting, for my lesson.
- I will scaffold my instruction by using instructional strategies and designing student activities that support my emerging-level English learner so that by the end of the lesson, she can ask and answer detailed questions in a small-group discussion on the key concepts I am presenting in my Algebra class with some prompting by me and/or the other students in the small group.

Example #2:

- I have several English learners in my 10th-grade World History class who have been identified at the emerging and expanding levels.
- From the ELD standards, I will choose the skill presenting to incorporate into my lesson.
- My emerging-level students can plan and deliver short oral presentations on familiar topics independently and automatically.
- My expanding-level students can plan and deliver oral presentations on grade-level topics that present evidence and facts to support their ideas independently and automatically.
- For my emerging English learners, I will choose the expanding-level skill described previously, plan and deliver oral presentations on grade-level topics that present evidence and facts to support their ideas.

- For my expanding English learners, I will choose the bridging-level skill, plan and deliver oral presentations on grade-level topics that express complex and abstract ideas that are well supported by evidence and reasoning.
- I will scaffold my instruction by using instructional strategies and designing student activities so that by the end of the lesson, my emerging English learners can present evidence and facts to support their ideas in an oral presentation on World War I in my World History class. My expanding English learners also will plan and deliver an oral presentation on World War I, but will be expected to support more complex and abstract ideas with evidence and reasoning.

After choosing ELD standards based on English learners' proficiency levels—one level above their current level—teachers write a language objective aligned to the standard that is observable and measurable. The next step is to design an assessment based on the language objective to determine if English learners have mastered the listening and speaking skill chosen for the lesson. In classes that enroll English learners at multiple proficiency levels, the assessment should be differentiated based on the skill level identified for each English learner in class (one level above their current proficiency level). Examples of how to differentiate assessments based on English learners' proficiency levels are described in each content area chapter (Chapters 6–9).

Incorporating Listening and Speaking Skills into Lessons Throughout the Year

Targeting instruction one proficiency level above an English learner's current level will increase his or her listening and speaking proficiency. English learners need to practice all the listening and speaking skills at the higher proficiency level throughout the year in order to become proficient. Throughout the year, content area teachers should continually incorporate into their lessons all the skills listed in Table 3.1 for middle school English learners and Table 3.2 for high school students. To facilitate this, a checklist of listening and speaking skills along with skills in the other language domains of reading and writing is provided in Appendix B. Next to each skill on the list are blank spaces for teachers to record the date that skill was taught. This gives teachers a guide to assist them in ensuring that all listening and speaking skills are repeatedly covered throughout the year and that they are not relying on one or two skills while neglecting others. The checklist will also assist teachers in tracking their English learners' progress on each of the listening and speaking skills, as well as the many subskills embedded within each skill (e.g., exchanging information and ideas) and determine which skills and subskills their English learners need to continually develop more fully as the year progresses.

Summary

As you reflect on the information provided in this chapter on listening/ speaking skills, keep in mind these main points:

- ELD/ELP standards present skills that English learners need to develop across the language areas, including listening and speaking, in order to become fully proficient in English.
- It is important to remember that middle and high school English learners need to continually develop their listening and speaking skills through out the year and across all content areas. Teachers should plan activities in their classes that help their English learner students practice all the listening and speaking skills so they can become proficient.
- Teachers need to learn their English learners' listening and speaking proficiency levels. Once they do so, they can differentiate their instruction so they are incorporating a variety of listening and speaking skills into their lessons that are just beyond their English learners' current level (what the student can currently do independently and automatically).

Applying What You Have Learned

In this chapter, you have learned about a variety of listening and speaking skills that English learners must develop in order to become proficient in English. Demonstrate your understanding of the chapter by participating in the following activities and responding to the corresponding questions.

- Determine which of your students are classified as English learners. Using the data provided by your school or district, determine each student's proficiency level in the area of listening/speaking. Review the listening and speaking skills presented in this chapter (exchanging information/ideas, supporting opinions and persuading others, adapting language choices, listening actively and presenting).
- What does each listening and speaking skill look like at my English learner students' different proficiency levels?
- What listening and speaking skills presented in this chapter can I incorporate into teaching for my English learner students? Identify at least three classroom activities you use in your teaching where you can incorporate one of the listening and/speaking skills presented in this chapter.
- For the listening and speaking skills you identified above to incorporate in your three classroom activities, how will you differentiate your instruction based on your English learners' listening and speaking proficiency level(s)?

chapter 4

Reading Skills

LEARNING OUTCOMES

- Discuss the reading skills English learners need.
- Describe what reading skills look like at the different proficiency levels.
- Describe how to differentiate instruction based on English learners' reading proficiency levels.

What Reading Skills Do My English Learners Need?

In the language domain of reading, English learners need to practice and master a variety of reading skills in order to attain English proficiency and ultimately to succeed in school. These skills range from analyzing an author's language choice to reading a text closely in order to explain inferences and conclusions. Using the California ELD standards as a base, this chapter outlines four broad reading skills, with the first skill divided into three subskills:

1. Reading and viewing closely
   a. Explain ideas, processes, and relationships
   b. Explain inferences and conclusions
   c. Understand morphology
2. Analyzing language choices
3. Evaluating language choices
4. Understanding cohesion in structuring texts

The reading skills outlined in the state standards represent those that are needed to be academically and socially successful in school and classroom contexts. Many nuances of the English language are not covered in standards and/or addressed in classroom settings; English learners may attain these subtleties, which will contribute to their overall reading proficiency in English in their lives outside of school.

How each of these reading skills is integrated into lessons depends on the content area, the specific lesson taught, and to a great extent, the vocabulary used in any given content area classroom. Introducing and continually practicing vocabulary words in the context they are used in English, mathematics, science, and social studies classrooms will help English learners understand reading passages and use vocabulary in the context in which it is presented. For example, a lesson for a biology class on genetics can introduce vocabulary words such as *melanin, phenotype,* and *genotype* within the context of a science class. Teachers can introduce these vocabulary words at the beginning of a lesson and then assign a reading passage from the textbook or from a supplemental text in which the vocabulary terms are used in context. The teacher can assess whether English learners understand the meaning of these words within the context of the lesson through a reading activity that focuses on the skill of reading/viewing closely—knowledge of morphology. Continually practicing these vocabulary words throughout the lesson and unit provides English learners with the opportunity to fully understand the definitions of these words in the context of science. It also helps students learn that vocabulary words may have multiple meanings depending on the context in which they are presented. Asking students to use vocabulary words in comprehensive and increasingly complex sentences and statements can be difficult for English learners who may translate language structures from their native language to English (for example, placing an adjective after a noun as is done in Spanish). These examples demonstrate the complexity of the English language and the importance to English learners of practicing vocabulary development through reading activities in content area classes. All the reading skills presented in this chapter should be incorporated into lessons over the course of the school year repeatedly so English learners have opportunities to develop their overall reading proficiency.

English learners may demonstrate their mastery of any reading skill through a listening, speaking, or writing activity. Because the ELD standards used in this book are aligned to the Common Core State Standards (CCSS), skills across all the language domains easily complement one another. For example in a 10th-grade English class, a teacher begins a poetry unit by introducing the topic and new vocabulary words through a partner activity where students can begin to negotiate the meaning of the vocabulary and/or content presented (listening and speaking: exchanging information and ideas). Students then read a series of poems focusing on the language choices the author made in each (reading: analyzing language choices). These activities can lead into a writing activity in which students write their own poems (writing: literary and informational texts). Incorporating these language skills into lessons gives English learners the tools they need to become proficient readers and to successfully master the skills outlined in the CCSS.

Reading Skills and the Common Core State Standards

The CCSS for Literacy in History/Social Studies, Science, and Technical Subjects cover reading skills in the following areas: key ideas and details, craft and structure, integration of knowledge and ideas, and range of reading and level of text complexity. In Table 4.1 (middle school, grade 7) and Table 4.2 (high school, grades 9–10), the reading skills outlined in the CCSS for Literacy in History/Social Studies, Science, and Technical Subjects are used as a foundation to frame the same skills from ELD/ELP state standards. To illustrate this connection, the California ELD standards are presented in the tables as they have been developed to align with the CCSS. For middle school (Table 4.1), the Grade 7 California ELD standards are used, and Grades 9–10 California ELD standards are used for high school (Table 4.2). To further demonstrate the alignment to the Common Core, some of the ELD/ELP standards are listed multiple times as they line up to several of the CCSS. In the tables, skills outlined for the reading standards at the two higher proficiency levels of expanding and bridging are presented.

Table 4.1 Reading Skills, Middle School (Grade 7)
CCSS Aligned to California ELD Standards at the Expanding and Bridging Levels

	Expanding	Bridging
CCSS—Key Ideas and Details		
ELD Standard/Skill **Reading/viewing closely:** explain ideas, processes, and relationships (CCSS 1 & 2)	Explain ideas, phenomena, processes, and text relationships based on close reading of grade-level texts and viewing of multimedia with moderate support	Explain ideas, phenomena, processes, and text relationships based on close reading of a variety of grade-level texts and viewing of multimedia with light support
ELD Standard/Skill **Reading/viewing closely:** explain inferences and conclusions (CCSS 3)	Express inferences and conclusions drawn based on close reading of grade-appropriate texts and viewing of multimedia using a variety of verbs	Express inferences and conclusions drawn based on close reading of grade-level texts and viewing of multimedia using a variety of precise academic verbs
CCSS—Craft and Structure		
ELD Standard/Skill **Analyzing language choices** (CCSS 4)	Explain how phrasing, different words with similar meanings, or figurative language produces shades of meaning and different effects on the audience	Explain how phrasing, different words with similar meanings, or figurative language produces shades of meaning, nuances and different effects on the audience

ELD Standard/Skill **Reading/viewing closely:** knowledge of morphology (CCSS 4)	Use knowledge of morphology, context, reference materials, and visual cues to determine the meanings of unknown and multiple-meaning words on familiar and new topics	Use knowledge of morphology, context, reference materials, and visual cues to determine the meanings, including figurative and connotative meanings, of unknown and multiple-meaning words on a variety of new topics
ELD Standard/Skill **Evaluating language choices** (CCSS 5 & 6)	Explain how well writers and speakers use specific language to present ideas or support arguments, and provide detailed evidence when provided with moderate support	Explain how well writers and speakers use language resources to present ideas or support arguments and provide detailed evidence when provided with light support
CCSS—Integration of Knowledge and Ideas *ELD Standard/Skill* **Reading/viewing closely:** explain inferences and conclusions (CCSS 7)	Express inferences and conclusions drawn based on close reading of grade-appropriate texts and viewing of multimedia using a variety of verbs	Express inferences and conclusions drawn based on close reading of grade-level texts and viewing of multimedia using a variety of precise academic verbs
ELD Standard/Skill **Evaluating language choices** (CCSS 8)	Explain how well writers and speakers use specific language to present ideas or support arguments, and provide detailed evidence when provided with moderate support	Explain how well writers and speakers use language resources to present ideas or support arguments, and provide detailed evidence when provided with light support
CCSS—Range of Reading and Level of Text Complexity *ELD Standard/Skill* **Understanding cohesion: structuring texts** (CCSS 9) (CCSS—10 in all)	Apply growing understanding of how ideas, events, or reasons are linked throughout a text using a variety of connecting words or phrases to comprehending texts and writing texts with increasing cohesion	Apply increasing understanding of how ideas, events, or reasons are linked throughout a text using an increasing variety of academic connecting and transitional words or phrases to comprehending texts and writing texts with increasing cohesion

Source: California Department of Education (2012b); Common Core State Standards (2010).

The tables provide a guide of what reading skills English learners need to attain in content area classes for proficiency in this language domain. While this chapter focuses on reading skills, the blended skills for all language domains—listening, speaking, reading, and writing—used in this book can be found in Appendix A.

Table 4.2 Reading Skills, High School (Grades 9–10)
CCSS Aligned to California ELD Standards at the Expanding and Bridging Levels

	Expanding	Bridging
CCSS—Key Ideas and Details		
ELD Standard/Skill **Reading/viewing closely:** explain ideas, processes, and relationships (CCSS 1 & 2)	Explain ideas, phenomena, processes, and relationships within and across texts based on close reading of a variety of grade-appropriate texts, presented in various print and multimedia formats, using increasingly complex sentences, and an increasing variety of general academic and domain-specific words	Explain ideas, phenomena, processes, and relationships within and across texts based on close reading of a variety of grade-level texts, presented in various print and multimedia formats, using a variety of detailed sentences, and a range of general academic and domain-specific words
ELD Standard/Skill **Reading/viewing closely:** explain inferences and conclusions (CCSS 3)	Explain inferences and conclusions drawn based on close reading of a variety of grade-appropriate texts and viewing of multimedia using a variety of verbs and adverbs	Explain inferences and conclusions drawn based on close reading of grade-level texts and viewing of multimedia using a variety of verbs and adverbs
CCSS—Craft and Structure		
ELD Standard/Skill **Analyzing language choices** (CCSS 4)	Explain how a writer's or speaker's choice of phrasing or specific words produces nuances and different effects on the audience	Explain how a writer's or speaker's choice of a variety of different types of phrasing or words produces nuances and different effects on the audience
ELD Standard/Skill **Evaluating language choices** (CCSS 5 & 6)	Evaluate how successfully writers and speakers structure texts and use language to persuade the reader or create other specific effects, with moderate support	Evaluate how successfully writers and speakers structure texts and use language to persuade the reader or create other specific effects, with light support
CCSS—Integration of Knowledge and Ideas		
ELD Standard/Skill **Reading/viewing closely:** explain inferences and conclusions (CCSS 7)	Explain inferences and conclusions drawn based on close reading of a variety of grade-appropriate texts and viewing of multimedia using a variety of verbs and adverbs	Explain inferences and conclusions drawn based on close reading of grade-level texts and viewing of multimedia using a variety of verbs and adverbs
ELD Standard/Skill **Evaluating language choices** (CCSS 8)	Evaluate how successfully writers and speakers structure texts and use language to persuade the reader or create other specific effects, with moderate support	Evaluate how successfully writers and speakers structure texts and use language to persuade the reader or create other specific effects, with light support
CCSS—Range of Reading and Level of Text Complexity		
ELD Standard/Skill **Understanding cohesion:** structuring texts (CCSS 9) (CCSS 10 in all)	Apply knowledge of familiar language resources for linking ideas, events, or reasons throughout a text to comprehending texts and to writing increasingly more cohesive texts for specific purposes and audiences	Apply knowledge of familiar language resources for linking ideas, events, or reasons throughout a text to comprehending grade-level texts and to writing clear and cohesive grade-level texts for specific purposes and audiences

Source: California Department of Education (2012b); Common Core State Standards (2010).

What Do Reading Skills Look Like at the Different Proficiency Levels?

The ELD standards compiled for this book are divided into five proficiency levels. The reading skills outlined in Tables 4.1 and 4.2 represent the two most prevalent proficiency levels for English learners in content area classes, expanding and bridging. The specific reading skill listed under each proficiency level represents the ELD standard for that level. At each level, English learners can independently and automatically perform each reading skill identified. Using the reading skill of evaluating language choices as an example, an expanding-level English learner in high school (grades 9–12) can evaluate how successfully an author structures texts and uses words and phrases to persuade the reader in providing reasoning and evidence to support claims. An expanding-level English learner is proficient enough in English to perform this skill independently and automatically, or without the assistance from a teacher or peers. In contrast, an English learner at the entering level of English proficiency may have the reading skills to understand the main ideas of the text, but only with considerable scaffolding from the teacher or his or her peers. Because the complexity of the reading skills an English learner can perform independently and automatically depends on his or her proficiency level, it is important for teachers to know their students' proficiency levels in each of the language domains.

In ELD or ELP standards for states that outline skills in five proficiency levels, a standard may not be stated for each reading skill. In the previous example the skill of evaluating language choices may only have standards listed for higher proficiency levels. English learners who are not as proficient—for example, those at the entering level, have not attained the level of proficiency needed to evaluate how an author has structured a text through his or her language choices as a means of persuading the reader. It is not considered a skill that English learners at the entering proficiency level can do independently and automatically. Following are snapshots of what English learners can do independently and automatically in reading skills at each proficiency level. The snapshots are not meant to be a comprehensive listing of all the elements within each reading skill; rather they should be used to paint a portrait of the general skills an English learner can perform at that level.

Middle School Grades 6–8

Entering At the entering level, English learners recognize and pronounce phonemes and most morphemes in phrases and simple sentences. They can retell stories using phrases and simple sentences and demonstrate understanding of new words by using one- or two-word-sentence responses. Entering-level English learners can point out text features such as the title, table of contents, and chapter headings. They can use pictures, charts, and tables in informational materials such as newspapers and magazines to identify factual meanings. Entering-level English learners can identify the main idea of a text and respond to factual questions about it by using key words and phrases. Entering students can orally identify examples of facts and opinions as well as cause and effect. They can orally identify different characters and settings in texts and create pictures, lists, charts, and tables to identify the sequence of events in simple literary texts.

Emerging At the emerging level, when reading grade-level texts English learners can explain ideas, phenomena, processes, and text relationships with support such as through graphic organizers. They can use frequently used verbs to express inferences and conclusions drawn from reading grade-level texts and viewing of multimedia, and they can use their knowledge of morphology (e.g., roots, base words), context, reference materials, and visual cues to determine the meanings of unknown and multiple-meaning words. Emerging-level students are able to explain how writers use language to support their ideas and arguments with details and evidence in grade-level texts when they are provided with background knowledge, visual supports, and similar scaffolds. They can explain how phrasing or common words with similar meanings used in texts have different effects on the reader.

Developing At the developing level, when reading grade-level texts English learners can explain ideas, phenomena, processes, and text relationships. They can use frequently used verbs to express inferences and conclusions drawn from reading grade-level texts and viewing multimedia, and they can use their knowledge of morphology (e.g., roots, base words) to determine the meanings of unknown and multiple-meaning words. Developing-level students are able to explain how writers use language to support their ideas and arguments with details and evidence in grade-level texts by using simple sentences. They can use detailed sentences, expanded vocabulary, and descriptive words to describe the main ideas, events, and characters of a text or piece of literature. They can explain how phrasing or common words with similar meanings used in texts have different effects on the reader.

Expanding English learners at the expanding level can explain ideas, phenomena, processes, and text relationships when reading grade-level texts with support such as using sentence starters. They can use a variety of verbs to express inferences and conclusions drawn from reading grade-level texts and viewing multimedia, and they can use their knowledge of morphology (e.g., roots, base words), context, reference materials, and visual cues to determine the meanings of unknown and multiple-meaning words used in familiar and new topics. Expanding-level students are able to explain how writers use language to support their ideas and arguments with details and evidence in a variety of grade-level texts when they are provided with supports such as graphic organizers. They can explain how phrasing or common words with similar meanings used in texts produce shades of meaning and have different effects on the reader.

Bridging English learners at the bridging level can explain ideas, phenomena, processes, and text relationships when reading a variety of grade-level texts with support such as using a word wall. They can use a variety of precise academic verbs to express inferences and conclusions drawn from reading grade-level texts and viewing multimedia, and they can use their knowledge of morphology (e.g., roots, base words), context, reference materials, and visual cues to determine the meanings, including figurative and connotative meanings, of unknown and multiple-meaning words on a variety of new topics. English learners at the bridging level are able to explain how writers use language to support their ideas and arguments with details and evidence in a variety of grade-level texts. Bridging-level students can explain how phrasing or different words with similar meanings used in texts produce shades of meaning and have different effects on the reader.

High School Grades 9–12

Entering At the entering level, English learners recognize and pronounce phonemes and most morphemes in phrases and simple sentences. They can read simple words aloud that are presented in literature and subject matter texts, demonstrate understanding with simple sentence responses, and recognize simple synonyms, antonyms, and affixes. Entering-level English learners can point out text features such as the title, table of contents, and chapter headings. They can identify the vocabulary, syntax, and grammar used in public documents such as speeches, debates, and laws. Entering-level students can identify the main idea and some details of familiar literature and informational texts by orally using key words and phrases in their descriptions. They can recognize a few specific facts in familiar expository and content area texts and recognize differences in points of view between first person and third person using phrases and simple sentences. Entering students can orally identify different characters and settings in texts and create pictures, lists, and charts to identify the sequence of events in simple literary texts.

Emerging At the emerging level, when reading a variety of grade-level texts, English learners can explain ideas, phenomena, processes, and text relationships presented in various print and multimedia formats by using phrases, short sentences, and select academic and content-specific vocabulary words. They can use familiar verbs to express inferences and conclusions drawn from reading grade-level texts and viewing multimedia. Emerging-level students are able to explain how an author structures texts and uses introductory words and phrases to show their reasoning and evidence to support claims. They can explain how an author's choice of phrasing or words produces a different effect on the reader. Emerging-level English learners apply knowledge of resources that make texts more cohesive to understand well-structured, grade-appropriate texts.

Developing At the developing level, when reading a variety of grade-level texts, English learners can explain ideas, phenomena, processes, and text relationships presented in various print and multimedia formats by using detailed sentences and select academic and content-specific vocabulary words. They can use an increasing number of verbs and simple sentences to express inferences and conclusions drawn from reading grade-level texts and viewing multimedia. Developing-level students are able to evaluate how an author structures texts and uses words and phrases to show their reasoning and evidence to support claims. They can explain how an author's choice of phrasing or words produces a different effect on the reader by using simple, detailed sentences. Developing-level English learners apply knowledge of resources that make texts more cohesive to understand well-structured, grade-appropriate texts.

Expanding English learners at the expanding level can explain ideas, phenomena, processes, and text relationships within and across a variety of grade-level texts that are presented in various print and multimedia formats by using increasingly complex sentences as well as a range of academic and subject matter words. They can use a variety of verbs and adverbs to explain inferences and conclusions drawn from reading grade-level texts and viewing multimedia. Expanding-level students are able to evaluate how an author structures texts and uses words and phrases to persuade the reader in providing reasoning and evidence to support claims. They can explain how an author's choice of phrasing or words produces a different effect on the reader. Expanding-level English learners apply knowledge of resources that make texts more cohesive in order to understand more complex grade-appropriate texts that accomplish different purposes.

Bridging English learners at the bridging level can explain ideas, phenomena, processes, and text relationships within and across a variety of grade-level texts that are presented in various print and multimedia formats by using a variety of detailed sentences and precise, nuanced academic and subject matter words. They can use a variety of verbs and adverbs to explain inferences and conclusions drawn from reading grade-level texts and viewing multimedia. Bridging-level students are able to evaluate how successfully an author structures texts and uses sets of related words and series of sentences to persuade the reader in providing reasoning and evidence to support claims. They can explain how well an author's choice of phrasing or words produces a different effect on the reader. Bridging-level English learners apply knowledge of resources that make texts more cohesive in order to understand complex grade-appropriate texts that accomplish different purposes.

How Can I Differentiate My Instruction Based on My English Learners' Reading Proficiency Levels?

Teachers can differentiate instruction in the language domain of reading for their English learners at any proficiency level. Using the four-step lesson planning process outlined in this book, incorporating reading skills into lessons is covered in the first two steps: know your English learners and chose standards for your lessons. Each of the steps in the process is described in detail in the Introduction (Chapter 1) as well as in Part 3 of the book (Chapters 6–9) in the context of planning and teaching lessons in content area classes. What follows is an expanded description of the first two steps in the lesson planning process to help teachers fully understand what they need to know about their English learners' language proficiency levels and how to use that information to accurately choose ELD or ELP standards for their lessons. Following these descriptions is an explanation of how teachers can use reading skills throughout the school year in their lessons.

Step 1: Know Your English Learners

Understanding your English learners' language proficiency levels is a key element in the process of learning about who your students are and is necessary so you can begin to plan and teach lessons that are equitable for all your students. In the language domain of reading, equitable planning and teaching starts with learning what skills English learners can do at each proficiency level. For the English learners in your class, teachers can identify their reading proficiency levels through standardized test scores, language proficiency test scores, discussions with the ELD coordinator at the school, or a combination of any these methods. States with a designated percentage of English learners in public schools will have a systematic method for assessing proficiency across the language domains. In California, for example, English learners take a statewide assessment annually, the California English Language Development Test (CELDT), to assess their proficiency level in each language domain. English learners' CELDT scores are determined at the state level, communicated to districts and schools, and then made available to teachers. While this example describes the assessment process in California, it is similar to the processes in other states that have English learner student populations. Depending on the state, English learners' proficiency is divided into multiple levels, usually a range of three to six levels. State departments of education have descriptions of each proficiency level as well as the ELD/ELP standards used available for teachers to view (generally accessible on their websites). Content area teachers can contact their school administrators and/or ELD coordinators at the school or district level for the methods and processes used to identify English learners who are enrolled in their classes. Once teachers understand the processes used to identify English learners' reading proficiency levels along with the identified proficiency levels for all English learners in their class, they can choose appropriate ELD or ELP standards for their lessons.

Step 2: Choose Standards for Your Lessons

After an English learner's reading proficiency level is determined, the next step in the planning process is to choose a reading ELD standard for the lesson. As described earlier in this chapter, an English learner can perform each reading skill outlined in the ELD or ELP standards for her or his identified proficiency level independently and automatically at that level. Therefore when lesson planning, teachers should choose the reading skill that is one level above the English learner's current proficiency level (i+1). English learners will use their current proficiency skills as a base to build on to continually develop their English language skills while learning knowledge in content area classes. For example, if an English learner is identified at the emerging level in the language domain of reading, then teachers should select the ELD standard at the expanding level for their lesson. Teachers will target their instruction at the expanding level by scaffolding instruction through strategies and activities that make the content accessible to emerging English learners (as described in the content chapters in Part 3).

Example #1:

- I have several English learners in my 6th-grade Earth Science class who have been identified at the emerging level.
- I will choose the skill of evaluating language choices to incorporate into my lesson.
- My emerging-level students can demonstrate evaluating language choices by explaining how well the author of the assigned text uses language to support her arguments with substantial support (i.e., through a graphic organizer) independently and automatically.
- I will choose the evaluating language choices skill at the expanding level (explain how well the author of the assigned text uses language to support her arguments) for my lesson.
- I will scaffold my instruction by using instructional strategies and designing student activities that support my emerging-level English learners so that by the end of the lesson, they have read the assigned text and can explain how well the author used language to support her argument by writing a paragraph using detailed sentences (as opposed to presenting the information in a graphic organizer).

Example #2:

- I have several English learners in my 10th-grade English class who have been identified at the emerging and expanding levels.
- From the ELD standards, I will choose the skill of reading/viewing closely: explain ideas, processes, and relationships to incorporate into my lesson.
- My emerging-level students can demonstrate reading/viewing closely independently and automatically by explaining ideas presented in the text by using a select set of academic words from the text in short sentences.

- My expanding-level students can explain ideas presented in the text by using a range of academic and subject matter words from the text in increasingly detailed sentences independently and automatically.
- For my emerging English learners, I will choose the expanding-level skill described above (explain ideas presented in the text by using a range of academic and subject matter words from the text in increasingly detailed sentences).
- For my expanding English learners, I will choose the bridging-level skill (explain ideas presented in the text by using a range of academic and subject matter words from the text in a variety of detailed sentences).
- I will scaffold my instruction by using instructional strategies and designing student activities so that by the end of the lesson, my emerging English learners can explain the ideas from the text by writing a summary paragraph using several academic words in complex sentences. My expanding English learners also will write a summary paragraph, but will be expected to use nuanced academic words in a variety of detailed sentences.

After choosing ELD standards based on English learners' proficiency levels one step above their current level, teachers write a language objective aligned to the standard that is observable and measurable. The next step is to design an assessment based on the language objective to determine if English learners have mastered the reading skill chosen for the lesson. In classes that enroll English learners at multiple proficiency levels, the assessment should be differentiated based on the skill level identified for each English learner in class (one level above their current proficiency level). Examples of how to differentiate assessments based on English learners' proficiency levels are described in each content area chapter (Chapters 6–9).

Incorporating Reading Skills into Lessons Throughout the Year

Targeting instruction at one proficiency level above an English learner's current level will increase his or her reading proficiency. English learners need to practice all the reading skills at the higher proficiency level throughout the year in order to become proficient. Content area teachers should continually incorporate all the skills listed in Table 4.1 for middle school English learners and Table 4.2 for high school students throughout the year into their lessons. To facilitate this, a checklist of reading skills along with skills in the other language domains of listening, speaking, and writing is provided in Appendix B. Next to each skill on the list, there are blank spaces for teachers to record the date that the skill was taught. This gives teachers a guide to assist them in ensuring that all reading skills are repeatedly covered throughout the year and that they are not relying on one or two skills while neglecting the others. The checklist will also assist teachers in tracking their English learners' progress on each of the reading skills, as well as on the many subskills embedded within each skill (e.g., reading/viewing closely: explain ideas, processes, and relationships) and determine which skills and subskills their English learners need to continually develop more fully as the year progresses.

Summary

As you reflect on the information provided in this chapter on reading skills, keep in mind these main points:

- ELD/ELP standards present skills that English learners need to develop across the language areas, including reading, in order to become fully proficient in English. In the area of reading, skills are aligned to the Common Core State Standards (CCSS) for English Language Arts, as well as for Social Studies and Science.
- It is important to remember that middle and high school English learners need to continually develop their reading skills through out the year and across all content areas. Understanding the variety and complexity of texts that are presented across content area classes can be difficult for English learners. Therefore, teachers should plan reading activities in their classes that help their English learners become proficient readers of all types of texts and multimedia.
- Teachers need to learn their English learners' proficiency levels in the area of reading. Once they do so, teachers can then differentiate their instruction so they are incorporating a variety of reading skills into their lessons that are just beyond their English learners' current level (what the student can currently do independently and automatically).

Applying What You Have Learned

In this chapter, you have learned about a variety of reading skills that English learners must develop in order to become proficient in English. Demonstrate your understanding of the chapter by participating in the following activities and responding to the corresponding questions.

- Determine which of your students are classified as English learners. Using the data provided by your school or district, determine each student's proficiency level in the area of reading. Review the reading skills presented in this chapter (Reading/viewing closely—explain ideas, processes, and relationships; reading/viewing closely—explain inferences and conclusion; reading/viewing closely—knowledge of morphology; analyzing language choices; evaluating language choices; and understanding cohesion).

- What does each reading skill look like at my English learner students' different proficiency levels?
- What reading skills presented in this chapter can I incorporate into teaching for my English learner students? Identify at least three classroom activities you use in your teaching where you can incorporate one of the reading skills presented in this chapter.
- For the reading skills you identified above to incorporate in your three classroom activities, how will you differentiate you instruction based on your English learners' reading proficiency level(s)?

chapter 5

Writing Skills

LEARNING OUTCOMES

- Discuss the writing skills English learners need.
- Describe what writing skills look like at the different proficiency levels.
- Describe how to differentiate instruction based on English learners' writing proficiency levels.

What Writing Skills Do My English Learners Need?

In the language domain of writing, English learners need to practice and master a variety of writing skills to become proficient in English and to attain overall academic success in school. These writing skills range from connecting ideas to justifying opinions and positions on academic topics across content area classes. Of the four language domains, more emphasis is placed on writing at the secondary level than on the other language skills because writing proficiency is an integral component of the academic rigor prevalent in all content area classes. Using the California ELD standards as a base, the eleven writing skills presented in this chapter are:

1. justifying/arguing—express opinions
2. justifying/arguing—justify opinions and positions
3. understanding text structure
4. writing literary and informational texts
5. writing summaries
6. interacting via written English
7. selecting language resources—using a variety of words
8. selecting language resources—using knowledge of morphology
9. understanding cohesion—applying knowledge of resources

10. connecting ideas
11. condensing ideas

Many subskills are embedded in these standards, particularly at the higher proficiency levels where each skill requires more complex writing abilities. Also of note, the writing skills outlined in the state standards represent those that are needed to be academically and socially successful in school and classroom contexts. Many nuances of the English language are not covered in standards and/or addressed in classroom settings; English learners may attain these subtleties, which will contribute to their overall proficiency in written English in their lives outside of school.

How each of these writing skills is integrated into lessons depends on the content area, the specific lesson taught, and, to a great extent, the vocabulary used in any given content area classroom. Introducing and continually practicing vocabulary words in the context they are used in English, mathematics, science, and social studies classrooms will help English learners become proficient in all the writing skills identified in this chapter. For example, a lesson for an 8th-grade algebra class on point-slope form can introduce vocabulary words such as *point* and *slope* within the context of a math class. Continually practicing these vocabulary words through such writing activities as writing summaries and selecting language resources—using knowledge of morphology gives English learners the opportunity to fully understand the definitions of these words in the context of a mathematics class. It also helps students learn that these vocabulary words have multiple meanings depending on the context in which they are presented. Additionally, using the vocabulary words in comprehensive and increasingly complex sentences and statements can be difficult for English learners who may translate language structures from their native language to English (for example, placing an adjective after a noun as is done in Spanish). These examples demonstrate the complexity of the English language and the importance for English learners to practice vocabulary development through writing activities in content area classes. All the writing skills presented in this chapter should be repeatedly incorporated into lessons over the course of the school year so English learners have opportunities to develop their overall proficiency in written English.

English learners also can develop their vocabulary, learn concepts introduced in content area classes, and engage in the Common Core State Standards (CCSS) through progressive and scaffolded use of the writing skills outlined in this book. For example, in a high school world history class, a teacher begins a unit on Southeast Asia and American Imperialism. In the first lesson of the unit, the teacher introduces the topic and new vocabulary words by incorporating partner work or small group discussions into the lesson so students can begin to negotiate the meaning of the vocabulary and/or content presented (interacting via written English). In a subsequent lesson, the teacher can ask students to summarize the information presented on American Imperialism in a paragraph using new vocabulary words and concepts they have learned (writing summaries). After the students have learned about American Imperialism, they can participate in small-group activities where they expand on their written paragraph summaries by focusing on text organization and development to write a research paper (writing literary and informational texts). This final writing activity can be aligned to skills outlined in the CCSS (writing standard #2). The scaffolded writing activities described here are designed to help English learners progress in their writing proficiency and ultimately participate in writing assignments as outlined in the CCSS.

Writing Skills and the Common Core State Standards

The CCSS for Literacy in History/Social Studies, Science, and Technical Subjects cover the following writing skills: text types and purposes, production and distribution of writing, research to build and present knowledge, and range of writing. In Table 5.1 (middle school, grade 7) and Table 5.2

Table 5.1 Writing Skills, Middle School (Grade7)
CCSS Aligned to California ELD Standards at the Expanding and Bridging Levels

	Expanding	Bridging
CCSS—Text Types and Purposes		
ELD Standard/Skill **Justifying/Arguing:** express opinions (CCSS 1)	Express attitudes and opinions or temper statements with a variety of familiar modal expressions	Express attitudes and opinions or temper statements with nuanced modal expressions
ELD Standard/Skill **Justifying/Arguing:** justify opinions and positions (CCSS 1)	Justify opinions or persuade others by providing relevant textual evidence or relevant background knowledge with moderate support	Justify opinions or persuade others by providing detailed and relevant textual evidence or relevant background knowledge with light support
ELD Standard/Skill **Understanding cohesion:** apply knowledge of resources (CCSS 1)	Apply knowledge of familiar language resources for referring to make texts more cohesive and to comprehending and writing texts with increasing cohesion	Apply knowledge of familiar language resources for referring to make texts more cohesive and to comprehending and to writing cohesive texts
ELD Standard/Skill **Selecting language resources:** using a variety of words (CCSS 2)	Use a growing set of academic words, domain-specific words, synonyms, and antonyms to create precision and shades of meaning when speaking and writing	Use an expanding set of general academic words, domain-specific words, synonyms, antonyms, and figurative language to create precision and shades of meaning when speaking and writing
ELD Standard/Skill **Understanding text structure** (CCSS 2)	Apply understanding of the organizational features of different text types to comprehending texts and to writing texts with increasingly clear and coherent arguments, informative/explanatory texts, and narratives	Apply understanding of the organizational features of different text types to comprehending texts and to writing clear and cohesive arguments, informative/explanatory texts, and narratives

	Expanding	Bridging
ELD Standard/Skill **Writing:** literary and informational texts (CCSS 2)	Write longer literary and informational texts collaboratively and independently using appropriate text organization	Write longer and more detailed literary and informational texts collaboratively and independently using appropriate text organization and a growing understanding of register
CCSS—Production and Distribution of Writing		
ELD Standard/Skill **Writing:** summaries (CCSS 4)	Write increasingly concise summaries of texts and experiences using complete sentences and key words	Write clear and coherent summaries of texts and experiences using complete and concise sentences and key words
ELD Standard/Skill **Interacting via written English** (CCSS 5)	Engage in longer written exchanges with peers and collaborate on more detailed written texts on a variety of topics, using technology when appropriate	Engage in extended written exchanges with peers and collaborate on complex written texts on a variety of topics, using technology when appropriate
CCSS–Research to Build and Present Knowledge		
ELD Standard/Skill **Selecting language resources:** using a variety of words (CCSS 7 & 8)	Use a growing set of academic words, domain-specific words, synonyms, and antonyms to create precision and shades of meaning when speaking and writing	Use an expanding set of general academic words, domain-specific words, synonyms, antonyms, and figurative language to create precision and shades of meaning when speaking and writing
ELD Standard/Skill **Selecting language resources:** use knowledge of morphology (CCSS 7 & 8)	Use knowledge of morphology to appropriately select affixes in a growing number of ways to manipulate language	Use knowledge of morphology to appropriately select affixes in a variety of ways to manipulate language
ELD Standard/Skill **Understanding cohesion:** apply knowledge of resources (CCSS 9)	Apply knowledge of familiar language resources for referring that make texts more cohesive to comprehending and writing texts with increasing cohesion	Apply knowledge of familiar language resources for referring that make texts more cohesive to comprehending and writing cohesive texts
CCSS–Range of Writing		
ELD Standard/Skill **Connecting ideas** (CCSS 10)	Combine clauses in an increasing variety of ways to make connections between and join ideas, for example, to express a reason or to make a concession	Combine clauses in a wide variety of ways to make connections and join ideas, for example, to show the relationship between multiple events or ideas or to evaluate an argument
ELD Standard/Skill **Condensing ideas** (CCSS 10) (CCSS 6 throughout)	Condense ideas in an increasing variety of ways to create precise and detailed sentences	Condense clauses in a variety of ways to create precise and detailed sentences

Source: California Department of Education (2012b); Common Core State Standards (2010).

Table 5.2 Writing Skills, High School (Grades 9–10)
CCSS Aligned to California ELD Standards at the Expanding and Bridging Levels

	Expanding	Bridging
CCSS–Text Types and Purposes		
ELD Standard/Skill **Justifying/Arguing:** express opinions (CCSS 1)	Express attitudes and opinions or temper statements with a variety of familiar modal expressions	Express attitudes and opinions or temper statements with nuanced modal expressions
ELD Standard/Skill **Justifying / Arguing:** justify opinions and positions (CCSS 1)	Justify opinions and positions or persuade others by making connections between ideas and articulating relevant textual evidence or background knowledge	Justify opinions and positions or persuade others by making connections and distinctions between ideas and texts and articulating sufficient, detailed, and relevant textual evidence or background knowledge using appropriate register
ELD Standard/Skill **Understanding cohesion:** apply knowledge of resources (CCSS 1)	Apply knowledge of a growing number of language resources for referring to make texts more cohesive to comprehending and writing increasingly cohesive texts for specific purposes and audiences	Apply knowledge of a variety of language resources for referring to make texts more cohesive to comprehending grade-level texts and to writing clear and cohesive grade-level texts for specific purposes and audiences
ELD Standard/Skill **Selecting language resources:** using a variety of words (CCSS 2)	Use an increasing variety of grade-appropriate general academic words and domain-specific academic words accurately and appropriately when producing increasingly complex spoken and written texts	Use a variety of grade-appropriate and domain-specific academic words and phrases, including persuasive language, accurately and appropriately when producing complex spoken and written texts
ELD Standard/Skill **Understanding text structure** (CCSS 2)	Apply analysis of the organizational structure of different text types to comprehending and writing increasingly clear and cohesive arguments, informative/explanatory texts and narratives	Apply analysis of the organizational structure of different text types to comprehending texts and to writing clear and cohesive arguments, informative/explanatory texts, and narratives
ELD Standard/Skill **Writing:** literary and informational texts (CCSS 2)	Write longer literary and informational texts collaboratively and independently using appropriate text organization and a growing understanding of register	Write longer and more detailed literary and informational texts collaboratively and independently using appropriate text organization and register
CCSS–Production and Distribution of Writing		
ELD Standard/Skill **Writing:** summaries (CCSS 4)	Write increasingly concise summaries of texts and experiences using complete sentences and key words	Write clear and coherent summaries of texts using complete and concise sentences and key words

	Expanding	Bridging
ELD Standard/Skill **Interacting via written English** (CCSS 5)	Collaborate with peers to engage in increasingly complex grade-appropriate written exchanges and writing projects, using technology as appropriate	Collaborate with peers to engage in a variety of extended written exchanges and complex grade-appropriate writing projects, using technology as appropriate
CCSS–Research to Build and Present Knowledge		
ELD Standard/Skill **Selecting language resources:** using a variety of words (CCSS 7 & 8)	Use an increasing variety of grade-appropriate general academic words and domain-specific academic words accurately and appropriately when producing increasingly complex spoken and written texts	Use a variety of grade-appropriate and domain-specific academic words and phrases, including persuasive language, accurately and appropriately when producing complex spoken and written texts
ELD Standard/Skill **Selecting language resources:** use knowledge of morphology (CCSS 7 & 8)	Use knowledge of morphology to appropriately select affixes in a growing number of ways to manipulate language	Use knowledge of morphology to appropriately select affixes in a variety of ways to manipulate language
ELD Standard/Skill **Understanding cohesion:** apply knowledge of resources (CCSS 9)	Apply knowledge of a growing number of language resources for referring to make texts more cohesive to comprehending and writing increasingly cohesive texts for specific purposes and audiences	Apply knowledge of a variety of language resources for referring to make texts more cohesive to comprehending grade-level texts and to writing clear and cohesive grade-level texts for specific purposes and audiences
CCSS–Range of Writing		
ELD Standard/Skill **Connecting ideas** (CCSS 10)	Combine clauses in a growing number of ways to create compound and complex sentences that make connections between and link concrete and abstract ideas, for example, to express a reason or to make a concession	Combine clauses in a variety of ways to create compound and complex sentences that make connections between and link concrete and abstract ideas, for example, to make a concession or to establish cause
ELD Standard/Skill **Condensing ideas** (CCSS 10) (CCSS 6 throughout)	Condense ideas in a growing number of ways to create precise and detailed simple, compound, and complex sentences	Condense ideas in a variety of ways to create precise simple, compound, and complex sentences that condense concrete and abstract ideas

Source: California Department of Education (2012b); Common Core State Standards (2010).

(high school, grades 9–10), the writing skills outlined in the CCSS for Literacy in History/Social Studies, Science, and Technical Subjects are used as a foundation to frame the same skills from ELD/ELP state standards. To illustrate this connection, the California ELD standards are presented in the tables as they were developed in alignment with the CCSS.

For middle school (Table 5.1), the Grade 7 California ELD standards are used, and Grades 9–10 standards are used for high school (Table 5.2). To further demonstrate the alignment to the Common Core, some of the ELD/ELP standards are listed multiple times as they line up to several of the CCSS. In the tables, skills outlined for the writing standards for the two "higher" proficiency levels of expanding and bridging are presented. The tables provide a guide to which writing skills English learners need to attain in content area classes for proficiency in this language domain. While this chapter focuses on writing skills, the blended skills for all language domains—listening, speaking, reading, and writing—used in this book can be found in Appendix A.

What Do Writing Skills Look Like at the Different Proficiency Levels?

The ELD standards compiled for this book are divided into five proficiency levels. The writing skills outlined in Tables 5.1 and 5.2 are used because they represent two common proficiency levels, expanding and bridging, of English learners in content area classes. The specific writing skill listed under each proficiency level represents the ELD standard for that level. At each level, English learners can independently and automatically perform each language skill identified. Using the writing skill of justifying/arguing–justify opinions and positions as an example, a bridging-level English learner in high school (grades 9–12) can justify opinions and persuade others by making connections and distinctions between ideas and texts and articulating sufficient, detailed, and relevant textual evidence using appropriate register. A bridging-level English learner is proficient enough in English to perform this skill independently and automatically, or without the assistance from a teacher or peers. In contrast, for the same writing standards, an English learner at the emerging level has attained a level of proficiency to justify opinions by articulating some textual evidence with visual support. Because the complexity of the writing skills an English learner can perform independently and automatically increases with each proficiency level, teachers need to know their students' proficiency levels in each of the language domains so they have an accurate portrait of what their students can do.

It should be noted that in ELD or ELP standards for states that outline skills in five proficiency levels, a standard may not be stated for each writing skill. English learners who are not as proficient—for example, those at the entering level—have not attained the level of proficiency needed to justify opinions and positions or persuade others in a writing assignment. It is not considered a skill that English learners at the entering proficiency level can do independently and automatically. Following are snapshots of what English learners can do independently and automatically in writing skills at each proficiency level. The snapshots are not meant to be a comprehensive listing of all the writing skills, but rather can be used to paint a portrait of the general skills an English learner can perform at that level.

Middle School Grades 6–8

Entering At the entering level, English learners can write simple sentences or phrases with some assistance. They can write brief narratives and stories as well as simple descriptions and compositions that include a main idea and some details but with little grammatical form. Entering-level English learners can organize and record information by displaying it in pictures, lists, charts, and tables. They can identify basic vocabulary words and mechanics in a piece of writing and can edit their own work to correct punctuation.

Emerging At the emerging level, English learners can create simple summaries of texts from their notes or graphic organizers individually and collaboratively with peers using technology when appropriate. They can write short informational and literary texts using models provided either collaboratively with peers or individually. Emerging-level students can express their attitudes or opinions with some basic modal expressions and justify their opinions by providing some evidence with visual supports. In their writing, they can use a select number of general academic and domain-specific words and use knowledge of morphology to appropriately select affixes in basic ways. They can understand how different text types are organized to express ideas in their own basic writing. Emerging English learners apply their knowledge of language resources to make texts they are writing more cohesive. They can connect their ideas, events, and reasons when they write by using words such as "and," "but," and "because."

Developing At the developing level, English learners can create summaries of texts from their notes or graphic organizers individually and collaboratively with peers using technology when appropriate. They can write informational and literary texts using complex vocabulary and sentences either collaboratively with peers or individually. Developing-level students can express their attitudes or opinions with some modal expressions and justify their opinions by providing evidence with visual supports. In their writing, developing-level students can use some general academic and domain-specific words and use knowledge of morphology to appropriately select affixes in basic ways. They can understand how different text types are organized to express ideas in their own writing of short compositions and reports with a clear purpose. Developing English learners apply their knowledge of language resources to make texts they are writing more cohesive and can connect their ideas, events, and reasons.

Expanding At the expanding level, English learners can create coherent summaries of texts on a variety of topics from their notes or graphic organizers individually and collaboratively with peers using technology when appropriate. They can write short informational and literary texts using appropriate text organization and development either collaboratively with peers or individually. Expanding-level students can express their attitudes or opinions with a variety of familiar modal expressions and justify their opinions and persuade others by providing relevant text evidence. In their writing, expanding-level students can use a growing set of academic and domain-specific words and use knowledge of morphology to appropriately select affixes in a growing number of ways to manipulate language. They can understand the stylistic and organizational features of different text types to express ideas in their own writing. Expanding English learners apply their knowledge of language resources to make texts they are writing more cohesive. They can combine clauses in an increasing variety of ways to make connections and join ideas, events, and reasons when they write by using phrases such as "as a result" and "on the other hand."

Bridging At the bridging level, English learners can create concise and coherent summaries of texts on a variety of topics from their notes using appropriate text organization and development using technology when appropriate. Bridging-level students can express their attitudes or opinions with nuanced modal expressions and justify their opinions and persuade others by providing detailed and relevant text evidence. In their writing, bridging-level students can use an expanded set of academic and domain-specific words, synonyms, antonyms, and figurative language and use knowledge of morphology to appropriately select affixes in a variety of ways to manipulate language. They can understand the stylistic and organizational features of different text types to write cohesive texts that maintain a consistent style and tone. Bridging-level English learners apply their knowledge of language resources to make texts they are writing more cohesive. When they write, they combine clauses in a wide variety of ways to make connections and join ideas, events, and reasons or to evaluate an argument by using phrases such as "consequently" and "in other words."

High School Grades 9–12

Entering At the entering level, English learners can write simple sentences or phrases with some assistance. They can write brief narratives and stories as well as simple descriptions and compositions that include a main idea and some details but with little grammatical form. Entering-level English learners can organize and record information by displaying it in pictures, lists, charts, and tables. They are able to identify basic vocabulary words and mechanics in a piece of writing and can edit their own work to correct punctuation, capitalization, and spelling.

Emerging At the emerging level, English learners can create short summaries of grade-appropriate texts using key words and phrases. They can write short informational and literary texts using models provided for support either collaboratively with peers or individually. Emerging-level students can express their attitudes or opinions with familiar modal expressions and justify their opinions by articulating textual evidence with visual supports. In their writing, emerging-level students can use familiar general academic and domain-specific words and use knowledge of morphology to appropriately select basic affixes. They can understand how different text types are organized by identifying basic and linguistic elements in them and apply that knowledge to their own basic writing.

Emerging-level English learners apply their knowledge of language resources to make texts they are writing more cohesive by sequencing and summarizing information. They can connect word, clauses, and phrases when they write by using words such as "and," "but," and "because."

Developing At the developing level, English learners can create summaries of grade-appropriate texts using key words and phrases and consistent grammatical form. They can write informational and literary texts that include a thesis and some supporting details either collaboratively with peers or individually. Developing-level students can express their attitudes or opinions with familiar modal expressions and justify their opinions and persuade others by articulating textual evidence with visual supports. In their writing, developing-level students can use general academic and domain-specific words and use knowledge of morphology to appropriately select basic affixes. They can explain how different text types are organized by identifying basic and linguistic elements in them and apply that knowledge to their own basic writing. Developing-level English learners apply their knowledge of language resources to make texts they are writing more cohesive and can connect word, clauses, and phrases in them.

Expanding At the expanding level, English learners can create increasingly concise summaries of grade-appropriate texts using key words and phrases. They can write informational and literary texts on a range of personal and academic topics using appropriate text organization and development either collaboratively with peers or individually. Expanding-level students can express their attitudes or opinions with a variety of familiar modal expressions and justify their opinions and persuade others by making connections between ideas and articulating relevant textual evidence. In their writing, expanding-level students can use a variety of general academic and domain-specific words accurately and appropriately and use knowledge of morphology to appropriately select affixes in a growing number of ways to manipulate language. They can analyze the stylistic and organizational features of various text types and apply that knowledge to writing increasingly cohesive narrative, explanatory, and persuasive texts on grade-appropriate topics that maintain a consistent style and tone. Expanding English learners apply their knowledge of language resources to make texts they read and are writing more cohesive. They can combine clauses in increasingly complex ways to create simple, compound, and complex sentences that describe, explain, and summarize information and ideas.

Bridging At the bridging level, English learners can create coherent and concise summaries of grade-appropriate texts using key words and phrases. They can write informational and literary texts on a range of personal and academic topics using appropriate text organization, development, and register depending on content area, topic, audience, and purpose either collaboratively with peers or individually. Bridging-level students can express their attitudes or opinions with nuanced modal expressions and justify their opinions or persuade others by making connections and distinctions between ideas and articulating sufficient, detailed, and relevant textual evidence. In their writing, bridging-level students can use a variety of grade-appropriate general academic and domain-specific words and phrases, including persuasive language, accurately and appropriately and use knowledge of morphology to appropriately select affixes in a variety of ways to manipulate language. They can analyze the stylistic and organizational features of various genres and apply that knowledge to writing increasingly cohesive narrative, explanatory, and persuasive texts on grade-appropriate topics that maintain a consistent style and tone. Bridging-level English learners apply their knowledge of language resources to make texts they read and are writing more cohesive. When they write, bridging-level students can combine clauses in complex ways to create simple, compound, and complex sentences that describe or link concrete and abstract ideas, explain procedures and sequences, summarize texts and ideas, and present and critique points of view.

How Can I Differentiate My Instruction Based on My English Learners' Writing Proficiency Levels?

Teachers can differentiate instruction in the language domain of writing for their English learners at any proficiency level. Using the four-step lesson planning process outlined in this book, incorporating writing skills into lessons is covered in the first two steps: know your English learners and choose standards for your lessons. Each of the steps in the process is described in detail in the Introduction (Chapter 1) as well as in Part 3 (Chapters 6–9) in the context of planning and teaching lessons in content area classes. Below is an expanded description of the first two steps in the lesson planning process to help teachers fully understand what they need to know about their English learners' language proficiency levels and how to use that information to accurately choose ELD or ELP standards for their lessons. Following these descriptions is an explanation of how to incorporate writing skills throughout the school year in your lessons.

Step 1: Know Your English Learners

Understanding your English learners' language proficiency levels is key in knowing who your English learners are so you can begin to plan and teach lessons that are equitable for all your students. In the language domain of writing, equitable planning and teaching starts with learning what skills English learners can do at each proficiency level. For the English learners in your class, you can identify students' writing proficiency levels through standardized test scores, language proficiency test scores, discussions with the ELD coordinator at your school, or a combination of any these methods. States with a designated percentage of English learners in public schools will have a systematic method for assessing proficiency in the language domains. In California, for example, English learners take a statewide assessment annually, the California English Language Development Test (CELDT), to assess their proficiency level in each language domain. English learners' CELDT scores are determined at the state level, communicated to districts and schools, and then made available to teachers. While this example describes the assessment process in California, it is similar to the processes in other states that have English learner student populations. Depending on the state, English learners' proficiency is divided into multiple levels, usually a range of three to six levels. State departments of education have descriptions of each proficiency level as well as the ELD/ELP standards used available for teachers to view (generally accessible on their websites). Content area teachers can contact their school administrators and/or ELD coordinators at the school or district level for the methods and processes used to identify English learners enrolled in their classes. Once teachers understand the processes used to identify English learners' writing proficiency levels along with the identified proficiency levels for all English learners in their class, they can choose appropriate ELD or ELP standards for their lessons.

Step 2: Choose Standards for Your Lessons

After an English learner's writing proficiency level is determined, the next step in the planning process is to choose a writing ELD standard for the lesson. As described earlier in this chapter, English learners can perform each writing skill outlined in the ELD or ELP standards for their identified proficiency levels independently and automatically at that level. Therefore when lesson planning, teachers should choose the writing skill that is one level above an English learner's current proficiency level (i+1). English learners will use their current proficiency skills as a base to build upon to continually develop their English language skills while learning knowledge in content area classes. For example, if English learners are identified at the emerging level in the language domain of writing, then teachers should select the ELD standard at the expanding level for their lesson. Teachers target their instruction at the expanding level by scaffolding their instruction through strategies and activities that make the content accessible to their emerging English learners (as described in the content chapters in Part 3).

After choosing ELD standards based on English learners' proficiency levels, one step above their current level, teachers then write a language objective aligned to the standard that is observable and measurable. The next step is to design an assessment based on the language objective to determine if English learners have mastered the writing skill chosen for the lesson. In classes that enroll English learners at multiple proficiency levels, the assessment should be differentiated based on the skill level identified for each English learner in class (one level above their current proficiency level). Examples of how to differentiate assessments based on English learners' proficiency levels are described in each content area chapter (Chapters 6–9).

Example #1:

- I have English learners in my 7th-grade English class who have been identified at the emerging level.
- I will choose the skill justifying/arguing—justify opinions and positions to incorporate into my lesson.
- My emerging-level students can demonstrate justify opinions and positions by providing some textual evidence with substantial support independently and automatically.
- I will choose the skill at the expanding level, justify opinions or persuade others by providing relevant textual evidence with moderate support, for my lesson.
- I will scaffold my instruction by using instructional strategies and designing student activities that support my emerging-level English learners so that by the end of the lesson, they can write a paper in which they justify their opinion and persuade others of their position by providing relevant evidence from the assigned text.

Example #2:

- I have several English learners in my 10th-grade World History class who have been identified at the emerging and expanding levels.
- From the ELD standards, I will choose the skill of writing summaries to use in my lesson.
- My emerging-level students can write brief summaries of texts and experiences using complete sentences and key words independently and automatically.
- My expanding-level students can write increasingly concise summaries of texts and experiences using complete sentences and key words independently and automatically.
- For my emerging English learners, I will choose the expanding-level skill described above, write increasingly concise summaries of texts and experiences using complete sentences and key words.
- For my expanding English learners, I will choose the bridging level skill, write clear and coherent summaries of texts and experiences using complex and concise sentences and key words.
- I will scaffold my instruction by using instructional strategies and designing student activities so that by the end of the lesson, my emerging English learners can write a concise summary using some key words and phrases on Imperialism in my World History class. My expanding English learners also will write a summary on Imperialism but will be expected to write a coherent and concise summary using key words and phrases.

Incorporating Writing Skills into Lessons Throughout the Year

Targeting instruction at one proficiency level above an English learner's current level will increase his or her writing proficiency. English learners need to practice all the writing skills at the higher proficiency level throughout the year in order to become proficient writers in English. Content area teachers should continually incorporate all the skills listed in Table 5.1 for middle school English learners and Table 5.2 for high school students into their lessons throughout the school year. To facilitate this, a checklist of writing skills along with skills in the other language domains of listening, speaking, and reading is provided in Appendix B. Next to each skill on the list, there are blank spaces for teachers to record the date the skill was taught. This gives teachers a guide to assist them in ensuring that all writing skills are repeatedly covered throughout the year and that they are not relying on one or two skills while neglecting the others. The checklist also assists teachers in tracking their English learners' progress on each of the writing skills, as well as on the subskills embedded within each skill. This checklist for writing skills is particularly important given the focus on writing in all content area classes in the CCSS. Teachers can refer to their checklist to determine which writing skills and subskills their English learners need to continually develop more fully as the year progresses.

Summary

As you reflect on the information provided in this chapter on writing skills, keep in mind these main points:

- Language development skills that English learners need to develop in order to become fully proficient in English, including skills in the area of writing, are presented in ELD/ELP standards. In the area of writing, the skills presented in ELD/ELP standards are aligned to the Common Core State Standards (CCSS) for English Language Arts, as well as the CCSS for Social Studies and Science.
- It is important to remember that middle and high school English learners need to continually develop their writing skills through out the year and across all content areas. English learners become proficient writers by going through a writing process where they continually write, edit, revise, and rewrite texts. While writing that is assigned in an English language arts class is different from an assignment in a mathematics class, English learners need to develop their writing skills across all content area classes. Therefore, teachers should plan writing activities in their classes that help their English learners become proficient writers of all types of texts.
- Teachers need to learn their English learners' proficiency levels in the area of writing. Once they do so, teachers can then differentiate their instruction so they are incorporating a variety of writing skills into their lessons that are just beyond their English learners' current level (what the student can currently do independently and automatically).

Applying What You Have Learned

In this chapter, you have learned about a variety of writing skills that English learners must develop in order to become proficient in English. Demonstrate your understanding of the chapter by participating in the following activities and responding to the corresponding questions.

- Determine which of your students are classified as English learners. Using the data provided by your school or district, determine each student's proficiency level in the area of writing. Review the reading skills presented in this chapter (justifying/arguing—express opinions; justifying/arguing—justify opinions; understanding text structure; writing—literary and informational texts; writing–summaries; interacting via written English; selecting language resources—using a variety of words; selecting language resources— use knowledge of morphology; understanding cohesion—apply knowledge of resources; connecting ideas; and condensing ideas).
- What does each writing skill look like at my English learner students' different proficiency levels?
- What writing skills presented in this chapter can I incorporate into teaching for my English learner students? Identify at least three classroom activities you use in your teaching where you can incorporate one of the writing skills presented in this chapter.
- For the writing skills you identified above to incorporate in your three classroom activities, how will you differentiate you instruction based on your English learners' writing proficiency level(s)?

part 3

Differentiated Instruction in Content Classrooms

Ian Wedgewood/Pearson Education

The four chapters presented in this section outline a process that middle and high school teachers can use to design lessons that incorporate language, literacy, and content objectives based on English language development (ELD) standards, Common Core State Standards, and content standards for their English learners. The chapters explain how to differentiate instruction and assessment based on English learners' language proficiency levels and then outline strategies teachers can use in their English language arts, mathematics, science, and social studies classrooms to help their students understand the content. Middle and high school content area classes can have enrollments that range from one or two English learners at the same proficiency level to an entire class or a vast majority of English learner students at various proficiency levels. The lesson planning process described in these chapters can be used in classes in any context with any number of English learners enrolled at a variety of proficiency levels.

The principle of backwards mapping is used in this book to design lessons. Following this principle, teachers start the lesson planning process by identifying the content and language standards to include in their lessons. Teachers then write content and language objectives based on those standards that are observable and measurable. Next, teachers design assessments that are aligned to standards chosen and objectives written for them. Finally, teachers select classroom activities that are aligned to the standards, objectives, and assessments that have been chosen and that are designed to help their English learners access the content presented. When possible, culturally relevant/multicultural resources should be incorporated into the lesson to help keep students engaged in the content.

Chapters in this section first present a detailed description of each step in the process to design content lessons that are equitable for English learners. To further exemplify how teachers can use this process, lesson examples that have been adapted from those designed and taught by middle and high school teachers and teacher candidates are provided. These examples are followed by an analysis of the content lessons that highlights the reasons why instructional strategies chosen, activities presented, and culturally relevant/multicultural resources selected in the lessons benefit English learners.

chapter 6

English Language Arts

Learning Outcomes and Focus Questions

STEP 1: Know your English learners

- What difficulties might my English learners have with the Common Core State Standards for English Language Arts?
- What do I need to know about my English learners to plan instruction?

STEP 2: Choose standards for your lessons

- What content standards will my lesson focus on?
- How do I design lessons that include language standards and objectives in my English language arts class?

STEP 3: Design differentiated assessments and student-centered activities

- How can I differentiate my assessments to accurately assess English learners?
- What strategies can I use to help English learners master the content I am teaching?
- What activities can I implement in my class to promote interactions between English learners and native-English speakers?

STEP 4: Select culturally relevant/multicultural materials and resources

- How can I find culturally relevant/multicultural resources to use in my English language arts class?

This chapter outlines a process middle and high school teachers can use to design lessons that incorporate language objectives based on ELD standards alongside content objectives from the Common Core State Standards (CCSS) for English Language Arts for their English learners. Much of the content in middle and high school English language arts classes is built on knowledge that has been taught in previous English language arts classes in elementary, middle, and high school. An English learner who immigrates to the United States in 9th grade may not have the same foundational knowledge in the English language as his or her peers and/or the knowledge of literature, stories, poems, and other texts that are familiar to students who have attended U.S. schools in elementary and middle school. The need for English learners to develop academic language skills in English language arts that they can transfer to other content classes is another critical element of their overall academic success in middle and high school. Content presented in middle and high school English language arts classes includes extensive vocabulary development, many complex and abstract concepts, and culturally specific contexts presented in literature that may be unfamiliar to immigrant students. It is therefore important to design scaffolded activities that help build that background base of knowledge for English learners and to teach them the processes and procedures used in your class so they have opportunities to expand their vocabulary and more time to fully process and learn the meaning of newly presented concepts. While it may seem challenging, teachers can design activities to give students the time and learning support they need to fully process the meaning of English language arts content and thus increase their opportunities to excel academically.

STEP 1: Know your English learners

What Difficulties Might My English Learners Have with the Common Core State Standards for English Language Arts?

The CCSS for English Language Arts are divided into four areas:

1. Reading—literature and information texts
2. Writing
3. Speaking and listening
4. Language

Within each area, there are corresponding standards. Ten standards in reading and writing fall into these categories:

Reading	Writing
Key ideas and details	Text type and purposes
Craft and structure	Production and distribution of writing
Integration of knowledge and ideas	Research to build and present knowledge
Range of readings and level of text complexity	Range of writing

The ten standards in reading and ten in writing are aligned to the CCSS for Literacy in History/Social Studies, Science, and Technical Subjects. Additionally, the CCSS for English Language Arts contain six standards in speaking and listening in the two areas of comprehension and collaboration and presentation of knowledge and ideas, as well as six standards in these areas of language: conventions of standard English, knowledge of language, and vocabulary acquisition and use. The speaking and listening and language standards are unique to the CCSS for English Language Arts; these language development areas are not covered in the CCSS for Literacy in History/Social Studies, Science, and Technical Subjects. The information presented in this chapter is not intended to be an extensive description of the CCSS for English Language Arts, but rather a discussion of the difficulties English learners may have with the standards.

The CCSS for English Language Arts are developmental standards that start in kindergarten and progress through the 12th grade. The literacy skills outlined in the standards for middle school (grades 6, 7, and 8) and high school (grades 9–10 and 11–12) for any given standard require advanced levels of language development that some English learner students may not have attained. For example, what follows is the progression of the literacy skills required by Reading Standard #7: Integration of knowledge and ideas for informational texts:

- *Grade 6:* **integrate** information presented in different media or formats as well as in words to develop a coherent understanding of the topic or issue
- *Grade 7:* **compare and contrast** a text to an audio, video, or multimedia version of the text, **analyzing** each medium's portrayal of the subject
- *Grade 8:* e**valuate** the advantages and disadvantages of using different mediums to present a particular topic or idea

A comparison of the 8th-grade CCSS skills in reading to the skills outlined in the corresponding ELD standards for interpretive—reading/viewing closely shows that the CCSS represent a more complex literacy skill of "evaluating" knowledge. (For the purposes of this example, California ELD standards are used. Please note that ELD standards from other states yield the same comparisons.) In middle school (grades 6–8), an English learner at the bridging level (the highest level) can perform the following reading skills independently or without the aid of a teacher:

> Interpretive—reading/viewing closely (bridging): **Explain** ideas, phenomena, processes, and text relationships (e.g., compare/contrast, cause/effect, problem/solution) based on close reading of a variety of grade-level texts and viewing of multimedia with light support.

It is clear that the skill of *explain* represents less complex literacy abilities than *evaluate* does. If English learners at the bridging level have not yet developed the literacy skills necessary to successfully master the CCSS, then the gap for English learners at lower proficiency levels is unattainable without explicit language development instruction and scaffolding by teachers.

A similar gap exists between the level of the literacy skills outlined in the CCSS for English Language Arts and those outlined in the corresponding California ELD standards (grades 11–12) for high school English learners. Consider the description of literacy skills for the same CCSS Reading Standard #7: Integration of knowledge and ideas for informational texts for high school students:

- *Grades 9–10:* **analyze** various accounts of a subject told in different mediums, determining which details are emphasized in each account
- *Grades 11–12:* **integrate and evaluate** multiple sources of information presented in different media or formats as well as in words in order to address a question or solve a problem

A high school English learner (grades 11–12) at the bridging level can independently perform the following skill in reading/viewing closely:

> **Explain** ideas, phenomena, processes, and relationships within and across texts (e.g., compare/contrast, cause/effect, themes) based on close reading of a variety of grade-level texts, presented in various print and multimedia formats, using a variety of detailed sentences, and precise, nuanced general academic and domain-specific words.

As with a middle school English learner, the gap between *explain* and *integrate and evaluate* is significant. Without explicit scaffolding and consistent language development by teachers, it will be extremely challenging for English learners to perform the skills outlined in the CCSS for English Language Arts. Similar issues exist in the area of writing, where the gap between the skills that English learners have attained and those outlined in the CCSS must be addressed.

Another matter to consider regarding English learners and the CCSS is the language skills they develop in English language arts classes that are necessary to succeed in other content area classes. The CCSS for Literacy in History/Social Studies, Science, and Technical Subjects cover reading and writing skills. However, to become proficient in English, English learners must fully develop their listening and speaking skills as well. Similarly, English learners need to develop knowledge of the English language and academic vocabulary in order to master the level of academic English needed to develop the skills outlined in the CCSS for Literacy in English Language Arts and other content areas. For English learners to attain these skills, English language arts teachers should explicitly teach these students how to transfer the listening, speaking, and language skills learned in their classes to other content area classes. Given these challenges, the role that English language arts teachers play in the overall academic success of middle and high school English learners cannot be overstated. English language arts teachers who differentiate their language instruction for English learners based on their proficiency levels and teach language development skills simultaneously with the literacy skills required in the CCSS are giving their English learner students the foundation they need to be successful in all content area classes.

What Do I Need to Know About My English Learners to Plan Instruction?

The more information you learn about your English learner students, the greater the opportunities they will have to be academically successful in your English language arts class. For example, learning about your students' academic knowledge of the English language, knowledge of literature, and self-identification of their strengths and weaknesses with the language and content can help you understand which concepts will be accessible to them and which will need to be scaffolded more explicitly. Along with academic knowledge, it will be helpful to gauge English learners' English language proficiency levels in the four language domains of listening, speaking, reading, and writing. How an English learner's proficiency levels in the language domains are determined is described in detail in Part 2 of this book. It is important to know your English learners' proficiency level in each of the language domains so you can choose an ELD standard for your lesson at the level needed to scaffold students' English language development. This information helps focus on addressing language issues English learners may have with English language arts content. A survey administered at the beginning of the year also can help you understand what languages are spoken at home, which languages students use to speak to their friends, what they know about the content you will teach, and what difficulties students feel they may have with the content and vocabulary of an English classroom. You can also ask questions to enhance your understanding of your English learners' interests, extracurricular activities, goals in the class, and broader goals they have for their lives.

Understanding your English learners' learning styles allows you to design lessons to include teaching strategies and student activities that build on students' strengths and help them develop in areas of weaknesses. For students who are visual learners, presenting information through modes such as pictures, graphic organizers, and charts will help them access the content you are presenting. Information presented in other formats such as through a lecture (auditory) should include opportunities for you to check with English learners with a visual learning preference to demonstrate they know the content. Finally, a familiarity with your English learners' (and all your students') backgrounds, interests, cultural and social affiliations, any other pertinent information that in combination makes your students "who they are" will help you plan lessons that include multicultural and culturally relevant literature and resources for them. The emphasis on identifying and using supplemental resources in the CCSS presents an opportunity to incorporate culturally relevant/multicultural literature and resources in your lessons. Doing so will help English learners make connections to the content and keep them engaged in all aspects of lessons.

STEP 2: Choose standards for your lessons

What Content Standards Will My Lesson Focus on?

The sequence of how you present content standards in your English language arts class is most likely determined locally by your department, school, or district. However the content standards are chosen for each lesson you teach, it is important to note that they represent the "what" of your lesson, the content being taught. The CCSS for Literacy in English Language Arts present many complex literacy skills that will require multiple opportunities for students to practice the skills in order to develop mastery of the standard. Once the content standard being taught is determined, the next step is to write an objective based on the standard to guide the lesson. A content objective should be measurable and observable and let you and your students know what they will be able to do by the end of the lesson.

Example:

- I am teaching a 7th-grade English class and have chosen the Reading Standard for Informational Text: Craft and Structure 6: "Determine an author's point of view or purpose in a text and analyze how the author distinguishes his or her position from that of others."
- I write a content objective for my lesson based on the standard: Students will be able to work with a partner to write a paragraph describing the author's point of view in the assigned article and provide 2–3 examples of how it differs from other positions presented in the previous assigned articles.

Because the CCSS for English Language Arts are performance-based, many of them are already observable and sometimes measurable. Therefore, an objective you write for your lesson may either be the standard itself or closely aligned to it. For example, most of the five specific standards for the Anchor Writing Standard 3 under Text Types and Purposes—"Write narratives to develop real or imagined experiences or events using effective technique, well-chosen details, and well-structured event sequences"—already are observable performances. If you are teaching a 10th-grade English class, you may choose to focus your lesson on standard d under CCSS Anchor Writing Standard 3: "Use precise words and phrases, telling details, and sensory language to convey a vivid picture of the experiences, events, setting, and/or characters."Thus, your objective can focus on all or part of the standard by adding measurability: "Students will be able to use 3 precise words or phrases and 2 telling details of the event in their descriptive paragraph." Other specific standards under the anchor standards can be taught at another time during the school year.

How Do I Design Lessons That Include Language Standards and Objectives in My English Language Arts Class?

If the content standards represent the "what" of any lesson, then the ELD standards represent the "how" for English learners—how they will master the content standard chosen at the appropriate proficiency level. The process for choosing ELD standards in the areas of listening, speaking, reading, and writing to include in lessons was outlined in detail in Part 2 of this book. Briefly, teachers should choose a language standard that complements the content standard addressed in the lesson. Once a standard is chosen, teachers then write a language objective for the lesson that outlines how students will demonstrate that they have met the standard.

Example:

- I have English learners at the expanding (exit stage) proficiency level in the language area of reading in my 10th-grade English class.
- I select the skill Reading—Analyze language choices to include in my lesson (from the ELD standards, Grades 9–10).
- I use the standard that is one level above my students' current proficiency level. The standard at the bridging level reads: "Explain how a writer's or speaker's choice of a variety of different types of phrasing or words produces nuances and different effects on the audience."
- I write a language objective based on the standard: After students have read the three assigned texts, they will be able to write a paragraph explaining two types of phrasing used by the author and the effect each has on the reader.

English learners should have as much practice as possible with the English language in order to become proficient in all four language domains and attain the academic English they need to succeed across all their content area classes. Teachers can choose activities that incorporate several language skills to include in their lessons to help English learners practice their language skills. However, it is recommended that each lesson focuses on one or two language standards. As assessment is aligned to the standards chosen, this allows the assessment to specifically focus on the one or two language skills so teachers can accurately assess if English learners have mastered them.

STEP 3: Design differentiated assessments and student-centered activities

How Can I Differentiate My Assessment to Accurately Assess English Learners?

Once English learners' proficiency levels are determined in any language domain, they can perform language skills at those levels independently and automatically. Targeting instruction one proficiency level above their current level helps English learners build their knowledge of the English language and attain overall language proficiency. Following this tenet, an accurate assessment for English learners should be targeted at one level above their current proficiency level as well. Using California ELD standards as an example, English learners who demonstrate exiting-stage skills at the emerging level should be assessed on the expanding standards. Similarly, using the World-Class Instructional Design and Assessment (WIDA) standards, English learners who are proficient at the developing level should be assessed at the expanding level (for both examples, one level above their current level). In either example, for an English learner at the emerging level, assessments designed at proficiency levels above the expanding level may contain language skills and knowledge that are too far beyond the English learners' current proficiency to be accurate assessments. While English learners may have a general understanding of the content, they may not be proficient enough in English to communicate their mastery of the content in either oral or written form.

Following the backwards mapping principle, assessment should be aligned to the content and language standards chosen for each lesson as well as for the corresponding objective written for each standard. English language arts teachers who have both native-English speakers and English learners in their class can create one assessment plan for the lesson that includes both language and content. While the language objectives are specifically designed for English learners in the class, the skills covered in the language standards may also be beneficial for native-English-speaking students. The following example shows how teachers can assess both English learners and native-English-speaking students on how well they communicate the key ideas and details in a reading passage by using the listening and speaking standard of presenting—in this case an oral presentation. Lessons designed to guide English learners to develop their listening, speaking, reading, and writing skills also help native-English-speaking students with their English language development. In English language arts classes, all students can improve their language skills in listening, speaking, reading, and writing as a result of the explicit focus teachers place on these skills for their English learner students.

Example:

- The English learners in my 9th-grade English Language Arts class are at the emerging (exit stage) and expanding (exit stage) levels.
- We are reading a literature passage, and the CCSS for English Language Arts standard for the lesson is Reading: Key Ideas and Details (Grades 9–10) Anchor Standard 1: "Cite strong and thorough textual evidence to support analysis of what the text says explicitly as well as inferences drawn from the text."
- I am using the California ELD standard for grades 10–11 on presenting so my English learners can practice their academic English skills by working collaboratively with peers to plan and deliver an oral presentation on the assigned literature passage. I choose the ELD standards that are one level above my students' current proficiency levels for my assessment.

  Expanding: Plan and deliver a variety of oral presentations and reports on grade-appropriate topics that present evidence and facts to support ideas using a growing understanding of register.

  Bridging: Plan and deliver a variety of oral presentations and reports on grade-appropriate topics that express complex and abstract ideas, are well supported by evidence and reasoning, and are delivered using an appropriate level of formality and understanding of register.
- My class is working in groups of four to collectively analyze the assigned literature passage, citing specific evidence to support their analyses and discussing inferences that can be drawn from the text. Drawing from their notes, class discussions, and these group discussions, groups then create a five-minute oral presentation for the class.
- I create a rubric for the lesson that includes both the content and language objectives.
- I assess my English learners on the language objective that is one level above their current level: expanding for my emerging level students (a 3 on the rubric) and bridging for students at the expanding level (a 4 on the rubric).
- I assess the language objective both informally during group work and formally during the oral presentations. I assess the CCSS for English Language Arts content standard based on the oral presentation the group creates using the criteria I have included in the rubric.

For English learners, the assessment is equitable in that it accurately assesses their presentation skills based on the language proficiency level that is one level above their current level, as shown in the rubric in Table 6.1.

Table 6.1 Sample Rubric That Differentiates Assessment for English Learners

	1	2	3	4
Language Development: Presenting (ELD standard)	Plan and deliver a short (2–3 minutes) presentation with no focus or clear thesis	Plan and deliver a short (3–4 minutes) presentation with focus and a clear thesis	Plan and deliver a 5-minute presentation following an organized process, presenting 1–2 facts to support their ideas	Plan and deliver a 5-minute presentation following an organized process, presenting 3–4 facts to support complex ideas
Content (CCSS): Cite strong and thorough textual evidence to support analysis and inferences drawn from the text.	1–2 sources of evidence provided to support explicit analysis drawn from the text	1–2 sources of evidence provided to support explicit analysis of the text AND to support inferences drawn from the text	2–3 strong sources of evidence provided to support explicit analysis of the text AND support inferences drawn from the text	3–4 strong and thorough sources of evidence provided to support explicit analysis of the text AND support inferences drawn from the text

What Strategies Can I Use to Help English Learners Master the Content I Am Teaching?

Underlying any strategy teachers use to help English learners in their English language arts classes is the principle that teachers have high expectations of their students. Displaying and explaining the lesson content and language objectives ensures that English learners understand your expectations and goals for the day and allows them to focus on the main idea of the lesson. English learners can learn literature and language content when it is presented through strategies such as SDAIE (specially designed academic instruction in English) designed to help make challenging content accessible to English learners in content area classrooms. Using multiple modes of presenting content, such as visuals, video, and multimedia, will give English learners a variety of methods to access the content. Additionally, teachers can use heterogeneous grouping strategies where English learners can learn from and share their knowledge with native-English speakers. If necessary, English learners should be given the opportunity to use their native language to negotiate the meaning of content with their peers and then translate that knowledge so they can fully participate in larger class discussions in English.

Let's look at how using graphic organizers can help make challenging content more accessible to English learners.

Graphic Organizers

Graphic organizers are used to visually present and organize information for students and can be utilized in any phase of a lesson to make the content accessible (Bromley, Irwin-DeVitis, & Modlo, 1995; Herrell & Jordan, 2012). Using graphic organizers with English learners helps them process

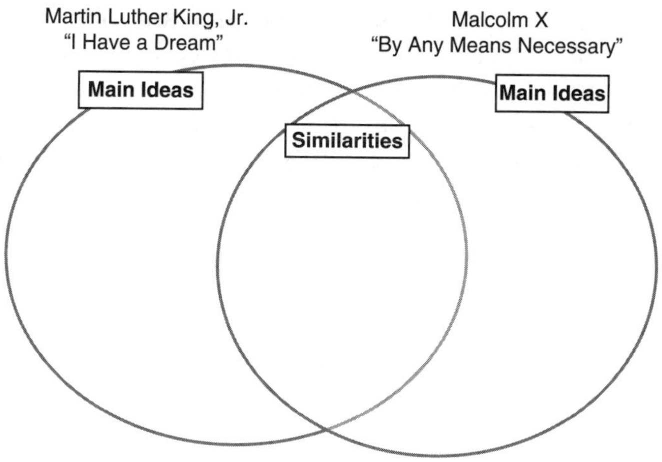

Figure 6.1 Example of a Venn Diagram from an 8th-Grade Lesson on Speech and Persuasion: African American Civil Rights Leaders—Martin Luther King, Jr., and Malcolm X

information, gives them a visual reference to use a guide, and provides them with necessary scaffolding. English learners at lower proficiency levels who may not yet have the skills to write an essay can use graphic organizers to demonstrate they understand a concept but cannot yet transfer their understanding into a coherent written format. There are countless types of graphic organizers, and teachers should choose whatever type fits the activity presented. For example, if students are comparing and contrasting information during the lesson, then a Venn diagram would be a good choice for a graphic organizer students can use to organize their ideas Figure 6.1. Whatever type of graphic organizer is used, English learners will benefit from seeing a visual representation of the information and concepts they are being taught.

In the *Into* phase of a lesson, graphic organizers can be used to organize new information (main idas) and/or vocabulary that will be taught during that lesson. In the *Through* phase of the lesson, graphic organizers can be used to organize information students will then use as a reference to write an essay or report. Finally, in the *Beyond* phase of the lesson, graphic organizers can provide a visual representation for information learned in the lesson or unit to be used as a study guide for an upcoming quiz or test.

What Activities Can I Implement in My Class to Promote Interactions Between English Learners and Native-English Speakers?

Using a variety of activities in English language arts classes allows students with different learning styles multiple ways to learn the content being presented. For English learners, designing lessons using activities that promote peer interactions allows them to communicate with their native-English-speaking peers. Students can learn from one another and learn the content while English learners have the added benefit of practicing their English, which leads to increased language development. English learners, like many students, need time to process new concepts learned and understand how these concepts are connected to and/or build on prior literature and/or language concepts presented in class. English learners also need as much time as possible to develop the academic language skills they will need to be successful across all their content classes. Designing activities so that English learners work with peers—with a partner or in small groups—gives them the necessary time to learn new concepts and practice vocabulary and academic English skills in the context of an English language arts class. Activities that promote peer interactions give English learners another method of equitable access to the same curriculum and core content as their native-English-speaking peers.

The following examples of jigsaw and quick write activities demonstrate how strategies like these can help achieve the goals of equal access to the core curriculum and increased peer interactions for English learners. Included in the appendices of this book is a list of all activities described in each content chapter (Chapters 6–9). These suggested activities for classroom use promote listening, speaking, reading, and writing skills for English learners. Numerous resources are available to teachers that outline effective classroom activities for English learners. Teachers should use classroom activities that they feel comfortable with and that match their teaching style and their students' learning styles. If students are familiar with an activity that has been used repeatedly in class and has proven effective in teaching content, teachers should continue to use it throughout the year. The routine of participating in familiar activities can help English learners focus on the content rather than on learning how to participate in a new activity.

Jigsaw Activity

A jigsaw activity is a cooperative learning technique in which students are given the opportunity to become "experts" on a piece of knowledge and then share their expertise with other students in the class (Aronson, 1978). In a class that enrolls English learners, a jigsaw activity is often used when a significant amount of text or a difficult text has been assigned. Students are divided into small groups (usually four per group), and each group is given a section of the text. Group members review the text and are assigned one of several reading tasks, such as:

- Answering questions about their section of the text
- Summarizing their section of the text
- Writing comprehension questions about their section of the text

Whatever task is chosen for the jigsaw activity, the goal is for all group members to understand what they have read and become experts on their section of text. When each group has completed their "expert" task, they will begin to teach the content of their section to the other groups. This can be done as group presentations to the whole class or as groups share their expert knowledge with one another. Teachers can also ask one member of each group to form a new group that will now consist of an "expert" on each topic the groups were asked to learn about. Each expert then shares his or her knowledge with one another in the new group. However teachers design their jigsaws, the activity allows English learners an opportunity to develop their English proficiency in all four language domains: listening, speaking, reading, and writing. Additionally, during a jigsaw activity, English learners can learn from and with their native-English-speaking peers.

Quick Write Activity

In a quick write activity, students begin to express their ideas on topics they are learning in class that can lead to a more structured writing assignment (Graves & Kittle, 2005). Students can complete a quick write activity during any phase of the lesson. As an *Into* activity, a quick write can be used as a review of information students have previously learned. Teachers can use the quick write to assess the amount and type of information students recall on the subject. Quick writes can also be used as a brainstorming tool to gauge how much students know about a topic that will be the focus of an upcoming lesson. As a *Through* activity, quick writes can serve as a foundation for a variety of writing activities, presentations, and discussions. As a *Beyond* activity, quick writes can be used as an assessment tool in many ways as students respond to a question about the lesson content, use vocabulary learned in the lesson, and recap key concepts.

- Present students with a topic, a question, and/or a statement and give them a minute or two to think about the topic. For example, as an *Into* activity, students can respond to a question that will help introduce the topic for that day's lesson on Martin Luther King's speech "I Have a Dream": What are some dreams you have for your future? As a *Beyond* activity, students can review the content they learned in that day's lesson: Write three main ideas you learned today about Emily Dickinson's poem "Tell all the Truth, but tell it slant."
- Ask students to write everything that comes to mind on the topic during a specified amount of time, generally two to five minutes, depending on the complexity of the topic.
- Students share their quick writes. Depending on the proficiency levels of English learners in the class and the amount of practice they need with their speaking skills, teachers can ask students to share their quick writes with a partner, then a small group, and finally with the whole class to give students multiple opportunities to share their work.
- During the discussions, students can add to and/or edit their quick writes so they have a complete description or response.
- Students can use their quick writes as a foundation for a more structured writing assignment, as notes on a topic to be covered in an upcoming lesson, or for a variety of other purposes.

STEP 4: *Select culturally relevant/multicultural materials and resources*

How Can I Find Culturally Relevant/Multicultural Resources to Use in My English Language Arts Class?

There are many opportunities to include relevant multicultural resources in English language arts classes. Throughout the CCSS, students are asked to identify, analyze, and evaluate multiple sources of information through reading and writing activities. This presents an opportunity for English language arts teachers to identify culturally relevant/multicultural resources that are aligned to their content and that reflect issues of diversity, equity, and social justice. The National Council for Teachers of English (NCTE, *www.ncte.org*) has an extensive collection of resources that help teachers incorporate relevant multicultural topics into their lessons. The organization Rethinking Schools offers resources on its website (*www.rethinkingschools.org*) to help teachers incorporate multicultural and social justice issues into English language arts classes. Teaching Tolerance (*www.tolerance.org*) has an extensive collection of resources on all multicultural topics. The resources are grouped by subject area, grade level, and a wide range of topics on diversity and social justice issues. Multicultural resources can also be found on the Multicultural Education Pavilion website (*www.edchange.org/multicultural/*), as well as through books, poems, and literature written by authors from diverse backgrounds. The Poetry Foundation's website (*www.poetryfoundation.org/*) offers numerous poems on culturally relevant topics from authors all over the world. Additionally, links to multicultural resources can be found on the National Education Association's website (*www.nea.org*). Finally, current topics, statistics, and opinion polls can be found in local, state, and national newspapers as well as on the Public Broadcasting Service website (*www.pbs.org*). Countless other websites provide multicultural and culturally relevant resources. The websites listed in this section can be thought of as a starting point for teachers to begin to search for culturally relevant/multicultural resources rather than a comprehensive list. The resources you choose to include in your lesson planning will depend on the information you have learned about your students (Step 1 of the process presented in this book) and how they best fit with the lesson content.

Annie Pickert Fuller/Pearson Education

English Language Arts Lesson Examples

Four lessons are presented in this section, two at the middle school level and two at the high school level. All four lessons are rewritten and adapted from lessons taught by either classroom teachers or teacher candidates to include content (CCSS for Literacy in English Language Arts) standards, language (ELD) standards and objectives, differentiated assessments aligned to the standards, student-centered activities, and culturally relevant resources. Teachers will most likely have lesson plans similar to these examples that can be easily adapted to incorporate the lesson planning process outlined in this book.

Middle School—8th-Grade English Language Arts

These lessons were originally designed in collaboration with a middle school teacher candidate in a secondary teacher credential program for an 8th-grade English language arts class. The author rewrote and then adapted the lessons to align them to CCSS and ELD standards. As the lessons were designed to be taught in a middle school in southern California, California ELD standards are included in the lesson for English learners; however, the process outlined in this book can be used with ELD standards from any state. For the purposes of designing lessons based on what teachers know about their students, the lesson in Figure 6.2 is for a class that enrolls English learners at the emerging and expanding levels, so the objectives, assessments, and activities are targeted one level up at the expanding and bridging levels. The lessons span two days, focus on speech and persuasion, and are both taught in 55-minute class sessions.

Figure 6.2
Sample English Lesson Plan–Speech & Persuasion (Day One)

Title of the Lesson Speech & Persuasion: African American Civil Rights Leader—Martin Luther King, Jr., and Malcolm X	**Class (Content Area) & Grade Level** English Language Arts 8th Grade English learners at the emerging and expanding levels
Content Standards *Grade 8* *Reading Standard for Informational Text—Integration of Knowledge and Ideas: #9* Analyze a case in which two or more texts provide conflicting information on the same topic and identify where the texts disagree on matters of facts or interpretation.	**ELD Standards** *Grade 8* *Reading/viewing closely* Express inferences and conclusions drawn based on close reading of grade-level texts and viewing of multimedia using a variety of verbs (e.g., suggests that). (Expanding level) Express inferences and conclusions drawn based on close reading of grade-level texts and viewing of multimedia using a variety of precise academic verbs (e.g., indicates that, influences) (Bridging level)
Content Objectives After reading the two speeches, students will be able to identify on their Venn diagrams the common themes of the speeches as well as points of disagreement.	**Language Objectives** Working in small groups, students will be able to discuss the conclusions they have drawn from comparing the common themes and differences in two speeches.

(continued)

Figure 6.2
(continued)

Assessment Plan *Informal:* Monitor small-group discussions by randomly asking students questions about their conclusions of the common themes and differences of each speech. *Informal*: At the end of the class, each group presents one common theme identified in the two speeches and one area of disagreement. English learners at the emerging level can use vocabulary terms and verbs such as "express" or "says" in their presentations. English learners at the expanding level are expected to use academic vocabulary terms and verbs in their presentations (the same expectation for native-English speakers). *Formal:* Students write the common themes of each speech on their Venn diagrams. Students' diagrams will be collected at the end of the class and graded before the next class session.
Instructional Strategies/Student Activities *Into/Through/Closure/Beyond* *INTO: Review Civil Rights Movement* (5 minutes) As students enter the room, ask them to read the content and language objective for the day (posted on the board). As the bell rings, randomly ask a student to read the content objective. Ask another student to restate the objective in his or her own words. Do the same for the language objective. Ask students to brainstorm what they learned about the civil rights movement in their social studies class. Name the key figures of the movement, the key events, the time frame, etc. As students are sharing responses, jot down their ideas and display them on the document camera. *THROUGH: Speeches by Martin Luther King, Jr., and Malcolm X* (25 minutes) Working in heterogeneous pairs (pairing English learners with native-English speakers when possible), students read "I Have A Dream" by Martin Luther King, Jr. Pairs write down the main ideas of the speech and any unfamiliar vocabulary. Display the text of the speech on the document camera and randomly call on pairs to identify the main idea of the speech. Clarify any unfamiliar vocabulary and ask questions to assess whether all pairs have identified the main idea of the speech. Working with the same partner, students read "By Any Means Necessary" by Malcolm X. Pairs write down the main ideas of the speech and any unfamiliar vocabulary words. Display the text of the speech on the document camera and randomly call on pairs to identify the main idea of the speech. Clarify any unfamiliar vocabulary and ask questions to assess whether all pairs have identified the main idea of the speech. *CLOSURE: Venn Diagrams* (15 minutes) Display a Venn diagram on the board. Model the activity by asking the class to choose one main idea from either speech the students have read. Ask the class to determine if the main idea is unique to one of the speeches or both. Then place the idea either in the center of the diagram (overlap of the two speeches) or in one of the circles (Martin Luther King, Jr., or Malcolm X). Students work in small groups to complete their Venn diagrams.

Figure 6.2
(continued)

As the students are completing their Venn diagrams, monitor the groups by randomly asking students comprehension questions about the speeches and where the students are placing their ideas on the diagrams. Students will complete their Venn diagrams and turn them in at the end of the class. *BEYOND: Class Discussion* (10 minutes) After students have completed their Venn diagrams, lead a class discussion on points (main ideas) of agreement and disagreement in the two speeches. Each group must share at least one idea. Write the similarities and differences the students identify on the document camera, and lead a discussion on the reasons the students believe that Martin Luther King, Jr., and Malcolm X had differing views on these points.
Key Vocabulary Unfamiliar vocabulary from each speech
Materials Needed "I Have A Dream" speech by Martin Luther King, Jr., and "By Any Means Necessary" speech by Malcolm X, document camera

During the second day of the lesson presented in Figure 6.3, students review the two speeches they read and analyzed the previous day by watching videos of them. In small groups, they review the Venn diagrams (graphic organizer) comparing and contrasting the speeches they completed the previous day. Students use these diagrams to write a persuasive essay outlining one main idea presented in each of the speeches. For the identified idea, students need to provide evidence from the speeches or other historical records demonstrating the similarities and differences of the perspective of each speaker on the chosen idea.

Figure 6.3
Sample English Lesson Plan—Speech & Persuasion (Day Two)

Title of the Lesson Speech & Persuasion: African American Civil Rights Leaders— Martin Luther King, Jr., and Malcolm X	**Class (Content Area) & Grade Level** English Language Arts 8th Grade English learners at the emerging and expanding levels
Content Standards *Grade 8* *Writing: Text Types and Purposes: #2.b.* Write informational/explanatory texts to examine a topic and convey ideas, concepts, and information through the selection, organization, and analysis of relevant content. Develop a topic with relevant, well-chosen facts, definitions, concrete details, quotations, or other information and examples.	**ELD Standards** *Grade 8* *Writing* Write longer literary and informational texts collaboratively and independently using appropriate text organization. (Expanding level) Write longer and more detailed literary and informational texts collaboratively and independently using appropriate text organization and a growing understanding of register. (Bridging level)

(continued)

Figure 6.3
(continued)

Content Objectives	Language Objectives
Students will be able to write an essay on one main idea from the two speeches, demonstrating the similarities and differences of each speaker's perspective on the selected idea.	Students will be able to write an essay (following the format used in class) using quotations and facts to support their claims on the selected main idea from the speeches.

Assessment Plan

Informal: Monitor the class discussion (review) by randomly asking students questions about the main ideas and critical details of each speech.

Informal: Monitor partners as students write their persuasive essays. Randomly check students' essays to ensure students have required elements in their essays.

Formal: Students will complete drafts of their essays during the class session, finalize them, and submit them for a grade the following day.

Emerging English learners: Essays should contain a clear thesis supported by at least one quote and one fact for each speaker's position (similarities and differences on the idea).

Expanding English learners: Essays should contain a clear thesis supported by at least two quotes and two facts for each speaker's position (similarities and differences on the idea). Native-English speakers' essays will be assessed at this level.

Instructional Strategies/Student Activities

Into/Through/Closure/Beyond

INTO: Review Speeches—Videos (10 minutes)

As students enter the room, ask them to read the content and language objective for the day (posted on the board). As the bell rings, randomly ask a student to read the content objective. Ask another student to restate the objective in his or her own words. Do the same for the language objective.

To review the two speeches, "I Have A Dream" by Martin Luther King, Jr., and "By Any Means Necessary" by Malcolm X, start by randomly asking students to consult their Venn diagrams to identify similarities and differences in the two leaders' perspectives.

Show YouTube videos of each of the speeches (students read texts of the speeches during the previous lesson). After watching the videos, discuss any questions the students have about the speeches.

THROUGH: Write Essays (25 minutes)

Review the required elements of a persuasive essay (from previous class sessions). The criteria for the essay's assessment should be posted on the board and reviewed with students. Using their Venn diagrams and any notes they have taken, students begin to write drafts of their persuasive essays. The students are working individually, but can ask their partners any clarifying questions they have.

As students are completing their essays, the teacher monitors the pairs by randomly asking students comprehension questions about the organization of their essays, the content of the two speeches, and the mechanics of the essays (grammar, vocabulary use, spelling, etc.).

CLOSURE: Sharing Essays/Editing (10 minutes)

Randomly select students to show the drafts of their essays on the document camera. The students read a paragraph of their essays and the class discusses any edits (spelling, grammar, content) each student can make. As students are reviewing the essays presented on the document camera, they are making similar edits to their own essays.

Figure 6.3
(continued)

BEYOND: Class Discussion (10 minutes) After the writing activity, students reconvene as a whole class. Post the following questions on the board and ask students to think of their responses: Do you think Martin Luther King, Jr.'s message (perspective) would be effective today? Why or why not? Do you think Malcolm X's message (perspective) would be effective today? Why or why not? Do you think Dr. King's "dream" for America has been achieved today? Why or why not? Ask students to share their responses with their partners and then with the class through a class discussion. (Think-Pair-Share) Homework—Students take the drafts of their essays home to complete a final version.
Key Vocabulary Unfamiliar vocabulary from each speech
Materials Needed "I Have A Dream" speech by Martin Luther King, Jr., and "By Any Means Necessary" speech by Malcolm X—text and on video (YouTube), document camera

High School—11th-Grade English Literature

The following English language arts lesson plans were originally developed in collaboration with a teacher candidate in a secondary credential program in southern California. The lessons were rewritten and further modified by the author to highlight language objectives and include the CCSS for English Language Arts. As the lessons were designed to be taught in a high school in southern California, California ELD standards are incorporated into the lesson for English learners; however, the process outlined in this book can be used with ELD standards from any state. In order to base the lesson on what teachers know about their students, the lesson presented in Figure 6.4 was designed to be taught in an 11th-grade English Literature class with an enrollment of 35 students, 10 of whom are English learners at the expanding level. The two lessons were originally taught during 50-minute class sessions at a high school in a mid-sized, suburban town in southern California.

During the second day of the lesson presented in Figure 6.5 on universal themes in poetry, students review the poems read the previous day and identify the universal themes in each poem (e.g., love, jealousy, truth). Using the sentences students wrote as their homework assignment as a foundation, students write their own poems on a universal theme of their choice, incorporating literary elements (figurative language, imagery, allegory, and symbolism) and read them aloud to their small groups.

The rubric presented in Table 6.2 is the differentiated assessment for the jigsaw activity in the high school universal themes in poetry (day one) lesson. The criteria for the language standards and objectives are derived from each proficiency level of the standard of Interpretive—Listening

Figure 6.4
Sample English Lesson Plan—Universal Themes in Poetry (Day One)

Title of the Lesson Universal Themes in Poetry	**Class (Content Area) & Grade Level** 11th-Grade English Literature English learners at the expanding level
Content Standards *Grades 11–12* *Reading Standards for Literature: Craft and Structure: #5* Analyze how an author's choices concerning how to structure specific parts of a text (e.g., the choice of where to begin or end a story, the choice to provide a comedic or tragic resolution) contribute to its overall structure and meaning as well as to its aesthetic impact.	**ELD Standards** *Grades 11–12* *Analyzing language choices* Explain how a writer's or speaker's choice of a variety of different types of phrasing or words (e.g., varying connotations, the cumulative impact of word choices) produces nuances and different effects on the audience. (Bridging level) *Listening attentively* Demonstrate comprehension of oral presentations and discussions on a variety of social and academic topics by asking and answering detailed and complex questions that show thoughtful consideration of the ideas or arguments with light support. (Bridging level)
Content Objectives Students will be able to identify 2–3 choices made by each author of the three poems to structure his or her poem that contribute to the poem's meaning.	**Language Objectives** Students will be able to identify at least two literary elements used by the author of each poem. Students will be able to use literary elements appropriately when presenting their poems to small groups by asking and answering at least two questions about each student's poem.

Assessment Plan

Informal: Monitor the groups as they are working on their presentations to one another during the jigsaw activity by randomly choosing students to ask comprehension questions about the main idea of their poems and the literary elements they will present.

Formal: During the jigsaw activity, each student will be assessed during his or her group's presentation on the two questions he or she asks about the two literary elements used appropriately to describe the assigned poem (using the rubric in Table 6.2).

(Expanding-level English learners will be assessed using the same criteria as native-English speakers.)

Formal: Students will select one poem and write sentences identifying 2–3 choices made by the author that contribute to the poem's meaning. (homework assignment)

Instructional Strategies/Student Activities

Into/Through/Closure/Beyond

INTO: Fame Is a Bee (by Emily Dickinson) (10 minutes)

As students enter the class, they read the following poem on the overhead:

Fame is a bee
It has a song-
It has a sting-
Ah too, it has a wing.

And write 2 sentences to respond to any of the following questions:
What do you think this means?
Do you agree or disagree?
Do you have any personal experiences with the theme of this poem?

Figure 6.4
(continued)

Randomly call on students to read their sentences. The class then reviews vocabulary terms: figurative language, imagery, allegory, and symbolism (all terms are listed and defined on a poster hanging on a wall in the class).

The teacher then randomly calls on students to read the content and language objectives for the day, and other students to restate the objectives in their own words.

THROUGH: Read Emily Dickinson Poem (15 minutes)
Read the poem, "Tell all the Truth, but tell it slant" by Emily Dickinson and ask students to listen carefully. Select a student to read the poem again, and ask students questions about the main idea of the poem.

Working in a small group (English learners working with native-English speakers when possible), students discuss their responses to the following questions (displayed on the overhead projector):
What does the poem remind you of?
What does the title reveal about the poem?
What are some literary devices that stood out to you the most? Why?
If someone asked you to paraphrase the main idea of the poem, what would you say?
How does the poem relate to your life?

After a few minutes, ask each group to share their discussion of one of the questions, ensuring that all questions have been addressed by the end of the discussion.

THROUGH: Jigsaw Activity of Selected Poems (20 minutes)
Divide the class into three groups of 12. Each group is then divided again into three groups (4 per group) and given a handout of one of the following three poems (downloaded from the Poetry Foundation website):
"How to write the great American Indian novel" by S. Alexie
"The Present" by J. Harrison
"Envying the Children of San Francisco" by G. Soto

Groups are given poster paper and told they are "experts" on the poem their group has been assigned and will teach the other groups about their poem. Group members read their poem and ask any clarifying questions they may have about the poem.

On their posters, each group responds to the questions used during the analysis of the Dickinson poem and adds any other pertinent information about their poem to the poster:
What does the poem remind you of?
What does the title reveal about the poem?
What are some literary devices that stood out to you the most? Why?
If someone asked you to paraphrase the main idea of the poem, what would you say?
How does the poem relate to your life?

Each group is given 3 minutes to teach the other two groups about their assigned poem so students in all groups have either read or learned about all three poems.

CLOSURE: Review of Jigsaw Activity/Selecting Poems (5 minutes)
Ask the "experts" of each poem (3 groups per poem) to review the information presented for their poem. Each student then chooses one of the three poems to focus on for the homework assignment. Let them know the poem will be the focus of a writing assignment in class tomorrow.

BEYOND: Homework
Students will select one poem and write sentences identifying 2–3 choices made by the author that contribute to the poem's meaning.

Key Vocabulary
Review of terms: figurative language, imagery, allegory, and symbolism
Unfamiliar vocabulary from the selected poems

Materials Needed
Poems from the Poetry Foundation website (*www.poetryfoundation.org/*), document camera and/or overhead projector, poster paper, 11th-grade literature textbook (Holt & Holt, 2009)

Figure 6.5
Sample English Lesson Plan—Universal Themes in Poetry (Day Two)

Title of the Lesson Universal Themes in Poetry	**Class (Content Area) & Grade Level** 11th-Grade English Literature English learners at the expanding level
Content Standards *Grades 11–12* *Writing—Research to build and present knowledge: #9.a* Draw evidence from literary or informational texts to support analysis, reflection, and research. Apply grades 11–12 Reading Standards to literature (Analyze how an author's choices concerning how to structure specific parts of a text [e.g., the choice of where to begin or end a story, the choice to provide a comedic or tragic resolution] contribute to its overall structure and meaning as well as to its aesthetic impact.)	**ELD Standards** *Grades 11–12* *Adapting language choices* Adjust language choices according to the task, context, purpose, and audience. (Bridging level) *Understanding Text Structure* Apply analysis of the organizational structure of different text types to comprehending texts and to writing clear and cohesive arguments and informative/explanatory texts. (Bridging level)
Content Objectives Students will be able to write an original poem on a universal theme and identify, in a paragraph accompanying the poem, the connections between choices they made to construct the poem with its overall meaning.	**Language Objectives** Students will be able to write an original poem that incorporates at least two literary elements (e.g., figurative language, imagery, allegory, symbolism). Students will be able to orally present their poems to their small groups, using intonation and speech patterns consistent with a poetry reading.
Assessment Plan *Informal:* Monitor the students as they write their poems in their small groups by randomly choosing students to ask comprehension questions about the main idea of the poem and the literary elements they will present. *Formal:* Each student will present his or her poem to a small group of peers using at least two literary elements (e.g., figurative language, imagery, allegory, symbolism). *Formal:* Students will turn in their original poems for a grade. Students' poems must incorporate at least two literary elements (e.g., figurative language, imagery, allegory, symbolism). Formal: Along with their poems, students will submit a paragraph identifying the connections between choices to construct the poem and its overall meaning.	
Instructional Strategies/Student Activities *Into/Through/Closure/Beyond* *INTO: Review of Universal Themes in Poems* (10 minutes) Randomly call on students to read the content and language objectives for the day and other students to restate the objectives in their own words. Show each of the four poems presented in class the day before on the document camera. For each poem, students describe the universal theme presented while you write the themes next to each poem. *THROUGH: Writing Original Poems* (20 minutes) Working in their small groups (table groups of 4), each student writes an original poem modeled after the poems presented in class. Students' poems must incorporate at least two literary elements (e.g., figurative language, imagery, allegory, symbolism). The universal themes identified in the four assigned poems from the previous day are still projected on the board, as well as the students' posters from the jigsaw activity.	

Figure 6.5
(continued)

As the students are working on their poems, they can ask their group members clarifying questions (a classroom norm established at the beginning of the year). Monitor students' progress on their poems by circulating the room asking and answering students' questions.

THROUGH: Presenting Original Poems (5 minutes)
After each student has finished his or her poem, the teacher models intonation and speech patterns consistent with a poetry reading. Each student then reads his or her poem to the small group of peers using appropriate intonation and speech patterns. If there is time, ask a few students to read their poems to the class (after all students have presented their poems to their groups).

CLOSURE: Analysis of Original Poems (10 minutes)
Students will write a paragraph that identifies the connections between choices they made to construct their poems with their overall meaning.

BEYOND: Discussion of Universal Themes (5 minutes)
Returning to the universal themes the students identified at the beginning of class, ask students to share examples of stories, poems, and books from their culture (or a culture they are familiar with) that present a universal theme.

Homework—If students do not complete their paragraphs, they can finish them as homework and submit them the following day.

Key Vocabulary
Review of terms: figurative language, imagery, allegory, symbolism
Unfamiliar vocabulary from the selected poems

Materials Needed
Poems from the Poetry Foundation website (*www.poetryfoundation.org/*), document camera, 11th-grade literature textbook (Holt & Holt, 2009)

Table 6.2 Rubric for Sample Lesson Plan on Universal Themes in Poetry—Jigsaw Group Presentations

	1	2	3	4
Language—Use literary elements appropriately	Does not identify a literary element used by the author	Partially identifies one literary element used by the author	Identifies one literary element used by the author (figurative language, imagery, allegory, and/or symbolism)	Identifies two literary elements used by the author (figurative language, imagery, allegory, and/or symbolism)
Ask and answer questions about each poem	Does not ask a question about the literary elements presented	Asks one question during the presentation that demonstrates partial knowledge of a literary element	Asks one question during the presentation that demonstrates knowledge of one literary element	Asks two questions during the presentation that demonstrate knowledge of both literary elements presented

attentively and analyzing language choices. Since the content standard is assessed during a writing assignment, this rubric will be used to assess the ELD standard and objective only. This streamlines the assessment for the teacher, who will use the rubric to assess each student's presentation. The criteria for the objectives are differentiated on a 1–4 scale, with 4 representing the criteria expected of expanding-level English learners and native-English speakers (the bridging level). English learners have many opportunities to access the content through the strategies and activities designed for the lesson before they are assessed.

Discussion of the Lessons

The English language arts lessons described in this chapter present challenging content to all students and use strategies and activities that allow English learners access to the content and opportunities to develop their English language skills.

Standards, Objectives, and Assessments

Using the backwards mapping principle, content (CCSS for English Language Arts) and language (ELD) standards have been chosen for each lesson. Because content and language are intertwined in English language arts, the two sets of standards and objectives complement one another. Generally, the content standard represents the "what" of the lesson, and the language standards represent the "how": How will English learners demonstrate mastery of the standard? For example, during the second day of the middle school lessons, students write a persuasive essay aligned to both the content and language standards chosen. The content objective describes the focus of the essay—the similarities and differences of one main idea of the two speeches (what)—while the language objective describes the specific elements required of the essay—a clear thesis and supporting evidence that is differentiated for English learners at various proficiency levels (how).

The next step in the process is to design an assessment plan aligned to standards and objectives. For all four lessons, there are informal and formal assessments and a description of the summative assessment for the overall unit. Continuously monitoring students' work during each assigned activity is a type of informal assessment threaded throughout all the lessons. In each lesson, the assessment for the language objective has differentiated levels of mastery for English learners targeted at one level above their current proficiency level. In the rubric provided for the jigsaw activity during the first day of the high school lesson on universal themes of poetry (Table 6.2), the criteria written for the levels of the rubric are taken directly from the ELD standard, ensuring that English learners are accurately assessed on the skill based on their proficiency level. As discussed previously, although the rubric is designed to measure mastery of the language standard and objective for English learners, native-English speakers can be held to the same criteria, and the same rubric can be used to assess their language abilities.

Instructional Strategies

In all the lesson examples, a variety of instructional strategies make the content accessible for all students and specifically scaffold instruction for English learners. Lessons include modeling, using multimedia in the forms of visuals and video, vocabulary development, graphic organizers, and strategies that give students time to process the information presented, such as brainstorming. These scaffolding strategies are designed to gradually move the lessons from teacher-directed instruction to student-centered activities. For example, during the first day of the middle school lessons on speech and persuasion, students read and analyze the two speeches through teacher-directed instruction of brainstorming, guided reading, posters of required essay elements, and modeling on how to fill out a Venn diagram. The scaffolds are gradually taken away during the second day of the lesson as students work individually, with a partner, and in small groups to write a persuasive essay. English learners and many native-English speakers can perform tasks (write an essay) independently when they have been provided with a variety of tools to draw from to assist them with the task.

Embedded in many of the instructional strategies presented in these lessons is the concept of repetition. The lessons are models for how the process of repetition and scaffolding instruction helps English learners access the content being taught while practicing their English proficiency skills. Concepts learned during the first day of the lesson or in previous lessons or curricular units are recalled during activities during the *Into* phases of the lesson. On the first day of the high school lessons on universal themes of poetry, students respond to questions that help them recall information learned previously about poetry and review applicable vocabulary they need to build on to fully participate in the lesson's activities.

Student Activities

In all the lesson examples, instructional strategies and student activities are aligned to the content and language standards and objectives and to the assessment plan. The activities are student-centered and give English learners the opportunity to practice their listening, speaking, reading, and writing skills and to access the core curriculum being taught. During the jigsaw activity of the high school lesson, students *read* their assigned poems, *write* their expert knowledge on poster paper, *present* their information to other group members, and *listen* attentively to the presentations on other poems. While students specifically are assessed on their presentations (listening and speaking skills), English learners have the opportunity to practice the reading and writing skills necessary to become fully proficient in English. Given the CCSS focus on literacy skill development in the content areas, the incorporation of reading and writing activities into every lesson will help students build and draw on a literacy knowledge base needed to be successful across all content classes.

Each lesson also includes a variety of student grouping activities, including partner small-group, and whole-classwork. As English learners work in groups with native-English speakers, they can learn the content presented from their peers as well as from the teacher. In the middle school lesson, students read the speeches with a partner, which gives them the opportunity to hear English spoken by a peer and to practice speaking themselves. Giving English learners opportunities to practice language skills multiple times with a partner and/or in a small group also allows them to self-correct their mistakes. The additional time to process information and practice their responses can give some English learners the confidence they need to actively participate in larger class discussions and activities.

Culturally Relevant/Multicultural Resources

The middle and high school lessons include culturally relevant/multicultural resources teachers have identified as topics their students would be interested in based on the information gathered on their students. The focus on speeches by Martin Luther King, Jr., and Malcolm X in the middle school lessons is intended to help students make connections between the tenets of the civil rights movement and current topics on issues of equality. In the high school lessons, students read poems by authors from diverse backgrounds that present their interpretation of universal themes. Students are given the opportunity to understand topics from multiple perspectives, including those of their peers. By learning about universal themes from a partner or small-group member who comes from a culturally and/or linguistically diverse background, all students can make connections with one another that may not happen otherwise. Promoting an understanding of diversity and choosing materials that are relevant to students' lives increases both student engagement and overall academic achievement.

Summary

As you reflect on how to design English language arts lesson plans for your English learner students, keep in mind the main interrelated points of this chapter:

- It is important to fully understand who your English learners are in order to include teaching strategies and student activities in your lessons that build on their strengths and help you address any areas of weakness they have. In addition to their English proficiency levels, prior knowledge they have with your subject area, and learning styles, understanding your English learners' backgrounds, interests, and cultures can help you choose multicultural resources to use in your lessons that are relevant to your students' lives.

- The objectives you write for your lesson should be based on the CCSS for English Language Arts and the ELD standards your state has adopted. The content standard generally represents the "what" of the lesson (what content is being taught), while the language standards represents "how" your English learners will master the content standard chosen at the appropriate proficiency levels for them.
- The assessments and activities you use should be aligned to the content and language objectives you have chosen so that you and your students understand the expectations for each lesson. It is important to use the information you have learned about your English learners in Step 1 of the lesson planning process to differentiate your assessments so they accurately reflect what your students are able to accomplish at the end of your lesson. You should also use the information you have learned about your students to design scaffolded activities that will help them learn the content you are presenting while simultaneously developing their English proficiency.

Applying What You Have Learned

In this chapter, you have learned how to provide equitable instruction for your English learner students by using a four-step lesson planning process. Demonstrate your understanding of the chapter by participating in the following activities and answering the corresponding questions.

STEP 1: Know your English learners

- What difficulties might English learners have with the CCSS for English Language Arts that you can take into account when designing your lessons?
- Explain ways you can obtain information about your English learners so that your lessons are aligned to their English proficiency levels, prior content knowledge, and learning styles.

STEP 2: Choose standards for your lessons

- In the lesson planning process presented in this chapter, you have learned that lessons should focus on CCSS for English Language Arts as well as ELD standards used in your state. Choose a CCSS for English Language Arts and a corresponding ELD standard. Write measurable and observable content (CCSS) and language (ELD) objectives based on the standards you have chosen.

STEP 3: Design differentiated assessments and student-centered activities

- You have learned how to differentiate your assessment to accurately assess English learners in your English language arts class. You have also learned how to use teaching strategies that can help your English learners access the content you are teaching. Additionally, you have learned specific student activities to use in your class that will promote interactions between English learners and native-English speakers. Using the content and language objectives you wrote in the Step 2 exercise, design the following components of a lesson plan:

- Assessments that will allow your students to demonstrate they have met the content and language objectives (Remember to differentiate your assessments based on your English learners' language proficiency levels.)
- A student activity that is aligned to the objectives you have written and the assessments you have designed
- An explanation of what teaching strategies you will use to ensure that your English learners understand and can complete the activity you have designed

STEP 4: Select culturally relevant/multicultural materials and resources

- List some national, state, and/or local organizations that provide culturally relevant/multicultural resources on their websites that can be incorporated into your English language arts lessons.

chapter 7

Mathematics

Learning Outcomes and Focus Questions

STEP 1: Know your English learners

- What difficulties might my English learners have with the Common Core State Standards for Mathematics?
- What do I need to know about my English learners to plan instruction?

STEP 2: Choose standards for your lessons

- What content standards will my lesson focus on?
- How do I design lessons that include language standards and objectives in my mathematics class?

STEP 3: Design differentiated assessments and student-centered activities

- How can I differentiate assessment to accurately assess my English learners?
- What strategies can I use to help English learners master the content I am teaching?
- What activities can I implement in my class to promote interactions between English learners and native-English speakers?

STEP 4: Select culturally relevant/multicultural materials and resources

- How can I find culturally relevant/multicultural resources to use in my mathematics class?

This chapter outlines a process middle and high school teachers can use to design lessons that incorporate language objectives based on ELD standards alongside content objectives from the Common Core State Standards (CCSS) for Mathematics for their English learner students. Much of the content in middle and high school mathematics classes is built on knowledge that has been taught in previous mathematics classes in elementary, middle, and high school. An English learner who immigrates to the United States in the 9th grade may not have the same foundational knowledge as his or her peers and/or may have learned how to solve math problems differently in his or her home country. It is crucial to design activities that help build that background for English learners and teach them the processes and procedures used in your class. Content presented in middle and high school mathematics classes also includes many complex and abstract concepts, along with vocabulary that oftentimes has a specific meaning in mathematics (e.g., sequence, series). While it may seem challenging, teachers can design their activities to give English learners the time they need to fully process the meaning of concepts presented to increase their opportunities to excel in class.

STEP 1: Know your English learners

What Difficulties Might My English Learners Have with the Common Core State Standards for Mathematics?

The CCSS for Mathematics contain standards for mathematical content that are focused on procedure and understanding. The standards for mathematical practice outline ways for students to engage with the content to become "mathematically proficient students." As is the case with the CCSS for English Language Arts and Literacy for History/Social Studies, Science, and Technical Studies, the CCSS for Mathematics are developmental and build on skills and knowledge learned in the previous grades. The information presented in this section is not intended to be an extensive description of the CCSS for Mathematics, but rather a discussion of the difficulties English learners may have with the standards so teachers can understand how to design their instruction in order to help their students overcome these challenges.

In both sets of standards in the CCSS for Mathematics, much of the knowledge or mastery of the standards is demonstrated through student activities such as explaining the steps, formulas, and equations represented in the standard. Given the complexity of the standards at the middle and high school levels, this involves levels of English language proficiency, particularly in speaking and writing, that may be beyond English learners' levels. Similarly, a "mathematically proficient student" as described in the eight Mathematics Practices is a student who has attained a fairly advanced level of English proficiency to be able to demonstrate the mathematical knowledge required. Although the level of English literacy required of these standards may be difficult for many students in a math class, the challenges for English learners must be addressed to ensure that they have access to the math content being taught. The CCSS for Mathematics can be accessible to English learners if math teachers teach them in conjunction with ELD standards. Using the ELD standards will ensure that English learners are developing their English proficiency skills at the level necessary to master the content of the CCSS for Mathematics.

The CCSS for Mathematics are designed so that students developmentally learn skills from kindergarten through high school. Some English learners who enter the U.S. school system in middle school or later will not have the benefit of building on the skills in the CCSS as other students in the class have. It may also be the case that an English learner who has attended U.S. schools since elementary school will have difficulties in your middle or high school mathematics class because he or she may not have the level of English language proficiency to express his or her knowledge of the content as it is prescribed in the CCSS for Mathematics. Along with incorporating ELD standards into lessons, you can design activities that are student-centered and promote peer interactions so that English learners have more opportunities to practice their English while learning content. Given the performance-based nature of the CCSS for Mathematics, student-centered activities and group work will help English learners, and all students become more active participants in their learning.

What Do I Need to Know About My English Learners to Plan Instruction?

The more information you have about your English learner students, the greater the opportunities they will have to be academically successful in your math classroom. For example, learning about your students' academic knowledge of mathematics and their self-identification of strengths and weaknesses with the subject can help you understand which concepts are accessible to them and which will need to be scaffolded more explicitly. Along with academic knowledge, understanding what your English learners' English language proficiency levels are in the four language domains of listening, speaking, reading, and writing can guide lesson planning. The process of assessing an English learner's language proficiency levels is described in detail in Part 2 of this book. It is important to know your English learners' proficiency levels in each of the language domains so you can choose an ELD standard for lessons at the level needed to scaffold students' English language development. This information can help you focus on addressing language issues English learners may have with mathematics content. A survey administered at the beginning of the year also can guide your understanding of what languages are spoken at home, which languages students use to speak to their friends, what they know about the mathematics content you will teach, and what difficulties students feel they may have with the content and vocabulary of a math classroom. You can also ask questions that will help you understand your English learners' interests, extracurricular activities, goals in the math class, and broader goals they have in their lives.

Understanding your English learners' learning styles allows you to design lessons to include teaching strategies and student activities that build on students' strengths and help them develop in areas of weaknesses. If you have English learner students who are visual learners, presenting information through modes such as pictures, graphic organizers, and charts will help them access the content you are presenting. For visual learners, information presented in other formats such as through a lecture (auditory) should include opportunities to continually check for understanding to ensure these students can demonstrate they know the content. Finally, knowing about your English learners' (and all your students') backgrounds, interests, cultural and social affiliations, and any other pertinent information that combined makes your students "who they are" helps you plan lessons that include multicultural and culturally relevant resources for them. Doing so will help English learners make connections to the content you are teaching and keep them engaged in all aspects of the lesson.

STEP 2: Choose standards for your lessons

What Content Standards Will My Lesson Focus On?

The sequence of how you present content standards in your mathematics class is most likely determined locally by your department, school, or district. However the content standards are chosen for each lesson you teach, it is important to note that they represent the "what" of your lesson—what content is being taught. The CCSS for Mathematics present many complex processes, so it may take more than one lesson for students to master the standard. Once the content standard being taught is determined, your next step is to write an objective based on the standard to guide the lesson. The objective should be measurable and observable and let you and your students know what they will be able to do by the end of the lesson.

Example:

- I am teaching a 7th-grade math class and have chosen the standard The Number System: "Apply and extend previous understandings of operations with fractions to add, subtract, multiply, and divide rational numbers. a. Describe situations in which opposite quantities combine to make 0" (7.NS.1.a).
- I write a content objective for my lesson based on the standard: Students will be able to work with a partner to describe 2–3 situations in which opposite quantities combine to make 0 in a short presentation to the class.

Because the CCSS for Mathematics are performance-based, many are already observable and sometimes measurable. Therefore, the objectives you write for your lesson may either be the standard itself or closely aligned to it.

How Do I Design Lessons That Include Language Standards and Objectives in My Mathematics Class?

If the content standards represent the "what" of any lesson, then the ELD standards represent the "how" for English learners—how they will master the content standard chosen at the appropriate proficiency level. The process for choosing ELD or language standards in the language domains of listening, speaking, reading, and writing to include in lessons was outlined in detail in Part 2 of this book. Briefly, teachers should choose a language standard that complements the content standard addressed in the lesson. Once a standard is chosen, teachers then write a language objective for the lesson that outlines how students will demonstrate that they have met the standard.

Example:

- I have English learners at the exiting stage of the emerging proficiency level in my 8th-grade Algebra class.
- I select the skill of exchanging information/ideas to include in my lesson.
- I use the standard that is one level above my students' current proficiency level. The standard at the expanding level reads: "Contribute to class, group, and partner discussions by following turn-taking rules, asking relevant questions, affirming others, adding relevant information, and paraphrasing key ideas."
- I write a language objective based on the standard: Students will be able to contribute to a partner discussion by asking at least 2 relevant questions and adding relevant information to each others' conjectures about point-slope formulas.

English learners benefit from as much practice as possible with the English language in order to become proficient. Teachers can choose activities that incorporate several language skills to include in their lessons to help English learners practice the language. However, it is recommended that each lesson focus on one or two language standards. Assessment is aligned to the chosen standards, so focusing on one or two language skills allows teachers to accurately assess if English learners have mastered them.

STEP 3: Design differentiated assessments and student-centered activities

How Can I Differentiate Assessment to Accurately Assess My English Learners?

Once English learners' proficiency levels are determined in any language domain, they can perform a language skill independently and automatically at those levels. Targeting instruction one proficiency level above their current level helps English learners build their knowledge of English language and attain overall language proficiency. Following this tenet, an accurate assessment for English learners should be targeted at one level above their current proficiency level as well. Using California ELD standards as an example, English learners who demonstrate exiting-stage skills at the emerging level should be assessed on the expanding-level standards. Similarly, using the World-Class Instructional Design and Assessment (WIDA) standards, English learners who are proficient at the developing level should be assessed at the expanding level (one level above their current level). In either example, assessments designed at proficiency levels above the expanding level may contain language skills and knowledge that are too far beyond the English learners' current proficiency to be accurate assessments. While English learners may have a general understanding of the math content, they may not be proficient enough in English to communicate their mastery of the content in either oral or written form.

Following the backwards mapping principle, assessment should be aligned to the content and language standards chosen for each lesson and to the objectives written for each standard. Mathematics teachers who have both native-English speakers and English learners in their class can create one assessment plan for their lesson that includes both language and content. While the language objectives are specifically designed for English learners, the skills covered in the language standards may also be beneficial for the native-English speaking students. In the following example, teachers can assess their native-English speakers on how well they are able to communicate content they have learned during a group work activity with their peers by using the standard identified for English learners—presenting or delivering an oral presentation. The listening and speaking skill (and/or reading and writing skills) designed for English learners to become proficient also help native-English speakers with their English language development and literacy skills. In math classes, all students can improve their language skills in listening, speaking, reading, and writing by the explicit focus teachers place on these skills for their English learner students.

Example:

- I have 10th-grade English learners in my mathematics class at the expanding and entering the bridging levels.
- My content area is geometry. The standard for the lesson is "Congruence: Develop definitions for rotations, reflections, and translations in terms of angles, circles, perpendicular lines, parallel lines, and line segments" (CCSS: G-CO, 4).
- I am using the California ELD standard for grades 9–10 on presenting so my English learners can practice the skill of presenting information in front of the class. I choose the ELD standards that are one level above my students' current expanding proficiency level for my assessment.

  Bridging: Plan and deliver a variety of oral presentations and reports on grade-appropriate topics that express complex and abstract ideas, are well supported by evidence and reasoning, and are delivered using an appropriate level of formality and understanding of register.
- My class is working in groups of four to collectively create an oral presentation on their definitions for rotations, reflections, and translations in terms of angles, circles, perpendicular lines, parallel lines, and line segments.

- I create a rubric for the lesson that includes both the content and language objective.
- I assess my English learners on the language objective that is one level above their current level—the entry stage of the bridging standard for emerging students and the exit stage of the bridging standard for students at the bridging level. This is done by increasing the academic criteria for students at each level on the rubric: A 3 on the rubric represents skills at the entry stage of the bridging standard for emerging students, and a 4 represents skills at the exit stage of the same standard for entry bridging-level English learners.
- I assess the language objective both informally during the group work and formally during the oral presentations. I assess the CCSS for Mathematics content standard based on the oral presentation the group creates using the criteria I have included in the rubric.

For English learners, the assessment is equitable in that it accurately assesses them based on the language proficiency level that is one level above their current level, as shown in the rubric in Table 7.1.

Table 7.1 Sample Rubric That Differentiates Assessment for English Learners

	1	2	3	4
Language Development: Presenting (ELD standard)	Planned and delivered a short presentation with no focus or clear thesis	Prepared and delivered a short presentation using a clear thesis, and 1 fact to support ideas	Prepared and delivered a presentation following an organized process, supported by 2–3 items of evidence	Prepared and delivered a presentation that followed an organized process and expressed abstract ideas supported by 2–3 items of evidence and reasoning
Content (CCSS): Vocabulary definitions in terms of angles, circles, perpendicular lines, parallel lines, and line segments	Partial definitions of vocabulary provided in terms of 1 key geometrical concept	Definitions of all vocabulary provided in terms of 2–3 key geometrical concepts	Definitions of all vocabulary provided correctly in terms of at least 4 key geometrical concepts	Definitions of all vocabulary provided correctly in terms of all 5 key geometrical concepts

What Strategies Can I Use to Help English Learners Master the Content I Am Teaching?

Underlying any strategy teachers use to help English learners in their mathematics classes is the principle that teachers have high expectations of their students. Displaying and explaining the lesson's content and language objectives ensures that English learners understand your expectations and the goals for the day and allows them to focus on the main idea of the lesson. English learners can learn mathematics content when it is presented through accessible strategies such as SDAIE (specially designed academic instruction in English) that help make challenging content accessible to English learners in content area classrooms. Using multiple modes of presenting content, such as visuals, graphic organizers, video, and multimedia, will give English learners a variety of formats to access the content. Additionally, teachers can use heterogeneous grouping strategies where English learners can learn from and share their knowledge with native-English speakers. If necessary, English learners should be given the opportunity to use their native language to negotiate the meaning of content with their peers and then translate that knowledge so they can fully participate in larger class discussions in English.

What Activities Can I Implement in My Class to Promote Interactions Between English Learners and Native-English Speakers?

Using a variety of activities in mathematics classes allows students with different learning styles multiple ways to learn the content being presented. For English learners, designing lessons using activities that promote peer interactions allows them to communicate with their native-English-speaking peers. Students can learn from one another and learn the content while English learners have the added benefit of practicing their English, which leads to increased language development. English learners, like many students, need time to process new concepts learned and understand how these concepts are connected to and/or build on prior mathematics concepts. Designing activities so that English learners work with peers, with a partner or in small groups, gives them the necessary time to learn new concepts and practice content area vocabulary in the context of a mathematics class. Activities that promote peer interactions give English learners another way to equitably access the same curriculum and core content as their native-English-speaking peers.

The following two examples of classroom activities achieve the goals of equal access to the core curriculum and increased peer interactions for English learners. The two classroom activities presented here are used in the lesson examples detailed later in this chapter. Included in the appendices is a list of all activities described in each content chapter of this book (Chapters 6–9). Together, these are suggested activities for teachers to use in classes that help promote listening, speaking, reading, and writing skills for English learners. Numerous resources are available to teachers that outline effective classroom activities for English learners. Teachers should use classroom activities that they feel comfortable with and that match their teaching style and their students' learning styles. If students are familiar with a certain activity that has been used repeatedly in a class and that is effective in teaching content, then teachers should continue to incorporate the activity into lessons throughout the year. The routine of using familiar activities helps English learners focus on the content rather than on learning the steps and expectations of a new activity.

Think-Pair-Share Activity

Think-Pair-Share is an excellent and quick activity that teachers can use to allow English learners time to process information they are asked to learn before participating in a class discussion (McTighe & Lyman, 1988). It can be used in any phase of the lesson. In the *Into* phase, Think-Pair-Share can help gauge the background knowledge students have of the content that will be presented in the lesson. In the *Through* phase of the lesson, the strategy is a good assessment tool teachers can use to monitor if students have fully understood the content or if material needs to be reinforced or retaught. Finally, in the *Beyond* or *Closure* phase of the lesson, a Think-Pair-Share activity allows students to share what they have learned in the lesson, which provides another assessment opportunity for teachers.

- Pose a question or present a concept to the students. For example, as an *Into* activity in a geometry class, you can ask students: "What do you know about patterns and sequences?" Or as a *Beyond* activity at the end of an algebra lesson, you can ask students to identify two things they learned about predicting unemployment rates.
- Give students a few minutes to individually think of and/or write an answer or form a statement about the concept. (Think)
- Pair up students and give them a few minutes to share their responses with one another. The partners should be instructed to discuss any similarities or differences in their responses. (Pair)
- Ask students to share their responses in a class discussion. (Share)

English learners need time to process information learned and to form grammatically correct sentences to answer the question posed or think about the concept presented. With a Think-Pair-Share activity, English learners have multiple opportunities to practice their responses as well as hear other students' responses to ensure they have comprehended the question posed and fully understand the concept. Purposely partnering English learners with native-English speakers can also create opportunities for English learners to interact with their peers to hear them speak English and to create a community of learners in the classroom.

Reciprocal Teaching Activity

Reciprocal teaching is a group reading activity in which each student is assigned a role based on the reading and is responsible to complete a task assigned to that role (Palinscar & Brown, 1984). In this activity, students are placed in groups of four. As is the case with other student activities described in this book, it is beneficial to group English learners with native English speakers. Begin by distributing a note card to each member of the group identifying each student's unique role: summarizer, questioner, clarifier, and predictor. Students read the assigned text or a few paragraphs of the text if it is a long passage. Encourage students to use note-taking strategies such as selective underlining or sticky notes to help them better prepare for their role in the upcoming group discussion.

- At a given stopping point, the summarizer begins the activity by highlighting the key ideas up to this point in the reading.
- The questioner then poses questions about the selection, such as unclear parts, puzzling information, or connections to other concepts already learned.
- The clarifier addresses confusing parts of the text and attempts to answer the questions that were just posed by other group members.
- The predictor can offer guesses about what the author will tell the group next, or if it is a literary selection, what the next events in the story will be.

The roles in the group then switch one person to the right, and the next selection is read. Students repeat the process using their new roles (e.g., the summarizer is now the questioner). If the text only consists of one selection, group members should switch roles the next time the activity is used in class. Teachers can purposefully assign roles to their English learner students based on the information they know about their language and content abilities. For example, an English learner at the expanding level may have the necessary English proficiency to be the summarizer or questioner but may not be proficient enough in reading to be the clarifier or predictor. However, as other students in the group discuss these aspects of the reading, English learners will benefit from a reciprocal teaching activity.

STEP 4: Select culturally relevant/multicultural materials and resources

How Can I Find Culturally Relevant/Multicultural Resources to Use in My Mathematics Class?

There are many opportunities to include relevant, multicultural resources into mathematics classes. Throughout the CCSS, students are asked to identify, analyze, and evaluate multiple sources of information through reading and writing activities. This presents an opportunity for mathematics teachers to identify culturally relevant/multicultural resources that are aligned to their content and that reflect issues of diversity, equity, and social justice. The National Council for Teachers of Mathematics (NCTM, *www.nctm.org*) has an extensive collection of resources that help teachers incorporate relevant, multicultural topics into their lessons. The organization Rethinking Schools offers resources on its website (*www.rethinkingschools.org*) focused on helping teachers incorporate multicultural/social justice issues into their mathematics classes; one example is the book *Rethinking Mathematics: Teaching Social Justice by the Numbers.* Teaching Tolerance (*www.tolerance.org*) maintains an extensive collection of resources on all multicultural topics. The resources are grouped by subject area, grade level, and a wide range of topics on diversity and social justice issues. Multicultural resources also can be found on the Multicultural Education Pavilion website (*www.edchange.org/multicultural*). Additionally, links to multicultural resources are available on the National Education Association's website (*www.nea.org*). Relevant topics to include in mathematics lessons also can be found in statistics and opinion polls in local, state, and national newspapers as well as on the Public Broadcasting Service website (*www.pbs.org*). Multicultural and culturally relevant resources can be found on countless other websites; the suggested sites listed in this section should be viewed as a starting point to begin your search for these resources rather than a comprehensive list of materials to use in a mathematics class. The resources you choose to include in your lesson planning will depend on the information you have learned about your students (Step 1 of the process presented in this book) and how they best fit in with the lesson content.

Annie Pickert Fuller/Pearson Education

Mathematics Lesson Examples

Four lessons are presented in this section, two at the middle school level and two at the high school level. All four lessons have been adapted from lessons taught by classroom teachers to include language standards and objectives, differentiated assessments aligned to the standards, student-centered activities, and culturally relevant resources. Teachers will most likely have lesson plans similar to the ones outlined in this chapter that can be easily adapted to incorporate the process outlined in this book.

Middle School—8th-Grade Algebra

The following lessons were originally designed by a middle school teacher for an 8th-grade Algebra I class. The author rewrote and adapted the lessons to align them with the CCSS for Mathematics and ELD standards. As the lessons were designed to be taught in a middle school in southern California, California ELD standards are incorporated into the lesson for English learners; however, the process outlined in this book can be used with ELD standards from any state. This sample lesson presented in Figure 7.1 is designed for a class with English learners at the emerging level who can perform language skills at the exit level of the standard, so the objectives, assessments, and activities are targeted at the expanding level (one level above their current proficiency level). The lessons span two days, focus on point-slope form, and are both taught during 1-hour class sessions.

Figure 7.1
Sample Mathematics Lesson Plan—Point-Slope Form (Day One)

Title of the Lesson Point-Slope Form	**Class (Content Area) & Grade Level** Algebra/8th Grade English learners at the emerging level
Content Standards *Grade 8—Expressions and Equations: Understand the connections between proportional relationships, lines, and linear equations* Graph proportional relationships, interpreting the unit rate as the slope of the graph. Compare two different proportional relationships represented in different ways. (8-EE,5)	**ELD Standards** *Exchanging information/ideas* Contribute to class, group, and partner discussions by following turn-taking rules, asking relevant questions, affirming others, adding relevant information, and paraphrasing key ideas. (Expanding level) *Writing* Write increasingly concise summaries of texts and experiences using complex sentences and key words (i.e., from notes or graphic organizers). (Expanding level)
Content Objectives Students will be able to understand the linear equations to help make predictions about consecutive unemployment figures and graph their data. Students will be able to research and familiarize themselves with U.S. unemployment numbers.	**Language Objectives** Students will be able to contribute to a partner discussion by asking at least 2 relevant questions and adding relevant information when discussing unemployment rates. Students will be able to use standard grammatical form to write summaries in their notebooks using the format outlined in the class.
Assessment Plan *Informal:* Monitor student discussion by assessing the questions students ask and adding relevant information to their partner's statements when they are discussing unemployment rates. *Formal:* Students' notebooks are checked every two weeks for use of the note-taking strategies and use of standard grammatical form to write summaries as outlined by the teacher (10 assignment points) *Formal:* As homework, students write equations in both point-slope form and slope-intercept form based on their research of unemployment percentages for two or more years. They will write equations to represent the real-life applications. (20 assignment points)	
Instructional Strategies/Student Activities *Into/Through/Closure/Beyond* *INTO: Review Point-Slope Formula* (5 minutes) Randomly call on students to read the content and language objectives for the day and other students to restate the objectives in their own words. The students attempt to derive the point-slope formula from the slope formula. Give them hints along the way if they have trouble with the task, and review vocabulary with them. This is a review of a lesson from the prior week. *THROUGH: Slope Formula and Point-Slope Formula Notes* (15 minutes) Working in pairs, students take notes on point-slope form as you present the material on an overhead projector. In their notes, they will write down the slope formula and the point-slope formula. Working with their partners, students will derive the point-slope formula from the slope formula they learned in a prior lesson. As students take notes on using the point-slope formula, they make conjectures about problems and share their conjectures with their neighbors. Students then take notes on how they could use the point-slope formula to derive a linear equation when given a slope and a point or when given two points. Students then share their ideas during a class discussion.	

Figure 7.1
(continued)

Give students several problems to work on either independently or with their partners while you monitor their learning by circulating the room and asking comprehension questions to random students. *THROUGH: Unemployment Percentages* (20 minutes) Students will go to the class computers and find U.S. unemployment percentages for any two-year period. When students have completed their Internet searches, direct them to make a graph of their information. They will independently make a coordinate plane and graph the unemployment numbers (two points) they found. The class will have a brief discussion about what size their graphs could be and what scale they could use. *CLOSURE: Finding Equations* (10 minutes) Students will then draw a line through the two points and find an equation for the line using the point-slope formula that represents the data they found. Then they will convert it to slope-intercept form. If the students have trouble with this task, model it by showing them an example of how to make an equation when given two points. *BEYOND: Making* Predictions (10 minutes) Using the equation they found, students will predict what the unemployment numbers will be on a future date. Homework–Students write equations to represent real-life applications in both point-slope form and slope-intercept form when given a slope and a point or just two points.
Key Vocabulary Point, slope, unemployment
Materials Needed Computers, overhead projector, textbook

The second day of this lesson on point-slope form presented in Figure 7.2 has been designed to allow students further opportunities to engage with the math content and practice their English language development skills in listening, speaking, and writing.

Figure 7.2
Sample Mathematics Lesson Plan—Point-Slope Form (Day Two)

Title of the Lesson Point-Slope Form	**Class (Content Area) & Grade Level** Algebra/8th Grade English learners at the emerging level
Content Standards *Grade 8–Expressions and Equations: Understand the connections between proportional relationships, lines, and linear equations* Graph proportional relationships, interpreting the unit rate as the slope of the graph. Compare two different proportional relationships represented in different ways. (8-EE,5)	**ELD Standards** *Exchanging information/ideas* Contribute to class, group, and partner discussions by following turn-taking rules, asking relevant questions, affirming others, adding relevant information, and paraphrasing key ideas. (Expanding level) *Productive: Writing* Write increasingly concise summaries of texts and experiences using complex sentences and key words (i.e., from notes or graphic organizers). (Expanding level)

(continued)

Figure 7.2
(continued)

Content Objectives	Language Objectives
Students will be able to compare and graph the unemployment rates from the two years they identified in their research. Students will understand linear equations that help them make predictions about consecutive unemployment figures, but not long-term unemployment figures.	Students will be able to contribute to a partner discussion by asking at least 2 relevant questions and adding relevant information when discussing unemployment rates. Students will be able to use standard grammatical form to write summaries in their notebooks using the format outlined in the class.

Assessment Plan

Informal: Monitor student discussion by assessing the questions students ask and adding relevant information to their partner's statements when they are discussing unemployment rates.

Formal: Students' notebooks are checked every two weeks for use of the note-taking strategies and use of standard grammatical form to write summaries as outlined by the teacher (10 assignment points)

Summative: Information learned during this two-day lesson will be included on the test at the end of the unit. (worth 100 quiz points and 100 test points)

Instructional Strategies/Student Activities

Into/Through/Closure/Beyond

INTO: Journal Writing (15 minutes)

Randomly call on students to read the content and language objectives for the day, and other students to restate the objectives in their own words.

The students will journal about the previous day's tasks in their spiral notebooks. They will answer the following questions: (1) What were two things you learned from the previous day's class? (2) What did your graph of the unemployment numbers you found look like? Did your line make a positive or negative slope, and what does that mean in relation to unemployment? (3) Write down the equations two of your classmates found. How do their equations differ from yours?

The teacher walks around the classroom and checks for understanding as students are journaling in their notebooks. Once students have answered the questions, have them share their responses with a partner and begin to make conjectures about possible differences in their responses.

THROUGH: Discussion (10 minutes)

Facilitate a discussion on differences and similarities between the students' equations and graphs.

Students participate in the class discussion about the differences and similarities between their equations and their classmates' equations. Students will make conjectures about why some students might have positive slopes and some might have negative slopes.

BEYOND: Graphing Unemployment Data (10 minutes)

Make and put up a giant graph in the front of the class for students to put their unemployment data on. The students will plot the points they found the previous day on the big graph.

Facilitate a class discussion about the new data on the graph in front of the class. Ask students why this data is not linear and when it would be useful to use linear equations with unemployment data.

Figure 7.2
(continued)

CLOSURE: Journal Writing (15 minutes) Make a line of best fit through the data and ask students to journal about the overall trend line and what it conveys about unemployment figures. The students will journal about what they see on the big graph when everyone's unemployment points are plotted. They will notice that the points are not linear. They will also journal about the trend line that represents the unemployment figures spanning several decades.
Key Vocabulary Point, slope, and vocabulary that may arise from the research and discussions about unemployment rates
Materials Needed Computers, overhead projector, textbook

High School—Algebra II

The mathematics lesson plans described in this section were originally developed by a high school teacher in southern California for her Algebra II class. The author rewrote and adapted the lessons to align them with the CCSS for Mathematics and to address the needs of English learners by including appropriate California ELD standards; however, note that the process outlined in this book can be used with ELD standards from any state. The Algebra II class featured in this example presented in Figure 7.3 enrolls students in grades 11–12 and has 11th-grade English learners at the emerging (exit) and expanding (entry) levels. The class is taught on a block schedule, so each lesson is approximately 1 hour, 45 minutes.

Figure 7.3
Sample Mathematics Lesson Plan—Arithmetic Sequences

Title of the Lesson Arithmetic Sequences	**Class (Content Area) & Grade Level** Algebra II–11th to 12th grade English learners–emerging (exit) and expanding (entry) levels
Content standards *Functions: Linear, Quadratic, and Exponential Models* Construct linear and exponential functions, including arithmetic and geometrical sequences, given a graph, a description of a relationship, or two input-output pairs. (F-LE,2)	**ELD standards** *Selecting Language Resources* Use an increasing variety of grade-appropriate general academic and domain-specific academic words accurately and appropriately when producing increasingly complex written and spoken texts. (Expanding level)
Content Objectives Students will be able to identify arithmetic sequences. Students will be able to use a formula to find the nth term of a sequence.	**Language Objectives** Students will be able to recognize and understand that words have a different meaning in mathematics (e.g., sequence, term) and use this knowledge to solve mathematical equations.

(*continued*)

Figure 7.3
(continued)

Assessment Plan
Informal: In small groups (3–4), students will be assessed on how well they are able to complete the classroom examples using the formulas presented. Ask students to explain their responses using the new vocabulary in context to the teacher during the group work activity. Emerging-level students will be assessed on their ability to use 1–2 vocabulary terms in their responses. Expanding-level students will be assessed on their ability to use all the vocabulary terms accurately and appropriately in their responses.

Formal: Students will be graded on their homework and quizzes (one per section).

Summative: Students will be graded on a chapter exam at the end of the unit.

Instructional Strategies/Student Activities
Into/Through/Closure/Beyond

INTO: Find the Patterns (15 minutes)
Randomly call on students to read the content and language objectives for the day and other students to restate the objectives in their own words.

Students are given a worksheet that explains patterns and sequences (from a previous lesson, accessing prior knowledge). They work independently on identifying patterns and sequences in the problems on the worksheet. Ask them to use formulas and complete sentences to explain their answers. Students are chosen randomly to go to the board to respond to a question. The class discusses each question and response and corrects any mistakes as a class.

THROUGH: Introduce Vocabulary—Pattern, Sequence, *and* Term (15 minutes)
Introduce the vocabulary words *pattern*, *sequence*, and *term* by modeling formulas on the board and explaining the step-by-step process. Students refer to examples in their textbook as you go through each one step by step and continue to use the new vocabulary. Each vocabulary word is written on the overhead, along with a sentence definition and a corresponding formula. Students copy all this information into their notebooks.

THROUGH: Recursive Formulas (15 minutes)
Start by asking students what "re-" means. Explain that a recursive formula entails using the previous term in the sequence. Using an example from the textbook as a model, describe each step of the formula as it is written on the board. Students copy the descriptions into their notebooks along with the definition provided for *recursive formula*.

Present 5 practice problems to students. In their small groups, students work to solve each equation using the formula provided. One student is selected randomly from the group to go to the board and write out the group's solution. Each student at the board is asked to describe the process used (how the formula was used) to solve the equation.

THROUGH: Explicit Formulas (15 minutes)
Begin by asking students to read the information in the textbook on explicit formulas.
Introduce *explicit formula* by going over:

$$a_n = n^2$$
$$A_n = n^2 + 1$$

Describe how to use the formula, going step by step through an equation. Students copy this example and the definition of explicit formula into their notebooks.

Show students 5 practice problems on explicit formulas. Students work in their small groups to solve the equations using the formula provided. One student is selected randomly from the group to go to the board to write the group's solution. Each student at the board is asked to describe the process used to solve the equation.

THROUGH: Difference Between Recursive and Explicit Formulas (5 minutes)
Point out the differences between *recursive* and *explicit formulas*. Do one example of each on the board and have students explain the step-by-step process in solving each equation.

Figure 7.3
(continued)

CLOSURE: Group Work (30 minutes) In small groups, students work on the 10 equations presented to the class (using recursive and explicit formulas). After 10 minutes, one student is chosen randomly from each group to write out his or her answer on the board. Each student is asked to explain each step used in calculating the equation. *BEYOND: Homework* (10 minutes) In their groups, students begin to work on homework problems collaboratively–recursive and explicit formulas and the differences between the two. They will complete homework problems individually before the next class.
Key Vocabulary Sequence, term, recursive formula, explicit formula
Materials Needed Algebra I worksheet on patterns and sequences, overhead projector or document camera, textbook

Following the lesson on arithmetic sequences, the second lesson outlined in Figure 7.4 focuses on geometric sequences. This lesson also is taught during a block period of 1 hour and 45 minutes.

Figure 7.4
Sample Mathematics Lesson Plan—Geometric Sequences

Title of the Lesson Geometric Sequences	**Class (Content Area) & Grade Level** Algebra II–11th to 12th grade English learners–emerging (exit) and expanding (entry) levels
Content Standards *Functions: Linear, Quadratic, and Exponential Models* Construct linear and exponential functions, including arithmetic and geometrical sequences, given a graph, a description of a relationship, or two input-output pairs. (F-LE,2).	**ELD Standards** *Justifying/arguing* Justify opinions and positions or persuade others by making connections between ideas and articulating relevant textual evidence or background knowledge. (Expanding level)
Content Objective(s) Students will be able to identify a geometric sequence and find the common ratio. Students will be able to distinguish between a geometric sequence, arithmetic sequence, or neither. Students will be able to find the missing term in a geometric sequence using the geometric mean.	**Language Objectives** As a homework assignment, students will be able to write a persuasive paragraph explaining whether the sequence presented to them is geometric, arithmetic, or neither.
Assessment Plan *Informal:* In small groups (3–4), students will be assessed on how well they are able to complete the classroom examples using the formulas presented. Students will be asked to explain their responses to the teacher during the group work activity. *Formal:* Students' persuasive essays will be assessed on a 1–4 scale using a rubric (Table 7.2). Emerging (exit-level) English learners are expected to perform at a 3 level, and expanding (entry-level) English learners are expected to perform at a 4 level for both the content and language objectives described in the rubric. *Formal:* Students will be graded on their homework and quizzes (one per section). *Summative:* Students will be graded on a chapter exam at the end of the unit.	

(continued)

Figure 7.4
(continued)

Instructional Strategies/Student Activities
Into/Through/Closure/Beyond

INTO: Geometric Patterns (15 minutes)
Randomly call on students to read the content and language objectives for the day and other students to restate the objectives in their own words.

Building on students' knowledge from the lesson on arithmetic sequences, show students pictures of Islamic art downloaded from the Metropolitan Museum of Art website. Give students a few minutes to read the three short paragraphs describing how geometric patterns are used in Islamic art. Give students instructions on the reciprocal teaching process (an activity they have done in the past with reading) and assign each group member a role. After the students have read the passage, each group will go through the reciprocal teaching process. As a class, ask a few comprehension questions to assess the groups' understanding of the text. Give each table a photo of Islamic art, also downloaded from the Metropolitan Museum of Art website. Examples are from architecture, ceramics, carpets, text, etc. Ask each table group to examine the photo and present to the class on what geometric pattern is used and how they identified the pattern.

THROUGH: Geometric Sequence and Common Ratio (20 minutes)
Show 4 sequences on the overhead projector. Students must find the pattern of the 4 given sequences (the pattern will involve multiplying the previous term by something to get to the next). Ask the students: Are any of the given sequences arithmetic? How do you know?

Introduce the formal definitions for GEOMETRIC SEQUENCE and COMMON RATIO. Use the sequence 5, 15, 45, 135, . . . to explain how to identify a geometric sequence, how to properly form a ratio, and what a common ratio looks like. Students will write the sequence and the definitions provided in their notebooks.

Ask students the following question:
Is the sequence 15, 30, 45, 60, . . . geometric? To ensure students' understanding, ask students: If the sequence goes up by 15, why isn't it geometric?

As a class, complete the following: Derive the formula for the general term for geometric sequences using: 1, 2, 4, 8, 16, ... Again, ask comprehension questions to ensure students understand how to derive formulas.

Give students several other examples to let them practice. They work in their small groups, and then one student from each group is randomly selected to go to the board and show how the group solved the equation. Discuss any questions and/or problems students have to ensure they understand geometric sequence and common ratio.

THROUGH: Bank of Formulas for Geometric Sequences (20 minutes)
Introduce BANK OF FORMULAS FOR GEOMETRIC SEQUENCES (recursive and explicit) using the definitions and examples presented in the textbook. Students write the formulas in their notebooks along with the definitions you have written.

Use the following sequence to practice using the formulas to find the next term of a geometric sequence to find the 19th term—11, 33, 99, 297, ... Give students time to work in their small groups to find the 19th term, and then discuss as a class how to use the formula. Again, check for understanding by asking several comprehension questions.

Showing students a sequence, ask them to find the 19th term of the sequence:
20, 17, 14, 11, 8, . . . (this one is not geometric, it is arithmetic, so students will have to think creatively). Again, give students time to work in their groups to solve this and figure out why it is not geometric.

Write several sequences on the board and have the groups determine if they are geometric, arithmetic, or neither, and support their answer for each one. The groups must be in agreement and may not ask any questions of the teacher or others in the class except for the students in their group. When reporting to the class, they must use the appropriate math vocabulary.

Give the groups a couple more sequences to work on to practice their knowledge.
Is the sequence geometric? What is r?
a. 1, -6, 36, -216, . . .
b. 2, 4, 6, 8, 10, . . .

Figure 7.4
(continued)

THROUGH: Geometric Mean (10 minutes) Introduce the GEOMETRIC MEAN and how to find it. Give several examples, and refer to the examples and definitions in the textbook. Students write the definition in their notebooks. In their groups, have students practice with the following: a) 20, _____, 80 b) 3, _____,18,75 c) 28, _____, 5103 Choose a student randomly from the groups to go the board and fill in the blanks. Ask each student to explain how he or she determined the geometric mean for the problem. *CLOSURE: Group Work* (30 minutes) In small groups, students work on the equations presented on the overhead projector (using geometric sequences, common ratio, and geometric mean). After 10 minutes, one student is chosen randomly from each group to write out his or her answer on the board. Each student is asked to explain each step he or she used in calculating the equation. As a class, discuss any questions students have or difficulties in solving problems. *BEYOND: Homework* (10 minutes) In their groups, students begin to work on homework problems collaboratively. They will complete homework problems individually before the next class, along with the persuasive essay.
Key Vocabulary geometric sequence, common ratio, geometric mean
Materials Needed Textbook, geometric patterns in Islamic art from the Metropolitan Museum of Art, 3 paragraphs of text, and several photo examples (plates, architecture, carpet) *http://www.metmuseum.org/toah/hd/geom/hd_geom.htm* *http://www.metmuseum.org/* (search term: Islamic art)

The rubric presented in Table 7.2 is the differentiated assessment for the persuasive writing activity in the second high school lesson example on geometric sequences. The criteria for the language standard and objective, write persuasive compositions, is derived from the proficiency

Table 7.2 Rubric for Sample Lesson Plan on Geometric Sequences—Persuasive Compositions

	1	2	3	4
Language Productive—Justifying/arguing	Write a persuasive paragraph that establishes a controlling idea with detailed evidence	Write a persuasive paragraph that establishes a controlling idea and supports arguments with 1 example (detailed evidence)	Write a persuasive paragraph that structures ideas and arguments in a logical way with consistent use of standard grammatical form, with 2 examples—detailed evidence	Write a persuasive paragraph that includes a clear thesis, describes organized points of support, and addresses counterarguments, with 3 examples—detailed evidence
Content Geometric or arithmetic sequences	Paragraph presents somewhat clear ideas with at least one key vocabulary term	Paragraph presents clear ideas, but key vocabulary is not consistently used	Paragraph presents clear ideas; 2–3 relevant points, but they are unstructured	Paragraph presents clear and focused information; 3–4 relevant points that are well supported

levels of the ELD standard. Similarly, the criterion for the content objective is differentiated on the same 1–4 scale as the language objective. English learners have many opportunities to access the content through the strategies and activities designed for the lesson before they are assessed.

To accurately assess English learners at one level above their current language proficiency level, emerging (exit-stage) English learners are expected to perform at a 3 level, and expanding (entry-stage) English learners are expected to perform at a 4 level for both the content and language objectives described in the rubric.

Discussion of the Lessons

The mathematics lessons described in this chapter present challenging content to all students, using strategies and activities that allow English learners to access the content and to help them develop their English language skills. English learners in these classes are identified at proficiency levels ranging from emerging to expanding levels.

Standards, Objectives, and Assessments

Using the backwards mapping principle, a content (CCSS for Mathematics) and English language development (ELD) standard are chosen for each lesson. Based on the standards, objectives are written to show how students will demonstrate mastery of the standards. An assessment plan is then developed. All four lessons include informal, formal, and summative assessments. In each lesson, the assessment for the language objective has differentiated levels of mastery for English learners targeted at one level above their current proficiency level. In the first day of the high school lesson, English learners will be assessed on the language objective in small groups of 3–4 on how well they are able to complete the classroom examples using the formulas presented. Students explain their responses to the teacher using the new vocabulary learned in the lesson in context during the group work activity. Emerging-level students are assessed on their ability to use 1–2 vocabulary terms in their responses, while expanding-level students are assessed on their ability to use all the vocabulary terms accurately and appropriately in their responses. In all the assessments outlined in the lesson examples, students have multiple ways to access the content prior to being assessed through instructional strategies, group work, and student-centered activities.

Instructional Strategies

In both the middle and high school lesson examples, the first lesson presented is an introductory lesson for the unit. Since the lessons introduce students to several new math concepts, a significant portion of the each lesson focuses on vocabulary and concept development. For example, Day Two of the high school lesson builds on vocabulary learned in previous lessons and allows students the opportunity to make connections between the content and relevant examples in their lives. Similarly, the middle school lessons introduce concepts in Day One of the lesson that are reinforced and extended in Day Two of the lesson. The lessons are models for how the process of repetition and scaffolding instruction helps English learners access the content being taught while practicing their English proficiency skills.

Student Activities

In all lesson examples, instructional strategies and student activities are aligned to the content and language standards and objectives as well as to the assessment plan. The activities are student-centered and give English learners the opportunity to practice their listening, speaking, reading, and writing skills. Given that the CCSS for Mathematics are performance-based and contain many literacy skills, these types of student-centered activities outlined in the middle and high school lessons are crucial for English learners to access the core curriculum. In each lesson, activities are focused on English language development beyond the skills chosen to be included in the assessment plan. For example, as students are working in small groups to solve equations, they are practicing many listening and speaking skills such as speaking to be understood and participating in academic and classroom discussions. As English learners work in groups with native-English speakers, they can learn the content presented from their peers as well as from the teacher. Also included in each lesson are activities focused on reading and writing development, which help English learners to practice the literacy skills they need to successfully meet the standards outlined in the CCSS. In each lesson, students are writing vocabulary definitions, formulas, and responses to questions and sentences to explain to how they solved an equation in their notebooks. Day Two of the high school lesson also includes a persuasive essay to allow English learners, and all students, the opportunity to enhance their writing proficiency.

Culturally Relevant/Multicultural Resources

The middle and high school mathematics lessons also include culturally relevant/multicultural resources that the teachers identified as topics their students would be interested in based on what they knew about who their students were. The middle school lessons on unemployment rates are intended to expose students to a topic that directly impacts many of their families and/or their friends and neighbors. Some students may not have considered unemployment figures before. They will have a chance to empathize with those who are unemployed. For other students, the unemployment rates will be more of a reality and may help them better understand their family's economic situation.

Summary

As you reflect on how to design mathematics lesson plans for your English learner students, keep in mind the main interrelated points of this chapter:

- It is important to fully understand who your English learners are in order to include teaching strategies and student activities in your lessons that build on their strengths and help you address any areas of weakness they have. There may be concepts and vocabulary specific to mathematics that are unfamiliar to English learners and thus more challenging for them to learn. In addition to their English proficiency levels, getting to know your English learners' prior knowledge of the subject area, learning styles, backgrounds, interests, and cultures can help you choose multicultural resources to use in your lessons that are relevant to your students' lives.
- The objectives you write for your lesson should be based on the CCSS for Mathematics content standards and the ELD standards your state has adopted. The content standard generally represents the "what" of the lesson—what content is being taught—while the language standards represent "how" your English learners will master the content standard chosen at the appropriate proficiency levels for them.
- The assessments and activities you use should be aligned to the content and language objectives you have chosen so that you and your students understand the expectations for each lesson. It is important to use the information you have learned about your English learners in Step 1 of the lesson planning process to differentiate your assessments so they accurately reflect what your students are able to accomplish at the end of your lesson. You should also use the information you have learned about your students to design scaffolded activities that will help them learn the content you are presenting while simultaneously developing their English proficiency.

Applying What You Have Learned

In this chapter, you have learned how to provide equitable instruction for your English learner students by using a four-step lesson planning process. Demonstrate your understanding of the chapter by participating in the following activities and answering the corresponding questions.

STEP 1: Know your English learners

- What difficulties might English learners have with the CCSS for Mathematics that you can take into account when designing your lessons?
- Explain how you can obtain information about your English learners so that your lessons are aligned to their English proficiency levels, prior content knowledge, and learning styles.

STEP 2: Choose standards for your lessons

- In the lesson planning process presented in this chapter, you have learned that lessons should focus on the CCSS for Mathematics as well as the ELD standards used in your state. Choose a CCSS for Mathematics and a corresponding ELD standard. Write content (CCSS) and language (ELD) objectives based on the standards you have chosen that are measurable and observable.

STEP 3: Design differentiated assessments and student-centered activities

- You have learned how to differentiate your assessment to accurately assess English learners in your mathematics class. You have also learned how to use teaching strategies that can help your English learners access the content you are teaching. Additionally, you have learned specific student activities to use in your class that will promote interactions between English learners and native-English speakers. Using the content and language objectives that you wrote in Step 2, design the following components of a lesson plan:
  - Assessments that will allow your students to demonstrate they have met the content and language objectives (Remember to differentiate your assessments based on your English learners' language proficiency levels.)
  - A student activity that is aligned to the objectives you have written and the assessments you have designed
  - An explanation of the teaching strategies you will use to ensure that your English learners understand and can complete the activity you have designed

STEP 4: Select culturally relevant/multicultural materials and resources

- List some national, state, and/or local organizations that provide culturally relevant/multicultural resources on their websites that can be incorporated into your math lessons.

chapter 8

Science

Learning Outcomes and Focus Questions

STEP 1: Know your English learners

- What difficulties might my English learners have with the Common Core State Standards for Literacy in Science?
- What do I need to know about my English learners to plan instruction?

STEP 2: Choose standards for your lessons

- What content standards and Common Core State Standards for Literacy in Science will my lesson focus on?
- How do I design lessons that include language standards and objectives in my science class?

STEP 3: Design differentiated assessments and student-centered activities

- How can I differentiate assessment to accurately assess my English learners?
- What strategies can I use to help English learners master the content I am teaching?
- What activities can I implement in my class to promote interactions between English learners and native-English speakers?

STEP 4: Select culturally relevant/multicultural materials and resources

- How can I find culturally relevant/multicultural resources to use in my science class?

This chapter outlines a process middle and high school teachers can use to design lessons that incorporate language objectives based on ELD standards alongside content objectives from science content standards and Common Core State Standards (CCSS) for Literacy in History/Social Studies, Science, and Technical Subjects for their English learners.

It explains how to differentiate instruction and assessment based on English learners' language proficiency levels and then outlines strategies science teachers can use in their classrooms to help their students understand the content. Much of the content in middle and high school science classes is built on knowledge that has been taught in previous classes in elementary, middle, and high school. An immigrant English learner may not have the same foundational knowledge of the English language as his or her peers and/or knowledge of the fields of science such as biology, earth science, and life science that students who have attended U.S. schools in elementary and middle school have. Content presented in middle and high school science classes includes extensive vocabulary development, complex and abstract concepts, and culturally specific contexts that may be unfamiliar to English learners. With the CCSS for Literacy in History/Social Studies, Science, and Technical Subjects, science classes will include an increased amount of reading and writing activities that are aligned to these standards. Designing scaffolded activities helps build a base of knowledge for English learners and teaches them the processes and procedures used in your class. Although this may seem challenging, you can design activities to give students the time they need to fully process the meaning of science concepts and thus increase their opportunities to excel in class.

STEP 1: Know your English learners

What Difficulties Might My English Learners Have with the Common Core State Standards for Literacy in Science?

The Common Core State Standards (CCSS) for Literacy in History/Social Studies, Science, and Technical Subjects focus on the two language domains of reading and writing, with ten reading standards and ten writing standards in the following categories:

Reading	**Writing**
Key ideas and details	Text type and purposes
Craft and structure	Production and distribution of writing
Integration of knowledge and ideas	Research to build and present knowledge
Range of readings and level of text complexity	Range of writing

The reading and writing standards are aligned to the reading and writing CCSS for English Language Arts. The information presented in this section is not intended to be an extensive description of the CCSS for Literacy in

History/Social Studies, Science, and Technical Subjects but rather a discussion of the difficulties English learners may have with the standards.

The CCSS for Literacy in History/Social Studies, Science, and Technical Subjects are progressive and developmental standards that begin in kindergarten and become increasingly more complex by the 12th grade. The literacy skills outlined in the standards for middle school (grades 6–8) and high school (grades 9–10 and 11–12) for any given standard require advanced levels of language development that some English learner students may not have attained. For example, Anchor Writing Standard #1, "Write arguments focused on discipline-specific content," is divided into five standards, each representing progressively complex literacy skills from middle to high school. Standard 1.a outlines the following skills:

- *Grades 6–8:* Introduce claim(s) about a topic or issue, acknowledge and distinguish claim(s) from alternate or opposing claims, and organize the reasons and evidence logically.
- *Grades 9–10:* Introduce **precise** claim(s), distinguish the claim(s) from alternate or opposing claim(s), and create an organization that **establishes clear relationships among the claim(s).**
- *Grades 11–12:* Introduce precise, **knowledgeable** claim(s), **establish the significance of the claim(s),** distinguish the claim(s) from alternate or opposing claims, and create an organization that **logically sequences the claim(s)**.

The text in bold demonstrates the progressive nature of the standards. Not only do the literacy skills become more complex with each grade span, but the skills are also more performance-based. When comparing the writing skills in the CCSS for Literacy in Science to those outlined in California ELD standards, it is clear that the skills required of English learners at the bridging level (the highest proficiency level) are not as advanced as the literacy levels defined in the CCSS for Literacy in History/Social Studies, Science, and Technical Subjects. The following California ELD standard in Writing—Justifying/arguing (presented at the bridging level) is aligned to CCSS Writing Standard 1.a:

- *Grade 8:* (a) **Express attitudes** and opinions or temper statements with nuanced modal expressions; (b) **Justify opinions** or persuade others by providing detailed and relevant textual evidence.
- *Grades 9–10:* (a) **Express attitudes** and opinions or temper statements with nuanced modal expressions; (b) **Justify opinions** or persuade others by making connections and distinctions between ideas and texts and articulating sufficient, detailed, and relevant textual evidence, using appropriate register.
- *Grades 11–12:* (a) **Express attitudes** and opinions or temper statements with nuanced modal expressions; (b) **Justify opinions** or persuade others by making connections and distinctions between ideas and texts and articulating sufficient, detailed, and relevant textual evidence, using appropriate register.

Because the writing skills in the CCSS are more complex than those outlined in the ELD standards, English learners need explicit scaffolding to move from "articulating sufficient, detailed and relevant opinions" to "creating an organization that establishes clear relationships among the claim(s)." A similar gap exists between the level of the reading skills outlined in the CCSS for Literacy in History/Social Studies, Science, and Technical Subjects and those outlined in the ELD standards. Skills outlined in the reading standards are performance-based and progressively more complex from middle to high school.

Another matter to consider is that the CCSS for Literacy in History/Social Studies, Science, and Technical Subjects only cover the language domains of reading and writing. To become fully proficient in English, English learners must develop their listening and speaking skills as well. Similarly, English learners need to acquire knowledge of the English language and academic vocabulary specific to the content area of science in order to attain the level of academic English needed to be successful. As these language development areas are not specifically in the CCSS for Literacy in History/Social Studies, Science, and Technical Subjects, teachers need to explicitly teach English learners listening and speaking skills and vocabulary development so they have the language and literacy skills needed to master these standards. Science teachers who differentiate language instruction for English learners based on their proficiency levels and teach language development skills simultaneously with the literacy skills required in the CCSS will be giving their English learner students the opportunity to attain the academic skills needed to be successful in their classes and in all content area classes.

What Do I Need to Know About My English Learners to Plan Instruction?

The more information teachers learn about English learner students, the greater the opportunities they will have to be academically successful in your science classroom. For example, learning about students' academic and background knowledge of the science content you are teaching and self-identification of their strengths and weaknesses with the language and content can help you understand which concepts will be accessible to them and which will need to be scaffolded more explicitly. Along with academic knowledge, assess your English learners' English language proficiency levels in the four language domains of listening, speaking, reading, and writing. How an English learner's proficiency levels in the language domains are determined is described in detail in Part 2 of this book. It is important to know your English learners' proficiency level in each language domain so you can choose an ELD standard for your lesson at the level needed to scaffold students' English language development. This information can help sharpen the focus on addressing language issues English learners may have with science content. A survey administered at the beginning of the year also can gather useful information about what languages are spoken at home, which languages students use to speak to their friends, what they know about the science content you will teach them in your class, and what difficulties students feel they may have with the content and vocabulary of a science classroom. You can also ask questions that will help you understand your English learners' interests, extracurricular activities, goals in your science class, and broader goals they have for their lives.

By identifying English learners' learning styles, you can better design lessons to include teaching strategies and student activities that build on students' strengths and help them develop in areas of weakness. If English learner students are visual learners, presenting information through modes such as pictures, graphic organizers, and charts will help them access the content you are presenting. For visual learners, when you present information in other formats such as through a lecture (auditory), continually check for understanding to ensure that English learner students can demonstrate they know the content. Finally, knowing about your English learners' (and all your students') backgrounds, interests, cultural and social affiliations, and other pertinent information that in combination makes your students "who they are" will help you plan lessons that include multicultural and culturally relevant literature and resources for them. Doing so will help English learners make connections to the content you are teaching and keep them engaged in all aspects of the lesson.

STEP 2: Choose standards for your lessons

What Content Standards Will My Lesson Focus On?

The sequence of how you present content standards in your science class is most likely determined locally by your department, school, or district. However the content standards are chosen for each lesson you teach, it is important to note that they represent the "what" of your lesson—what content is being taught. In addition to content standards, the CCSS for Literacy in History/Social Studies, Science, and Technical Subjects represent what literacy skills your lesson will address. The CCSS present many complex literacy skills, so it will take multiple lessons for students to develop mastery of the standard. For example, Anchor Writing Standard #1 is divided into five separate developmental standards that together represent the writing skills a student needs to perform to demonstrate mastery of the standard. Once the content standard and CCSS for Literacy in History/Social Studies, Science, and Technical Subjects being taught is determined, the next step is to write an objective based on each standard to guide the lesson. Content and CCSS objectives should be measurable and observable and allow you and your students to know what they will be able to do by the end of the lesson.

Example:

- I am teaching a 6th-grade Earth Science class and have chosen State Standard 6-1.g (California Content): "Students know how to determine the epicenter of an earthquake and know that the effects of an earthquake in any region vary, depending on the size of the earthquake, the distance from the epicenter, the local geology, and the type of construction in the region."
- I write a content objective for my lesson based on the standard: Upon completion of the Japan/Haiti earthquake comparison activity, students will be able to identify the differing effects of both earthquakes based on the size of the earthquakes, distance from the epicenter, and construction in both regions.
- I choose the following CCSS for Literacy in Science—Grades 6–8 standard: Reading: Integration of Knowledge and Ideas, Standard 9: "Compare and contrast the information gained from experiments, simulations, video, or multimedia sources with that gained from reading a text on the same topic."
- I write a literacy objective based on the CCSS for Literacy in Science: Students will be able to identify 2 pieces of information that compare or contrast the effects of earthquakes in Haiti and Japan from videos and news articles.

Because the CCSS for Literacy in Science are performance-based, many of them are already observable and sometimes measurable. Therefore, the literacy objectives you write for your lesson may either be the standard itself or closely aligned to it. The same may be true for some science content standards. The key is to write your measurable and observable objectives so that they are aligned to the standard, thus allowing you to demonstrate with your assessment that your students have mastered the standard chosen for the lesson.

How Do I Design Lessons That Include Language Standards and Objectives in My Science Class?

If the content standards represent the "what" of any lesson, then the ELD standards represent the "how" for English learners—how they will master the content standard chosen at the appropriate proficiency level. The process for choosing language standards (ELD) in the areas of listening, speaking, reading, and writing to include in lessons was outlined in detail in Part 2 of this book. Briefly, teachers should choose a language standard that complements the content standard addressed in the lesson. Once a standard is chosen, teachers then write a language objective for the lesson that outlines how students will demonstrate that they have met the standard.

Example:

- I have 10th-grade English learners at the emerging (exit-stage) proficiency level in the language area of reading in my high school Biology class.
- I select the California ELD standard on reading/viewing closely (Grades 9–10) to include in my lesson.
- I use the standard that is one level above my students' current proficiency level, the expanding level: "Explain ideas, phenomena, processes, and relationships within and across texts, based on close reading of a variety of grade-appropriate texts, presented in various print and multimedia formats, using increasing variety of general academic and domain-specific words."
- I write a language objective based on the standard: "Students will be able to use at least 2–3 new vocabulary words correctly in detailed sentences when describing the main idea of the reading passage (and the video) in a small-group discussion activity."

English learners should have as much practice as possible with the English language in order to become proficient in all four language domains. Teachers can choose activities that incorporate several language skills to include in their lessons to help English learners practice the language. However, it is recommended that each lesson focus on one or two language standards. As assessment is aligned to the standards chosen, focusing the assessment on one or two language skills permits an accurate evaluation of the extent to which English learners have mastered them.

STEP 3: Design differentiated assessments and student-centered activities

How Can I Differentiate Assessment to Accurately Assess My English Learners?

Once English learners' proficiency levels are determined in any language domain, they can perform language skills at those levels independently and automatically. Targeting instruction one proficiency level above their current level helps English learners build knowledge of the English language that will help them attain overall language proficiency. Following this tenet, an accurate assessment for English learners should be targeted at one level above their current proficiency level as well. Using California ELD standards as an example, English learners who demonstrate exiting-stage skills at the emerging level should be assessed on the expanding standards. Similarly using the World-Class Instructional Design and Assessment (WIDA) standards, English learners who are proficient at the developing level should be assessed at the expanding level (one level above their current level). In either example, assessments designed at proficiency levels above the expanding level may contain language skills and knowledge that are too far beyond the English learners' current proficiency to be accurate assessments. While English learners may have a general understanding of the content, they may not be proficient enough in English to communicate their mastery of the content in either oral or written form.

Following the backwards mapping principle, assessment should be aligned to the content, CCSS, and language standards chosen for each lesson, as well as the objectives written to align to them. Science teachers who have both native-English speakers and English learners in their class can create one assessment plan for their lessons that includes both language and content. Although the language objectives are specifically designed for English learners, the skills covered in the language standards may also be beneficial for the native-English-speaking students. In the following example, the criteria used in the rubric from the ELD standards to assess the writing assignment highlights the writing skills needed to create coherent essays and thus can be used with English learners and native-English speakers to improve their language and literacy skills. In science classes, all students can improve their language skills in listening, speaking, reading, and writing by the explicit focus teachers place on these skills for English learner students.

Example:

- I have 6th-grade English learners in my middle school Science class at the expanding (exit stage) levels.
- My content area is Earth Science. The content standard for the lesson is: "Students know how to determine the epicenter of an earthquake and know that the effects of an earthquake of any region vary, depending on the size of the earthquake, the distance from the epicenter, the local geology, and the type of construction in the region" (Grade 6—1.g, California Content)
- I am using the CCSS for Literacy in Science, Writing Standard under Text Types and Purposes, 1.a (Grades 6–8): "Write arguments on discipline-specific content—Introduce claim(s) about a topic or issue, acknowledge and distinguish the claim(s) from alternate or opposing claims, and organize the reasons and evidence logically."
- I am using the ELD writing standard: "Write clear and coherent summaries of texts and experiences using complete and concise sentences and key words" (bridging level).
- Students will be writing essays on the factors that affect how a country recovers from an earthquake. The assessment will be based on organization of the content—a clear thesis supported by quotes and facts and proper grammatical form (complete sentences, spelling, and word choice).

  (Additional assessments on the content standard are outlined in the lesson plan examples in Figures 8.2 and 8.3).
- I create a rubric for the lesson that includes criteria to assess the content (state content standards and CCSS) and language objectives.

- I assess my English learners on the language objective that is one level above their current level, bridging. My English learners will be expected to earn a 4 on the rubric, representing the bridging level.
- Since the writing activity is fully scaffolded during the two-day lesson, I also expect that my English learners can earn a 4 on the rubric for the content objective criteria (state content standards and CCSS for Literacy in Science). I will assess my native English speakers' essays using the same rubric.

For English learners, the assessment is equitable in that it accurately assesses them based on the language proficiency level that is one level above their current level, as shown in the rubric in Table 8.1.

What Strategies Can I Use to Help English Learners Master the Content I Am Teaching?

Underlying any strategy teachers use to help English learners in their science classes is the principle that teachers have high expectations of their students. Displaying and explaining the lesson's content and language objectives ensures that English learners understand your expectations and goals for the day and allows them to focus on the main idea of the lesson. English learners can learn science content when it is presented through accessible strategies such as SDAIE (specially designed academic instruction in English) that help make challenging content accessible to English learners in content area classrooms. Using multiple modes of presenting content, such

Table 8.1 Sample Rubric That Differentiates Assessment for English Learners

	1	2	3	4
Language Development: Write concise and cohesive summaries	The essay does not have a clear thesis and has incomplete sentences, with 2–3 errors in spelling and word choice.	The essay is organized and has a clear thesis with some complete sentences and 2–3 errors in spelling and word choice.	The essay is organized, has a clear thesis, and uses complete sentences, with 2–3 errors in spelling and word choice.	The essay is organized, has a clear thesis, and uses complete sentences, spelling, and correct word choice.
Content: State Standard and CCSS for Literacy Write an essay on factors that affect how a country recovers from an earthquake, citing evidence from the Haiti and Japan earthquakes	The essay outlines factors that affect recovery from an earthquake in Japan or Haiti, which are not supported by quotes or facts.	The essay outlines factors that affect recovery from an earthquake in Japan or Haiti, supported by 1 quote or fact.	The essay outlines factors that affect recovery from an earthquake in Japan and Haiti, supported by 2 quotes or facts.	The essay outlines factors that affect recovery from an earthquake in Japan and Haiti, supported by 3 or more quotes or facts.

as visuals, graphic organizers, video, and multimedia, gives English learners a variety of methods to access the content. Additionally, teachers can use heterogeneous grouping strategies where English learners can learn from and share their knowledge with native-English speakers. If necessary, English learners should be given the opportunity to use their native language to negotiate the meaning of content with their peers and then translate their knowledge so they can fully participate in larger class discussions in English.

What Activities Can I Implement in My Class to Promote Interactions Between English Learners and Native-English Speakers?

Using a variety of activities in science classes allows students with different learning styles multiple ways to learn the content being presented. For English learners, designing lessons using activities that promote peer interactions allows them to communicate with their native-English-speaking peers. Students can learn from one another and learn the content, while English learners have the added benefit of practicing their English, which leads to language development. English learners, like many students, need time to process new concepts learned and understand how these concepts are connected to and/or built on prior science concepts presented in class. Designing activities so that English learners work with peers, with a partner, or in small groups gives them time to learn new concepts and practice content area vocabulary in the context of a science class. Activities that promote peer interactions give English learners another way to equitably access the same curriculum and core content as their native-English-speaking peers.

The following two examples of classroom activities, both used in the science lesson examples presented in this chapter, achieve the goals of equal access to the core curriculum and increased peer interactions for English learners. Included in the appendices of this book is a list of all activities described in each content chapter (Chapters 6–9). Together, these suggested activities help promote listening, speaking, reading, and writing skills for English learners. Numerous resources are available to teachers that outline effective classroom activities for English learners. Teachers should use classroom activities that provide a comfortable fit with their teaching style and students' learning styles. If students are familiar with a certain activity that has been used repeatedly in a class and that is effective in teaching content, teachers should continue to incorporate the activity into lessons throughout the year. The routine of using familiar activities helps English learners focus on the content rather than on learning the steps and expectations of a new activity.

SQP2RS Reading Activity

SQP2RS, or Survey, Question, Predict, Read, Respond, and Summarize, is a reading activity that can be used during assigned readings of any type of text, such as textbooks, articles, research reports, and novels (Vogt, 2000). Students can participate in a SQP2RS or "Squeepers" activity individually, with a partner, in small groups, or as a whole class. The activity gives English learners the opportunity to learn how to engage with the text so they can read with a purpose. Teaching English learners SQP2RS or any other reading activity gives them a valuable academic tool they can use to read text across all content area classes, first with the aid of a teacher (scaffolded instruction) and eventually as an independent reading activity. To begin a SQP2RS activity, a teacher can give students a handout (or show it on an overhead projector) with the following information down the left-hand column, leaving space next to each step for students to respond:

- Survey: (Before you read) Think about or discuss what this reading assignment will be about. Look at titles, headers, pictures, etc., for clues.
- Question: (Before you read) Write one to three questions you believe you will be able to answer from the reading.
- Predict: (Before you read) Can you predict one to three things we will learn?
- Read: (You don't need to write anything in this space.)
- Respond: (After you read) Try to answer your questions. Modify, add, or drop questions you wrote above.
- Summarize: (After you read) Write a four-sentence summary. Sentence 1: Identify the main idea of what you read. Sentences 2–4: State details, reasons, examples, and facts from the text to support the main idea.

Like many other reading activities, SQP2RS can help English learners read with a purpose. Reading activities can also help English learners focus on the main ideas in the text while understanding that supporting details are important but often not as critical.

Vocabulary Four Square Activity

Vocabulary Four Square is a vocabulary development activity students can use across all content area classes. It gives English learners the opportunity to engage with vocabulary in ways that enhance their ability to not just learn new vocabulary terms but also use the vocabulary in the context presented. Once students complete this activity, they will have a vocabulary "bank" they can continue to add to during the course of the academic year. The following steps describe the activity as a pen-and-paper activity. Along with other vocabulary development activities, Vocabulary Four Square can also be done electronically through a variety of software programs.

- Students divide a piece of paper into four squares.
- In the upper left-hand corner or square, students write the vocabulary term.
- In the upper right-hand corner or square, students write the definition of the vocabulary term. You can provide a definition for the term or develop one as a class. The key to this step is that you and your students write the same definition in this square.

Annie Pickert Fuller/Pearson Education

- In the lower left-hand corner or square, students write their own original sentence using the vocabulary term in the specified context. For example, if the vocabulary term is *table* and students are in a science class, their sentences should refer to a scientific table or a table used to present data rather than a dining room table.
- In the lower right-hand corner or square, students can draw a picture of the vocabulary term or any other visual or mnemonic device that helps them remember it.

In any content area class, students need to learn a multitude of vocabulary terms, so it may be unrealistic to use this vocabulary activity with every term you present in class. Instead, this activity should be used for vocabulary terms that represent the main ideas of the lesson and those that are necessary for students to bridge concepts from one lesson or unit to the next. By doing so, English learners will understand which vocabulary terms to focus on.

STEP 4: Select culturally relevant/multicultural materials and resources

How Can I Find Culturally Relevant/Multicultural Resources to Use in My Science Class?

There are many opportunities to include relevant, multicultural resources in science classes. Throughout the CCSS, students are asked to identify, analyze, and evaluate multiple sources of information through reading and writing activities. This presents an opportunity for science teachers to identify culturally relevant/multicultural resources that are aligned to their content and that reflect issues of diversity, equity, and social justice. The National Science Teachers Association (NSTA, *www.nsta.org*) has a good collection of resources that help teachers incorporate relevant multicultural topics into their lessons, including contributions to the field from scientists from diverse backgrounds. The organization Rethinking Schools offers resources on its website (*www.rethinkingschools.org*) to help teachers incorporate multicultural and social justice issues into their science classes, as does the Multicultural Education Pavilion (*www.edchange.org/multicultural/*). Teaching Tolerance (*www.tolerance.org*) has an extensive collection of resources on all multicultural topics. The resources are grouped by subject area, grade level, and a wide range of topics on diversity and social justice issues. Additionally, links to multicultural resources can be found on the National Education Association's website (*www.nea.org*). Finally, current science topics, statistics, and opinion polls can be found in local, state, and national newspapers and on the Public Broadcasting Service website (*www.pbs.org*). Countless other websites provide multicultural and culturally relevant resources. Think of the websites listed in this section as a starting point for teachers to begin to search for culturally relevant/multicultural resources rather than as a comprehensive list. The resources you choose to include in your lesson planning will depend upon the information you have learned about your students (Step 1 of the process presented in this book) and how they best fit with the lesson content.

Science Lesson Examples

Four lessons are presented in this section, two at the middle school level and two at the high school level. All four lessons have been rewritten and adapted from lessons designed to be taught by classroom teachers or teacher candidates to include language, content, and CCSS standards and corresponding objectives; differentiated assessments aligned to the standards; student-centered activities; and culturally relevant/multicultural resources. Teachers will most likely have lesson plans similar to these examples that can be easily adapted to align with the process outlined in this book.

Middle School—6th-Grade Earth Science

The lessons presented in this section were originally designed collaboratively with a middle school teacher candidate for a 6th-grade class. The author rewrote and adapted the lessons to include CCSS for Literacy in History/Social Studies, Science, and Technical Subjects and ELD standards. The lessons focus on earthquakes around the world and were originally designed for a middle school class in southern California to meet California State Science Standards in Earth Science. As the lessons were designed for a middle school in southern California, California ELD standards have been incorporated into the lesson for English learners; however, the process outlined in this book can be used with ELD standards from any state. In a previous lesson on the topic of earthquakes, students learned how to determine an epicenter of an earthquake. Continuing with content standard 6.1, the two lessons presented here focus on the effects of two earthquakes in Haiti and Japan. For the purposes of planning instruction based on what teachers know about their students, the lesson presented in Figure 8.1 is for a class that enrolls 34 students with 20 English learners at the expanding level (exit stage), so the objectives, assessments, and activities are targeted at the bridging level (one level above the students' current proficiency level). The lessons are taught during two 55-minute class sessions.

Figure 8.1
Sample Science Lesson Plan—Earthquakes (Day One)

Title of the Lesson Earthquakes Around the World	**Class (Content Area) & Grade Level** 6th Grade—Earth Science English learners at the expanding level
Content Standards *Grade 6—1.g (California Content)* Students know how to determine the epicenter of an earthquake and know that the effects of an earthquake in any region vary depending on the size of the earthquake, distance from the epicenter, local geology, and type of construction in the region. *CCSS for Literacy in Science* *Grades 6–8* *Reading: Integration of Knowledge and Ideas, Standard 9* Compare and contrast the information gained from experiments, simulations, video, or multimedia sources with that gained from reading a text on the same topic.	**ELD Standards** *Grade 6* *Exchanging information/ideas* Contribute to class, group, and partner discussions by following turn-taking rules, asking relevant questions, affirming others, adding relevant information and evidence, paraphrasing key ideas, building on responses, and providing useful feedback. (Bridging level)
Content Objectives Upon completion of the Japan/Haiti earthquake comparison activity, students will be able to identify the differing effects of both earthquakes based on the size of the earthquakes, distance from the epicenter, and construction in both regions. Students will be able to identify 2 pieces of information that compare or contrast the effects of earthquakes in Haiti and Japan from videos and news articles.	**Language Objectives** Upon completion of the Japan/Haiti earthquake comparison activity, students will be able to participate in conversations with their peers (in a small group) by writing and asking 4 relevant questions about the comparison and answering at least 4 questions written and asked by their peers.
Assessment Plan *Informal:* Monitor students' participation in the small-group discussions on the Japan/Haiti comparison activity by assessing the questions students ask and respond to for relevance to the topic and correct grammar. *Formal:* Students' notebooks are checked every two weeks. At the end of the unit on earthquakes, the following information will be graded: SQP2RS reading activity, Venn diagrams, 4 student-written questions on the comparison activity, and responses to at least 4 questions by written their peers.	

(*continued*)

Figure 8.1
(continued)

Instructional Strategies/Student Activities
Into/Through/Closure/Beyond

INTO: Review Earthquake Vocabulary (5 minutes)
Randomly call on students to read the content and language objectives for the day and other students to restate the objectives in their own words.

The students review vocabulary from the previous lesson on earthquakes: epicenter, seismograph, Richter scale, Ring of Fire. Ask students what (if anything) they know about the recent earthquakes in Japan and Haiti. Create two columns on the board (one for Haiti and one for Japan) and write down their brainstorming under the appropriate column.

THROUGH: Read Articles on the Haiti and Japan Earthquakes (20 minutes)
Present a brief PowerPoint® presentation on the earthquakes in Haiti and Japan, covering the size of each earthquake, the geology of the regions, and the type of construction in each country. Students take notes during the presentation. As an example of the comparison of the two earthquakes, students learn that while the Japan earthquake was much stronger than the Haiti quake, the death toll was higher in Haiti (even when factoring in the tsunami in Japan).

Working in pairs (English learners paired with native-English speakers, when possible), students read articles on the Japan and Haiti earthquakes using the SQP2RS strategy (displaying a poster on each step in this strategy may be helpful). With their partners, students write their SQP2RS responses in their notebooks.

As students are completing their SQP2RS responses, monitor the pair work by listening to the questions students are asking and respond to any questions the pairs have about the reading.

When students have completed the readings, randomly select pairs to share their responses. Go back to the responses from the brainstorming activity so students can add, delete, and modify their earlier responses based on the information they learned from the articles.

Using the two columns of responses (brainstorming) for the Haiti and Japan earthquakes, students create Venn diagrams in their notebooks and begin to fill them out based on the information on the two earthquakes.

THROUGH: Video Clips on the Two Earthquakes (10 minutes)
Returning to the PowerPoint presentation, students watch videos of the Haiti and Japan earthquakes. Include quotes from survivors of each earthquake on the presentation slides. Randomly select students to read the quotes.

Students return to their Venn diagrams and add any additional information based on the video clips and survivor quotes.

CLOSURE: Small-Group Discussions (15 minutes)
Using their SQP2RS responses, notes from the PowerPoint presentation, and their Venn diagrams, each student writes at least 4 questions comparing the two earthquakes in Haiti and Japan in their notebooks. Model a question on the board and show the students that the question is a complete sentence and uses correct grammatical form. Students must follow the model for their own questions.

In their table groups (small groups of 4), students take turns asking one of their questions and responding to their peers' questions. Students must choose 4 questions written by their peers to add to their notebooks (they should be different from the ones they created).

As students are asking and answering their questions, walk around the room monitoring students' participation in the small-group discussions on the Japan/Haiti comparison activity by assessing the questions students ask and respond to for relevance to the topic and correct grammar.

Figure 8.1
(continued)

BEYOND: What Affects Recovery After an Earthquake? (5 minutes) Lead a short discussion on the long-term effects of an earthquake with questions like these: What affects rebuilding—infrastructure, buildings, economy—after an earthquake? Can you think of other earthquakes around the world and how the countries are recovering? (Offer examples: Turkey, New Zealand, Chile)
Key Vocabulary epicenter, seismograph, Richter scale, Ring of Fire (review)
Materials Needed Newspaper articles and video clips on the Haiti and Japan earthquakes from the BBC website (*www.bbc.co.uk/news*), computer with Internet access, PowerPoint presentation

The second day of this lesson on comparing the effects of the earthquakes in Haiti and Japan is presented in Figure 8.2. The lesson gives students further opportunities to engage more deeply with the content and explore some of the economic and social factors that contribute to the short-term and long-term effects of earthquakes.

Figure 8.2
Sample Science Lesson Plan—Earthquakes (Day Two)

Title of the Lesson Earthquakes Around the World	**Class (Content Area) & Grade Level** 6th Grade—Earth Science English learners at the expanding level
Content Standards *Grade 6—1.g (California Content)* Students know how to determine the epicenter of an earthquake and know that the effects of an earthquake in any region vary, depending on the size of the earthquake, distance from the epicenter, local geology, and type of construction in the region. *CCSS for Literacy in Science Grades 6–8* *Writing: Text Types and Purposes, Standard 1.a* Write arguments on discipline-specific content—Introduce claim(s) about a topic or issue, acknowledge and distinguish the claim(s) from alternate or opposing claims, and organize the reasons and evidence logically.	**ELD Standard(s)** *Grade 6* *Adapting Language Choices* Adjust language choices according to purpose (e.g., facilitating a science experiment, providing peer feedback on written assignment), task, and audience. (Bridging level) *Writing* Write clear and coherent summaries of texts and experiences using complete and concise sentences and key words. (Bridging level)
Content Objectives Upon completion of the Japan/Haiti earthquake comparison activity, students will be able to identify the differing effects of both earthquakes based on the size of the earthquakes, distance from the epicenter, and construction in both regions. Students will be able to write an essay on factors that affect how a country recovers from an earthquake, citing evidence from the Haiti and Japan earthquakes.	**Language Objectives** Students will be able to work in small groups to revise their essays by using appropriate word choice, organization, and correct grammatical forms and spelling in a peer feedback activity. Students will be able to write an essay summarizing the effects of earthquakes that has a clear thesis supported by using quotations and facts appropriately.

(continued)

Figure 8.2
(continued)

Assessment Plan
Informal: Monitor pairs and small groups during student discussions and editing activity by assessing the questions students ask each other and asking comprehension questions on the claims students are making regarding what affects recovery from an earthquake.

Formal: Students' essays on factors that affect how a country recovers from an earthquake are submitted for a grade. The assessment will be based on organization of content: a clear thesis supported by quotes and facts, and grammatical forms (complete sentences, spelling, and word choice).
See rubric (Table 6.1 for specific assessment criteria)

Summative: Information learned about earthquakes in these lessons will be included on the quiz given at the end of the unit.

Instructional Strategies/Student Activities
Into/Through/Closure/Beyond

INTO: Quick Write (10 minutes)
Randomly call on students to read the content and language objectives for the day and other students to restate the objectives in their own words. Reading the objectives will serve as a brief review of the previous day's lesson on the earthquakes in Haiti and Japan.

Ask students to take out their Venn diagrams, SQP2RS notes, and questions from the previous lesson. The chart comparing the Haiti and Japan earthquakes from the previous lesson is still on the board. Using all this information, ask students to complete a quick write responding to the following questions: How do you think Japan is recovering from its earthquake? What are some challenges Japan still faces? How do you think Haiti is recovering from its earthquake? What are some challenges Haiti still faces? (time this activity—2 ½ minutes per response)

Walk around the classroom to check for understanding as the students are writing. Answer any questions students may have and ensure they understand the questions.

THROUGH: Quick Write Class Discussion (5 minutes)
Facilitate a discussion on the students' quick write responses. Tell students they will use their quick writes as a draft to write an essay on factors that affect how a country recovers from an earthquake, citing evidence from the Haiti and Japan earthquakes. Review with students the required elements of an essay with pointers on a poster.

THROUGH: Essay Writing (25 minutes)
Using their Venn diagrams, notes, quick writes, and the articles from the previous lesson, students begin writing their essays. Students are sitting in their table groups of 4 (English learners are paired with native-English speakers, when possible) and can ask their peers questions.

After 5 minutes, ask for volunteers to present the sentences with their thesis statements (usually the first or second sentence of the essay) on the document camera and read them to the class. Help the volunteers craft grammatically correct sentences (if necessary). Students check their thesis statements compared to models provided by volunteers.

After 5 minutes (10 minutes into the activity), ask for a volunteer to present his or her first paragraphs on the document camera and read them to the class, helping with edits if needed. Each student checks his or her work compared to the model provided.

This pattern is followed (a volunteer sharing his or her work on the document camera) throughout the essay-writing activity.

Figure 8.2
(*continued*)

During the writing activity, walk around the room monitoring students' essays, ensuring that they use appropriate word choice, organization, and correct grammatical forms and spelling and answering any clarifying questions students may have about their essays. *BEYOND: Group Editing Activity* (10 minutes) In their table groups, the students set up for the group editing activity. Each student in the table group is responsible for one aspect of the editing process: (1) appropriate word choice, (2) organization, (3) correct grammatical forms, and (4) spelling. Instruct each table group to exchange essays with another table group. Students read an essay and make any corrections based on their assigned aspect and then pass it to the student on the right to make corrections based on his or her assigned aspect. Once all students in the group have edited all four essays, they exchange the essays with another group. At the end of the process, each student should have read eight essays and made corrections on the essays based on his or her aspect. The essays are then returned to their owners. *CLOSURE: Review* (5 minutes) Students review some of the factors (e.g., social, economic) that affected the recovery from the earthquakes in Japan and Haiti. Ask students what role (if any) other countries in the world should play in rebuilding a nation after an earthquake (or other natural disaster). Homework: Students will complete final drafts of their essays as homework and submit them during the following class session.
Key Vocabulary epicenter, seismograph, Richter scale, Ring of Fire (review)
Materials Needed Newspaper articles and video clips on the Haiti and Japan earthquakes from the BBC website (*www.bbc.co.uk/news*), computer with Internet access, PowerPoint presentation

High School—Biology

The biology lesson plans described in this section were originally developed in collaboration with a teacher candidate in a secondary credential program for a biology class (grades 9–12) in a suburban high school in southern California. As the lessons were designed to be taught in a high school in southern California, California ELD standards have been incorporated into the lesson for English learners; however, the process outlined in this book can be used with ELD standards from any state. The lessons were rewritten and modified by the author to explicitly include the following: language objectives based on ELD standards; literacy objectives based on the CCSS for Literacy in History/Social Studies, Science, and Technical Subjects; differentiated assessments and student-centered activities; and culturally relevant resources. The two-day lesson plan is part of a larger unit on genetics. Prior to these lessons, students have learned about Mendelian genetic laws, practiced Punnett squares on one and two traits, and completed genetic practice problems. The biology class enrolls 38 students, with 10 English learners—4 at the emerging level (exit stage) and 6 at the expanding level (exit stage). Each class lasts 55 minutes. The first lesson presented in Figure 8.3 is on the genetics of skin color.

Figure 8.3
Sample Biology Lesson Plan—Genetics of Skin Color (Day One)

Title of the Lesson The Genetics of Skin Color: The Case of Desiree's Baby	**Class (Content Area) & Grade Level** Biology—Grades 9–12 English learners—emerging and expanding levels
Content Standards *Science (California State Standards): Biology, 3.a* Students know how to predict the probable outcome of phenotypes in a genetic cross from the genotypes of the parents and mode of inheritance. *CCSS for Literacy in Science Grades 9–10* *Reading: Key Ideas and Details, Standard 2* Determine the central ideas or conclusions of a text: Trace the text's explanation or depiction of a complex process, phenomenon, or concept; provide an accurate summary of the text.	**ELD Standards** *Grades 9–10* *Reading/viewing closely* Explain ideas, phenomena, processes, and relationships within and across texts, based on close reading of a variety of grade-appropriate texts, presented in various print and multimedia formats, using increasingly detailed sentences and an increasing variety of general academic and domain-specific words. (Expanding level) Explain ideas, phenomena, processes, and relationships within and across texts, based on close reading of a variety of grade-level texts, presented in various print and multimedia formats, using a variety of detailed sentences and a range of general academic and domain-specific words. (Bridging level)
Content Objectives After reading and class discussion, students will be able to predict possible phenotypes based on the parents' genotypes for polygenetic traits. After reading the passage, students will be able to determine the main idea by orally providing an accurate summary of the text.	**Language Objectives** Students will be able to use at least 2–3 new vocabulary words correctly in detailed sentences when describing the main idea of the reading passage in their small groups.

Assessment Plan

Informal: As students are reading the text passage, walk around the room and ask groups reading comprehension questions.

Formal: Students will be assessed during small-group presentations based on their ability to use at least 2–3 new vocabulary words correctly when describing the main idea of the reading passage.
A rubric will be used to assess the participation points earned (presented in Table 6.2).

Emerging-level English learners are expected to use 2 new vocabulary words correctly in their sentences when describing the main idea of the reading.

Expanding-level English learners are expected to use 3 new vocabulary words correctly in their detailed sentences when describing the main idea of the reading.
(participation points)

Summative: Students will be graded on the vocabulary and concepts learned in this lesson on the end-of-unit quiz.

Instructional Strategies/Student Activities
Into/Through/Closure/Beyond

INTO: Designer Babies (10 minutes)
Randomly calls on students to read the content and language objectives for the day and other students to restate the objectives in their own words. Ask students if they know what a "designer baby" is. Write their responses on the board (brainstorming).

Figure 8.3
(continued)

Students then watch a short interview (4 minutes from *CBS This Morning*, June 8, 2012) with Dr. Eric Schadt, chairman of the Genetics Department at New York's Mount Sinai Medical Center, discussing the medical benefits and risks (social implications) of designing babies
(*http://www.youtube.com/watch?v=yJB7PP6TGxQ*).
http://www.cbsnews.com/8301-505269_162-57449437/expert-on-gene-test-baby-designing-a-real-risk/

Students add to their brainstorming about designer babies.

THROUGH: Introduce vocabulary (10 minutes)
Introduce the following vocabulary words: melanin, polygenetic, genotype, phenotype, homozygote, heterozygote. Use the Vocabulary Four Square activity (vocabulary word, definition, use it in sentence, draw a picture/representation). Using a document camera, randomly select students to present their sentences and pictures/representations. Also ask comprehension questions to ensure students understand the new vocabulary terms and their relationship to concepts and vocabulary learned previously in the unit.

THROUGH: Read "Desiree's Baby" short story (20 minutes)
Students read the story "Desiree's Baby" with a partner. One student reads 2–3 paragraphs aloud and his or her partner paraphrases them. The students switch roles until the entire passage is read. Students may not understand some of the vocabulary words in the text, but the goal is for students to comprehend the main ideas of the story. Students take notes on the main ideas of the text in their interactive notebooks.

As students are reading in pairs, walk around the room monitoring students' learning by asking comprehension questions about the sections they are reading.

Once all partners have completed reading the story, ask the class to discuss the first 3 comprehension questions provided (question 4 will be discussed at the end of class).

CLOSURE: Small-Group Discussions of the Story (10 minutes)
In small groups (students are seated in assigned table groups of 4), students discuss the story. Each student is required to use at least 3 new vocabulary words correctly when describing the main idea of the reading passage to the small group. If needed, students can write out sentences of their contributions to the discussion and read them when it is their turn to contribute.

As the groups are discussing the story, the teacher assesses each student's participation in the discussion by assessing whether he or she is using vocabulary words correctly when discussing the main idea of the story.

BEYOND: Biracial Individuals (5 minutes)
The teacher projects the following question on the board (from the "Desiree's Baby" handout) for a class discussion: Consider the skin pigmentation of biracial individuals, such as Halle Berry, Lenny Kravitz, Mariah Carey, or the Rock. Can these phenotypes (skin colors) be explained by the same Mendelian model?

Key Vocabulary
melanin, polygenetic, genotype, phenotype, homozygote, heterozygote

Materials Needed
RACE: The Power of an Illusion, "Episode 1: The Difference Between Us" (on video or DVD from PBS, *www.pbs.org*), "Desiree's Baby" article and other handouts
available from PBS, document camera or overhead projector, computer with Internet connection

The second day of this lesson on genetics presented in Figure 8.4 focuses on race. Students will complete the handout "Skin Color Is a Polygenetic (Multiple Gene) Trait," watch a segment of the video *Race: The Power of Illusion* as an extension of the prior day's lesson, and then participate in a writing activity.

Figure 8.4
Sample Biology Lesson Plan—Genetics of Skin Color (Day Two)

Title of the Lesson The Genetics of Skin Color: The Case of Desiree's Baby	**Class (Content Area) & Grade Level** Biology—Grades 9–12 English learners—emerging and expanding levels
Content Standards *Science (California State Standards): Biology, 3.a* Students know how to predict the probable outcome of phenotypes in a genetic cross from the genotypes of the parents and mode of inheritance. *CCSS for Literacy in Science* *Grades 9–10* *Writing: Production and Distribution of Writing, Standard 5* Develop and strengthen writing as needed by planning, revising, editing, rewriting, or trying a new approach, focusing on addressing what is most significant for a specific purpose and audience.	**ELD Standards** *Grades 9–10* *Writing* Write longer literary and informational texts collaboratively and independently using appropriate text organization and growing understanding of register. (Expanding level) Write longer and more detailed literary and informational texts collaboratively and independently on a range of personal and academic topics using appropriate text organization and register. (Bridging level)
Content Objectives Students will be able to complete the handout "Skin Color Is a Polygenetic (Multiple Gene) Trait" to predict the probable outcomes of phenotypes in a genetic cross. Students will be able to use their notes and quick writes to write a summary of the main ideas they have learned about designer babies.	**Language Objectives** Students will be able to use their notes and drafts to write an organized summary of the main ideas they have learned about designer babies.
Assessment Plan *Informal:* Assess students' participation in the editing (writing process) small-group activity. Are they editing their own summaries as well as their peers' summaries? *Formal:* Students' organized summaries on the main ideas they have learned about designer babies will be assessed. Present a rubric outlining the required elements of the summaries (used previously in class) as a writing guide, and use the rubric to assess the essays. Emerging-level English learners: Summaries will be organized, and 2–3 grammatical errors will be accepted. Expanding-level English learners: Summaries will be organized and present a clear topic and supporting evidence. *Formal:* Students will be graded on the completeness of the skin color/genetics handout. *Summative:* Students will be graded on the vocabulary and concepts learned in this lesson on the end-of-unit quiz.	

Figure 8.4
(continued)

Instructional Strategies/Student Activities
Into/Through/Closure/Beyond

INTO: Video Clip on Race (10 minutes)
Randomly call on students to read the content and language objectives for the day and other students to restate the objectives in their own words. Reading the objectives will serve as a brief review of the previous day's lesson on the genetics of skin color.

Students will watch a video clip from *RACE: The Power of an Illusion*, "Episode 1: The Difference Between Us" (an approximately 5-minute clip on skin color) and take notes on the main ideas of the clip. After watching the video, students will discuss the clip using the new vocabulary words they learned the previous day.

THROUGH: Skin Color Is a Polygenetic Trait Handout (15 minutes)
Display a Punnett square showing the possible offspring from a cross between two individuals of intermediate skin color. Each parent produces eight different types of gametes, which can combine in 64 different ways. Using the Punnett square, the students will determine how many of the 64 possible offspring have skin that is darker than their parents. Model the first combination and then give students the handout "Skin Color Is a Polygenetic (Multiple Gene) Trait," so they can work in small groups to determine the rest.

All groups will submit their handout at the end of the activity for a participation grade.

THROUGH: Writing—Summarize Main Ideas of "Designer Babies" (20 minutes)
Students complete a quick write (2 minutes) on what they feel are the main ideas of what they learned about designer babies. They then turn to their partners and share their ideas. Randomly select a few students to share their ideas with the class.

Students use their quick writes and notes from "Desiree's Baby," the video clip, and their vocabulary words to write a summary of what they feel are the main ideas they learned about designer babies.

As the students are writing their summaries, monitor their learning by asking comprehension questions about students' summaries and answering clarifying questions.

CLOSURE: Group Editing Work (10 minutes)

In their table groups, the students set up for the group editing activity. Each student in the table group is responsible for one aspect of the editing process: (1) appropriate word choice, (2) organization, (3) correct grammatical forms, and (4) spelling. The teacher instructs each table group to exchange essays with another table group. Students read an essay and make any corrections based on their assigned aspect and then pass it to the student on their right to make corrections based on his or her assigned aspect. Once all students in the group have edited all four essays, they exchange the essays with another group. At the end of the process, each student should have read eight essays and made corrections on the essays based on his or her assigned aspect. The essays are then returned to their owners.

BEYOND: Homework
Students complete their summaries and submit them for a grade during the following class session.

Key Vocabulary
melanin, polygenetic, genotype, phenotype, homozygote, heterozygote

Materials Needed
RACE: The Power of an Illusion, "Episode 1: The Difference Between Us" (on video or DVD from PBS, *www.pbs.org*), "Desiree's Baby" article and other handouts available from PBS, document camera or overhead projector, computer with Internet connection

Table 8.2 Rubric for Sample Lesson Plan on Genetics of Skin Color—Small-Group Discussions on the Main Ideas of the Reading

	1	2	3	4
Language (ELD standard) Use new vocabulary words correctly and in detailed sentences	In his or her description, student uses 1 new vocabulary word incorrectly in one sentence	In his or her description, student uses 1 new vocabulary word correctly in one sentence	In his or her description, student uses 2 new vocabulary words correctly in at least two sentences	In his or her description, student uses 3 new vocabulary words correctly in detailed sentences
Content (CCSS for Literacy in Science) Provide an accurate summary of the text—the main idea	Summary provided in the discussion is inaccurate and does not focus on the main ideas of the reading	Summary provided in the discussion partially focuses on one main idea of the reading	Summary provided in the discussion focuses on one main idea of the reading	Summary provided in the discussion focuses on both main ideas of the reading

The rubric presented in Table 8.2 is the differentiated assessment for the small-group discussion activity in the first high school lesson *Genetics of Skin Color*. The criteria for the language standard and objective are taken from the ELD standard reading/viewing closely (Grades 9–10). English learners at the emerging level are expected to receive a 3 on the rubric, representing skills at the expanding level, and English learners at the expanding level are expected to receive a 4 on the rubric, representing skills at the bridging level. The criterion for the content objective based on the CCSS for Literacy in History/Social Studies, Science, and Technical Subjects is differentiated on the same 1–4 scale as the language objective, and the expectations for English learners will also be a 3 for students at the emerging level and a 4 for students at the expanding level. (Note: The state science content standard is assessed during a different student activity.) Native-English speakers' participation in the discussion will be assessed using the same rubric.

Discussion of the Lessons

The science lessons described in this chapter present challenging content to all students, using strategies and activities that allow English learners access to the content while developing their English language skills.

Standards, Objectives, and Assessments

Using the backwards mapping principle, content (state science and CCSS for Literacy in History/Social Studies, Science, and Technical Subjects) and language (ELD) standards have been chosen for each lesson. Generally, the content standard represents the "what" of the lesson, and the language standards represent the "how"—how English learners will demonstrate mastery of the standard. For example, during the second day of the middle school lessons on earthquakes, students write an essay aligned to both the content (CCSS) and language standards chosen. The content objective describes the focus of the essay—factors that affect how a country recovers from an earthquake, citing evidence from the Haiti and Japan earthquakes (what)—while the language objective describes the specific elements required of the essay—a clear thesis and supporting evidence—that is differentiated for English learners at various proficiency levels (how).

The next step in the process is to design an assessment plan aligned to the standards and objectives. All four lessons entail informal and formal assessments and a description of the summative assessment for the overall unit. Continuously monitoring students' work during each assigned activity is a type of informal assessment threaded throughout all the lessons. In each lesson, the assessment for the language objective has differentiated levels of mastery for English learners targeted at one level above their current proficiency level. In the rubric provided for the jigsaw activity (see Chapter 6) during the first day of the high school lesson on small-group discussions on the main idea of the reading (Table 8.2), the criteria written for the levels of the rubric are taken directly from the ELD standard, ensuring that English learners are accurately assessed on the skill based on their proficiency level. As discussed previously, although the rubric is designed to measure mastery of the language standard and objectives for English learners, native-English speakers can be held to the same criteria, using the same rubric for assessment.

Instructional Strategies

All the lesson examples employ a variety of instructional strategies that make the content accessible for all students and specifically scaffold instruction for English learners. Lessons include modeling; using multimedia in the forms of visuals, video, and PowerPoint presentations; vocabulary development; graphic organizers; and strategies that give students time to process the information presented, such as brainstorming. These scaffolding strategies are designed to gradually move the lessons from teacher-directed instruction to student-centered activities. For example, during the first day of the high school biology lessons on the genetics of skin color, the students are introduced to the topic through teacher-directed instruction and brainstorming, introduction to and review of vocabulary, presentation of a video clip, and modeling of the guided reading activity. The scaffolds are gradually taken away during the lesson when students work with a partner to complete the assigned reading and then write sentences with new vocabulary words learned based on the reading to participate in small-group discussions. Students are assessed during small-group presentations based on their ability to use at least two or three new vocabulary words correctly when describing the main ideas of the reading passage. English learners, as well as many native-English speakers, can perform tasks (participate in a small-group discussion) independently when they have been provided with a variety of tools to draw from to assist them with the task.

Embedded in many of the instructional strategies presented in these lessons is the concept of repetition. The lessons are models for how the process of repetition and scaffolding instruction helps English learners access the content being taught while practicing their English proficiency skills. Concepts learned during the first day of the lesson or in previous lessons or curricular units are recalled in activities during the *Into* phases of the lesson. During the first day of the high school lessons on earthquakes, students review vocabulary and participate in a brainstorming activity that helps them recall information learned previously about earthquakes that they need to build on to fully participate in the lesson's activities.

Student Activities

In all the lesson examples, instructional strategies and student activities are aligned to the content and language standards and objectives, as well as to the assessment plan. The activities are student-centered and give English learners the opportunity to practice their listening, speaking, reading, and writing skills, along with access to the core curriculum being taught. In the high school lesson, during the small-group discussion of the reading passage "Desiree's Baby," students are required to use new vocabulary words to participate in the discussion. They can write their definitions and read them during the discussion. While students specifically are assessed on their participation using new vocabulary words (listening and speaking skills), English learners also have the opportunity to practice reading and writing skills they need to become proficient in English. Given the CCSS focus on literacy skill development in the content areas, the incorporation of reading and writing activities into every lesson will help students build and draw on a literacy knowledge base to be successful across all content classes.

Each of the lessons also includes a variety of student grouping activities, including partner work, small groups, and whole class. As English learners work in groups with native-English speakers, they are able to learn the content presented from their peers as well as from the teacher. In the middle school lesson, students read the lesson content with a partner, giving them the opportunity to hear English spoken by a peer as well as to practice speaking themselves. Giving English learners opportunities to practice language skills multiple times with a partner and/or in a small group also allows them to self-correct their mistakes. The additional time to process information and practice their responses can give some English learners the confidence they need to actively participate in larger class discussions and activities.

Culturally Relevant/Multicultural Resources

The middle and high school lessons include culturally relevant/multicultural resources teachers have identified as topics their students would be interested in based on information gathered about who their students are. The focus on the effects of earthquakes in Japan and Haiti in the middle school lessons is intended to help students think critically about economic, political, cultural, and social class issues that affect recovery from a natural disaster. In the high school lessons, students learn about the genetics of skin color and the broader topic of race—what it mean to be biracial, for example, and what the term *race* actually means. Students have an opportunity to understand topics from multiple perspectives, including those of their peers. By discussing topics that represent universal themes with a partner or small-group member who comes from a culturally and/or linguistically diverse background, all students can make connections with one another that may not happen otherwise. Promoting an understanding of diversity and choosing materials that are relevant to students' lives increases student engagement and their overall academic achievement.

Summary

As you reflect on how to design science lesson plans for your English learner students, keep in mind the main interrelated points of this chapter:

- It is important to fully understand who your English learners are in order to include teaching strategies and student activities in your lessons that build on their strengths and help you address any areas of weakness they have. In addition to their English proficiency levels, prior knowledge they have with your subject areas, and learning styles, understanding your English learners' backgrounds, interests, and cultures can help you choose multicultural resources to use in your lessons that are relevant to your students' lives.
- The objectives you write for your lesson should be based on CCSS standards, science content standards, and the ELD standards your state has adopted. The CCSS standards and the science content standards generally represent the "what" of the lesson—what content is being taught—while the language standards represent "how" your English learners will master the content standard chosen at the appropriate proficiency levels for them.
- The assessments and activities you use should be aligned to the content and language objectives you have chosen so that you and your students understand the expectations for each lesson. It is important to use the information you have learned about your English learners in Step 1 of the lesson planning process to differentiate your assessments so they accurately reflect what your students are able to accomplish at the end of the lesson. You should also use the information you have learned about your students to design scaffolded activities that will help them learn the content you are presenting while simultaneously developing their English proficiency.

Applying What You Have Learned

In this chapter, you have learned how to provide equitable instruction for your English learner students by using a four-step lesson planning process. Demonstrate your understanding of the chapter by participating in the following activities and answering the corresponding questions.

STEP 1: Know your English learners

- What difficulties might English learners have with the CCSS for Literacy in History/Social Studies, Science, and Technical Subjects that you can take into account when designing your lessons?
- Explain ways you can obtain information about your English learners so that your lessons are aligned to their English proficiency levels, prior content knowledge, and learning styles.

STEP 2: Choose standards for your lessons

- In the lesson planning process presented in this chapter, you have learned that lessons should focus on CCSS for Literacy in History/Social Studies, Science, and Technical Subjects; science content standards; and the ELD standards used in your state. Choose a CCSS for science, a corresponding ELD standard, and a science content standard. Write content (CCSS and science) and language (ELD) objectives based on the standards you have chosen that are measurable and observable.

STEP 3: Design differentiated assessments and student-centered activities

- You have learned how to differentiate your assessment to accurately assess English learners in your science class. You have also learned how to use teaching strategies that can help your English learners access the content you are teaching. Additionally, you have learned specific student activities to use in your class that will promote interactions between English learners and native English speakers. Using the content and language objectives that you wrote in Step 2, design the following components of a lesson plan:
  - Assessments that will allow your students to demonstrate they have met the content and language objectives (Remember to differentiate your assessments based on your English learners' language proficiency levels.)
  - A student activity that is aligned to the objectives you have written and the assessments you have designed
  - An overview of the teaching strategies you will use to ensure that your English learners understand and can complete the activity you have designed

STEP 4: Select culturally relevant/multicultural materials and resources

- List some national, state, and/or local organizations providing culturally relevant/multicultural resources on their websites that can be incorporated into your science lessons.

chapter 9

Social Studies

Learning Outcomes and Focus Questions

STEP 1: Know your English learners

- What difficulties might my English learners have with the Common Core State Standards for Literacy in History/Social Studies?
- What do I need to know about my English learners to plan instruction?

STEP 2: Choose standards for your lessons

- What content standards and Common Core State Standards for Literacy in History/Social Studies will my lesson focus on?
- How do I design lessons that include language standards and objectives in my social studies class?

STEP 3: Design differentiated assessments and student-centered activities

- How can I differentiate assessment to accurately assess my English learners?
- What strategies can I use to help English learners learn the content I am teaching?
- What activities can I implement in my class to promote interactions between English learners and native-English speakers?

STEP 4: Select culturally relevant/multicultural materials and resources

- How can I find culturally relevant/multicultural resources to use in my social studies class?

This chapter outlines a process that middle and high school teachers can use to design lessons that incorporate language objectives based on ELD standards alongside social studies content standards and Common Core State Standards (CCSS) for Literacy in History/Social Studies, Science, and Technical Subjects for their English learners. It explains how to differentiate instruction and assessment based on English learners' language proficiency levels and then outlines strategies that social studies teachers can use in their classrooms to help their students understand the content. Much of the content in middle and high school social studies classes is built on knowledge that has been taught in previous social studies lessons in elementary school and classes in middle and high school. An English learner who immigrates to the United States in the 9th grade may not have the same foundational knowledge in the English language as his or her peers and/or the knowledge of topics such as U.S. history and geography that students who have attended U.S. schools in elementary and middle school have. Content presented in middle and high school social studies classes also includes extensive vocabulary development, complex and abstract concepts, and culturally specific contexts that may be unfamiliar to English learner students. Additionally, students who have attended schools in another country may have learned about events in history from a different perspective than what is presented in U.S. textbooks. It is therefore important to design scaffolded activities that help build that background base of knowledge for English learners and that teach them the processes and procedures used in your class. While this may seem challenging, social studies teachers can design scaffolded activities to give English learners the time and support they need to understand the content and thus increase their opportunities to excel in class.

STEP 1: Know your English learners

What Difficulties Might My English Learners May Have with the Common Core State Standards for Literacy in History/Social Studies?

The CCSS for Literacy in History/Social Studies, Science, and Technical Subjects focus on the two language domains of reading and writing. The ten standards in each domain fall into these categories:

Reading	Writing
Key ideas and details	Text type and purposes
Craft and structure	Production and distribution of writing
Integration of knowledge and ideas	Research to build and present knowledge
Range of readings and level of text complexity	Range of writing

The reading and writing standards for these content areas are aligned to the reading and writing CCSS for English Language Arts. The information presented in this section is not intended to be an extensive description of the CCSS for Literacy in History/Social Studies, Science, and Technical

Subjects but rather a discussion of the difficulties English learners may have with the standards.

The CCSS for Literacy in History/Social Studies, Science, and Technical Subjects are progressive and developmental standards that begin in kindergarten and become increasingly more complex by the 12th grade. The literacy skills outlined in the standards for middle school (grades 6–8) and high school (grades 9–10 and 11–12) for any given standard require advanced levels of language development that some English learners may not have attained. For example, what follows is the progression of the literacy skills required of Anchor Reading Standard 3 (under Key Ideas and Details):

- *Grades 6–8:* **Identify** key steps in a text's description of a process related to history/social studies.
- *Grades 9–10:* **Analyze** in detail a series of events described in a text; determine whether earlier events caused later ones or simply preceded them.
- *Grades 11–12:* **Evaluate** various explanations for actions or events and determine which explanations best accords with textual evidence, acknowledging where the text leaves matters uncertain.

The text in bold demonstrates the progressive nature of the standards. Students move from identifying key steps to evaluating various explanations through the grade levels. A comparison of the CCSS skills in reading to those outlined in ELD standards shows that the CCSS represent more complex literacy skills. The following reading standard from the California ELD standards is specifically aligned to the CCSS for Literacy presented previously. The standard is at the bridging level, representing the highest proficiency level of the ELD standards, and indicates what an English learner can perform independently or without the aid of a teacher in the area of reading:

- *Grade 8:* Reading/viewing closely—**Explain** ideas, phenomena, processes, and relationships within and across texts based on close reading of a variety of grade-level texts, presented in various print and multimedia formats, using a variety of detailed sentences and a range of general academic and domain-specific words.
- *Grades 9–10:* Reading/viewing closely—**Explain** ideas, phenomena, processes, and relationships within and across texts based on close reading of a variety of grade-level texts, presented in various print and multimedia formats, using a variety of detailed sentences, and general academic and domain-specific words.
- *Grades 11–12:* Reading/viewing closely—**Explain** ideas, phenomena, processes, and relationships within and across texts based on close reading of a variety of grade-level texts, presented in various print and multimedia formats, using a variety of detailed sentences, and precise, general academic and domain-specific words.

The skill *explain* represents less complex literacy abilities than the skill *evaluate* does. While the skills outlined in the ELD standard represent a solid progression of language development, English learners at this level (the highest proficiency level) have not yet developed the literacy skills necessary to master the CCSS. A similar gap exists between the level of the writing skills outlined in the CCSS for Literacy in History/Social Studies, Science, and Technical Subjects and those outlined in ELD standards.

Another matter to consider is that the CCSS for Literacy in History/Social Studies, Science, and Technical Subjects only cover the language domains of reading and writing. To become proficient in English, English learners must also develop their listening and speaking skills as well. Similarly, English learners need to acquire knowledge of the English language and academic vocabulary specific to the content area of history/social studies in order to attain the level of mastery of academic English needed to be successful. As these language development areas are not specifically in the CCSS for Literacy in History/Social Studies, Science, and Technical Subjects, teachers need to explicitly teach English learners listening and speaking skills and vocabulary development so they have the language and literacy skills needed to master these standards. History/social studies teachers who differentiate their language instruction for English learners based on their proficiency levels and teach language development simultaneously with the literacy skills required in the CCSS will be giving their English learner students the opportunity to attain the academic skills needed to be successful in their classes and all content area classes.

What Do I Need to Know About My English Learners to Plan Instruction?

The more information teachers learn about English learner students, the greater the opportunities they will have to be academically successful in your social studies classroom. For example, learning about students' academic and background knowledge of the English language, their perspective of historical events, and self-identification of their strengths and weaknesses with the language and content can help teachers understand which concepts will be accessible to them and which will need to be scaffolded more explicitly. Along with academic knowledge, teachers must understand what their English learners' English language proficiency levels are in the four language domains of listening, speaking, reading, and writing. How an English learner's proficiency levels in the language domains are determined is described in detail in Part 2 of this book. It is important to know your English learners' proficiency levels in each of the language domains so you can choose an ELD standard for your lesson at the level needed to scaffold students' English language development. This information can help you focus on addressing language issues English learners may have with social studies content. A survey administered at the beginning of the year also can gather useful information about what languages are spoken at home, which languages students use to speak to their friends, what they know about the social studies content they will learn in your class (and from which perspective the content has been learned in students' home countries), and what difficulties students feel they may have with the content, vocabulary, and cultural knowledge of a social studies classroom. You can also ask questions about your English learners' interests, extracurricular activities, and goals in the class as well as their broader goals in life.

Understanding English learners' learning styles facilitates designing lessons to include teaching strategies and student activities that build on students' strengths and help them develop in areas of weakness. For English learner students who are visual learners, presenting information through modes such as pictures, graphic organizers, and charts helps them access the content you are presenting. For visual learners, information presented in other formats such as through a lecture (auditory) should include opportunities for you to continually check for understanding to ensure that your English learner students can demonstrate they know the content. Finally, knowing about your English learners' (and all your students') backgrounds, interests, cultural and social affiliations, and any other pertinent information that combines to make your students "who they are" will help you plan lessons that include multicultural and culturally relevant resources for them. Doing so helps English learners make connections to the content being taught and keeps them engaged in all aspects of the lesson.

STEP 2: Choose standards for your lessons

What Content Standards Will My Lesson Focus On?

The sequence of how you present content standards in your social studies class is most likely determined locally by your department, school, or district. However the content standards are chosen for each lesson you teach, it is important to note that they represent the "what" of your lesson, the content being taught. In addition to content standards, the CCSS for Literacy in History/Social Studies, Science, and Technical Subjects represent the literacy skills students will develop as part of your lessons. The CCSS present many complex literacy skills, so it will take multiple lessons for students to master the standards. For example, Anchor Writing Standard 1 is divided into five separate developmental standards that together represent the writing skills a student needs to perform in order to demonstrate mastery of the standard. Once the content standard and CCSS for Literacy in History/Social Studies being taught is determined, teachers then write an objective based on each standard to guide the lesson. Content and CCSS for Literacy in History/Social Studies, Science, and Technical Subjects objectives should be measurable and observable and let you and your students know what they will be able to do by the end of the lesson.

Example:

- I am teaching a 10th-grade world history class and have chosen the standard, Grade 10—World History, Culture and Geography (California State Content Standards) 10.4.3: "Explain imperialism from the perspective of the colonizers and the colonized, and the varied immediate and long-term responses by the people under colonial rule."
- I write a content objective for my lesson based on the standard: After analyzing and discussing political cartoons, students will be able to explain at least two conflicting points of view Americans had about imperialism by creating their own political cartoons.
- I choose the following CCSS for Literacy in History/Social Studie—Grades 9–10 under Reading: Craft and Structure, Standard 4: "Determine the meaning of words and phrases as they are used in a text, including vocabulary describing political, social, or economic aspects of history/social studies."
- I write a literacy objective based on the CCSS for Literacy in History/Social Studies: Students will be able to demonstrate they can determine the meaning of vocabulary words in political cartoons by using at least 2 vocabulary terms in the political cartoons they create.

Because the CCSS for Literacy in History/Social Studies, Science, and Technical Subjects are performance-based, many of them are already observable and sometimes measurable. Therefore, the literacy objectives you write for your lesson may either be the standard itself or closely aligned to it. The same may be true for some social studies content standards. The key is to write measurable and observable objectives so that they are aligned to the standard, thus allowing students to demonstrate they have mastered the knowledge and skills outlined in the standard chosen for the lesson through the assessment plan.

How Do I Design Lessons That Include Language Standards and Objectives in My Social Studies Class?

If the content standards represent the "what" of any lesson, then the ELD standards represent the "how" for English learners—how they will master the content standard chosen at the appropriate proficiency level. The process for choosing ELD standards in the areas of listening, speaking, reading, and writing to include in lessons was outlined in detail in Part 2 of this book. Briefly, teachers should choose a language standard that complements the content standard addressed in the lesson. Once a standard is chosen, teachers then write a language objective for the lesson that outlines how students will demonstrate that they have met the standard.

Example:

- I have English learners at the expanding (exit-stage) proficiency level in the language area of reading in my 11th-grade History class.
- I select the skill (Reading) Evaluating language choices to include in my lesson from the California ELD standards, Grades 11–12.
- I use the standard that is one level above my students' current proficiency level. The standard at the bridging level reads: "Explain how successfully writers and speakers structure texts and use language to persuade the reader or create other specific effects, with light support."
- I write a language objective based on the standard: After students have read two assigned narrative accounts of the civil rights movement, they will work with a partner to evaluate the structure and format of the text to identify 1–2 features the author uses to persuade the reader to support his or her claims.

English learners need as much practice as possible with the English language to become proficient in all four of the language domains. Teachers can choose activities that incorporate several language skills to include in their lessons to help English learners practice the language. However, it is recommended that each lesson focuses on one or two language standards. As assessments are aligned to the standards chosen, the assessment should specifically focus on one or two language skills so teachers can accurately assess if English learners have mastered them.

STEP 3: Design differentiated assessments and student-centered activities

How Can I Differentiate Assessment to Accurately Assess My English Learners?

Once English learners' proficiency levels are determined in any language domain, they can perform language skills at those levels independently and automatically. Targeting instruction one proficiency level above their current level helps English learners build their knowledge of the English language to attain overall language proficiency. Following this tenet, an accurate assessment for English learners should be targeted at one level above their current proficiency level. Using California ELD standards as an example, English learners who demonstrate exiting-stage skills at the emerging level should be assessed on the expanding standards. Similarly using the World-Class Instructional Design and Assessment (WIDA) standards, English learners who are proficient at the developing level should be assessed at the expanding level (one level above their current level). In either example, assessments designed at proficiency levels above the expanding level may contain language skills and knowledge that are too far beyond the English learners' current proficiency to be accurate assessments. Although English learners may have a general understanding of the content, they may not be proficient enough in English to communicate their mastery of the content in either oral or written form.

Following the backwards mapping principle, assessment should be aligned to the content, CCSS, and language standards chosen for each lesson and to the objectives written to align to them. Social studies teachers who have both native-English speakers and English learners in their class can create one assessment plan for their lessons that includes both language and content. While the language objectives are specifically designed for English learners in the class, the skills covered in the language standards may also be beneficial for the native-English-speaking students. In the following example, the criteria used in the rubric from the ELD standards to assess the writing assignment highlights the writing skills needed to create persuasive essays and thus can be used with English learners and native-English speakers to improve their language and literacy skills. In social studies classes, all students can improve their language skills in listening, speaking, reading, and writing by the explicit focus teachers place on these skills for their English learner students. This example is designed from the sample 8th-grade U.S. history lesson plan on "North and South: Differing Opportunities for Women and African Americans" presented later in this chapter.

Example:

- I have English learners in my 8th-grade Social Studies class at the expanding (exit-stage) level.
- My content area is U.S. History. The standard for the lesson is United States History and Geography (California State Content Standards) 8.7-4: "Compare the lives of and opportunities for free blacks in the North with those in the South."
- I am using the CCSS for Literacy in History/Social Studies, Grades 6–8, Writing: Text Types and Purposes, Standard 2.b: "Write informative/explanatory texts, including the narration of historical events, scientific procedures/experiments, or technical processes; develop the topic with relevant, well-chosen facts, definitions, concrete details, quotations, or other information and examples."
- I am using the ELD standard for Grade 8 on Justifying/arguing (writing) so my English learners can practice their persuasive writing. I choose the ELD standard one level above my students' current proficiency levels for my assessment.

  Bridging level: Justify opinions or persuade others by providing detailed and relevant textual evidence or relevant background knowledge with light support.
- My class has read text, worked in small groups to create posters, and participated in discussions on the lesson's topic, "North and South: Differing Opportunities for Women and African Americans." For the culminating activity, students write a persuasive essay.

- I create a rubric for the lesson that includes both the content and language objective.
- I assess my English learners on the language objective that is one level above their current level of bridging (a 4 on the rubric) and use the same criteria for native-English speakers.
- I assess the content objective and the CCSS for Literacy in History/ Social Studies using criteria that is included on the rubric. For English learners at the expanding level, I expect they can earn a 3 based on their current proficiency level.

For English learners, the assessment is equitable in that it accurately assesses them based on the language proficiency level that is one level above their current level, as shown in the rubric provided in Table 9.1.

Table 9.1 Sample Rubric That Differentiates Assessment for English Learners

	1	2	3	4
Language Development—ELD Standard Elements of Persuasive Essay	Essay does not contain any relevant facts, details, and/or quotes.	Essay contains 1 relevant fact, detail, or quote to support the comparisons.	Essay contains 2 relevant facts, details, and/or quotes to support the comparisons.	Essay contains 3 relevant facts, details, and/or quotes to support the comparisons.
Content and CCSS for Literacy Persuasive essays comparing opportunities	Essay does not compare the opportunities of women or African Americans.	Essay compares the opportunities of either women or African Americans with a weak thesis.	Essay compares opportunities of women and African Americans with a weak thesis.	Essay compares opportunities of women and African Americans with a strong, cohesive thesis.

What Strategies Can I Use to Help English Learners Master the Content I Am Teaching?

Underlying any strategy teachers use to help English learners in their social studies classes is the principle that teachers have high expectations of their students. Displaying and explaining the lesson's content and language objectives ensures that English learners understand your expectations and the goals for the day and allows them to focus on the main idea of the lesson. English learners can learn social studies content when it is presented through accessible strategies such as SDAIE (specially designed academic instruction in English) that make challenging content accessible to English learners in content area classrooms. Using multiple modes of presenting content, such as visuals, graphic organizers, video, and multimedia, gives English learners a variety of methods to access the content. Additionally, you can use heterogeneous grouping strategies so that English learners can learn from and share their knowledge with native-English speakers. If needed, English learners should be given the opportunity to use their native language to negotiate the meaning of content with their peers and then translate that knowledge so they can fully participate in larger class discussions in English.

What Activities Can I Implement in My Class to Promote Interactions Between English Learners and Native-English Speakers?

Using a variety of activities in social studies classrooms allows students with different learning styles multiple ways to learn the content being presented. For English learners, designing lessons using activities that promote peer interactions allows them to communicate with their native-English-speaking peers. Students can learn from one another and learn the content while English learners have the added benefit of practicing their developing English language skills, which leads to increased language development. English learners, like many students, need time to process new concepts learned, to understand how these concepts are connected to and/or built on prior concepts, and to learn how these concepts fit into social, cultural, and/or historical contexts. Activities wherein English learners work with peers, with a partner or in small groups, gives them time to learn new concepts and practice content area vocabulary in the context of a social studies class. Activities that promote peer interactions give English learners another way to equitably access the same curriculum and core content as their native-English-speaking peers.

The following example of a classroom activity used in the lesson examples presented in this chapter achieves the goals of equal access to the core curriculum and increased peer interactions for English learners. Included in the appendices of this book is a list of all activities described in each content chapter (Chapters 6–9). Together, these suggested activities for teachers to use in classes help promote listening, speaking, reading, and writing skills for English learners. Numerous resources are available to teachers that outline effective classroom activities for English learners. Teachers should use classroom activities they feel comfortable with and that match their teaching style and students' learning styles. If students are familiar with a certain activity that has been used repeatedly in a class and is effective in teaching content, teachers should continue to incorporate the activity into lessons throughout the year. The routine of using familiar activities helps English learners focus on the content rather than on learning the steps and expectations of a new activity.

"Mix and Mingle" Party Activity

A "mix and mingle" party (sometimes referred to as a "tea party") is an activity in which English learners can practice listening, speaking, reading, and writing skills as they interact with their native-English-speaking peers. The activity described here has been adapted from one presented by Kylene Beers in her book *When Kids Can't Read* (2003). The description of the activity provided here is based on its use with an 11th-grade history class at the end of a unit on the civil rights movement. The activity serves as an assessment of what students learned about key individuals of the movement and as a review for an upcoming unit test.

- Students are seated in groups of four or five, depending on class size. Each group is assigned an individual whom they have learned about during the unit on the civil rights movement.
- Students in the small group are given note cards and instructed to write a description and a quote for their individual. Each note card must have the same information on it, so students must agree what to include on their note cards before writing on them.
- Students are told they will be participating in a "party" where they are required to meet and learn about the perspective of all individuals at the party. They are given the following directions:
  - As you "work the room," introduce yourself to someone by describing who you are and then reading your quote and description to that person.
  - After you have finished, the other person should do the same.
  - Find someone else, and introduce yourself to him or her. Continue to work the room until you have met all the people at the party.
  - Return to your seat. Describe and sum up each person's perspective and contribution to the civil rights movement by writing a complete sentence for each person.
- As students are participating in the activity, the names of all the civil rights activists should be projected on the overhead. NOTE: There will be multiple students (from each small group) reading the quote and description of one civil rights leader. Students should be instructed that if they meet a repeat civil rights individual, they do not need to hear the quote and description a second time. However, some English learners may need to hear the quote and description multiple times for full comprehension.
- Once students have returned to their seats and have written their sentences describing each civil rights leader, the teacher leads a small-group discussion on what they have learned about each individual. Teachers can ask students which individuals from the civil rights movement were not invited to the mix and mingle party (the activity focuses on key figures only).

Annie Pickert Fuller/Pearson Education

A mix and mingle party activity can be used in any content area in lessons where multiple perspectives, outcomes, situations, or definitions are presented. For example, students can engage in a mix and mingle party activity in a math class where each group of students is assigned an equation. Group members write explanations of how they solved equations on their note cards and then share their work with students from other groups. In an English language arts class, students can be assigned characters in a novel, play, or other literature and asked to write a quote and description of their characters on the note card. However teachers use a mix and mingle party activity in class, English learners have multiple opportunities to develop their English proficiency across all the language domains. For English learners at lower proficiency levels, teachers can assign them to be a character and write a description with less complex language so they can participate in all aspects of the activity. Purposely partnering English learners with native-English speakers can also create opportunities for English learners to interact with their peers so they can hear them speak English and to create a community of learners in the classroom.

STEP 4: Select culturally relevant/multicultural materials and resources

How Can I Find Culturally Relevant/Multicultural Resources to Use in My Social Studies Class?

There are many opportunities to include culturally relevant, multicultural resources into social studies classes. Throughout the Common Core State Standards, students are asked to identify, analyze, and evaluate multiple sources of information through reading and writing activities. This presents an opportunity for social studies teachers to identify culturally relevant/multicultural resources that are aligned to their content and that reflect issues of diversity, equity, and social justice. The National Council for the Social Studies (NCSS, *www.socialstudies.org/*) offers an extensive collection of resources that help teachers incorporate relevant, multicultural topics into their lessons. The organization Rethinking Schools has resources on its website (*www.rethinkingschools.org*) focused on helping teachers incorporate multicultural and social justice issues into their social studies classes. Teaching Tolerance (*www.tolerance.org*) has an extensive collection of resources on all multicultural topics. The resources are grouped by subject area, grade level, and a wide range of topics on diversity and social justice issues. Multicultural resources can also be found on the Multicultural Education Pavilion (*www.edchange.org/multicultural/*) as well as through books, historical accounts, and narratives written by authors from diverse backgrounds. The Stanford History Education Group's website (*http://sheg.stanford.edu/?q=node/45*) offers numerous *Reading Like a Historian* lessons that include primary source documents representing multiple perspectives of historical events. Digital History (*www.digitalhistory.uh.edu/*) also offers primary source documents and articles explaining them. Additionally, links to multicultural resources can be found on the National Education Association's website (*www.nea.org*). Finally, current topics, statistics, and opinion polls can be found in local, state, and national newspapers as well as on the Public Broadcasting Service website (*www.pbs.org*). Countless other websites provide culturally relevant/multicultural resources. Use the websites in this section as a starting point as you begin to search for culturally relevant/multicultural resources. The resources you choose to include in your lesson planning will depend on what you have learned about your students (Step 1 of the process presented in this book) and how these resources best fit with the lesson content.

Social Studies Lesson Examples

Four lessons are presented in this section, two at the middle school level and two at the high school level. All four lessons have been rewritten and adapted from lessons designed or taught by classroom teachers and teacher candidates to include CCSS for Literacy in History/Social Studies, Science, and Technical Subjects; language standards (ELD) and objectives; differentiated assessments aligned to the standards; student-centered activities; and culturally relevant/multicultural resources. Teachers will most likely have lesson plans similar to the ones outlined here that can be easily adapted to align with the lesson planning process presented in this book.

Middle School—8th-Grade History

The lessons presented in this section were originally designed by a middle school teacher for an 8th-grade social studies (U.S. history) unit and then rewritten and adapted by the author to include ELD standards and CCSS for Literacy in History/Social Studies, Science, and Technical Subjects. As the lessons were designed for a middle school in southern California, California ELD standards are incorporated into the lesson for English learners; however, note that the process outlined in this book can be used with ELD standards from any state. For the purposes of planning lessons based on what teachers know about students, all students in the class are English learners at the expanding level (exit stage), so the objectives, assessments, and activities are targeted at the bridging level (one level above their current proficiency level). The first lesson is presented in Figure 9.1. The lessons span two days and focus on "North and South: Differing Opportunities for Women and African Americans"; both lessons are taught in 1-hour class sessions.

Figure 9.1
Sample Social Studies Lesson Plan—North and South (Day One)

Title of the Lesson North and South: Differing Opportunities for Women and African Americans	**Class (Content Area) & Grade Level** 8th Grade—U.S. History English learners—expanding level
Content Standards *Grade 8—United States History and Geography (California State Content Standards) 8.7: Students analyze the divergent paths of the American people in the South from 1800 to the mid-1800s and the challenges they faced.* #4. Compare the lives of and opportunities for free blacks in the North with those in the South. *CCSS for Literacy in History/Social Studies—Grades 6–8* *Reading: Craft and Structure, Standard 4* Determine the meaning of words and phrases as they are used in a text, including vocabulary specific to domains related to history/social studies.	**ELD Standards** *Grade 8* *Listen actively* Demonstrate active listening in oral presentation activities by asking and answering detailed questions with minimal prompting and support. (Bridging level) *Reading/viewing closely* Use knowledge of morphology, context, reference materials, and visual cues to determine the meanings, including figurative and connotative meanings, of unknown and multiple-meaning words on a variety of new topics. (Bridging level)
Content Objectives Students will be able to demonstrate their understanding of the different opportunities for women and African Americans in the North and South through a poster presentation. Students will be able to use vocabulary terms accurately in the historical context presented in the text during their poster presentations.	**Language Objectives** Students will be able to ask detailed questions using at least 1 vocabulary term and answer questions using at least 2 vocabulary terms during the poster presentations. Students will be able to use their Guide to Reading Notes to decode the text and accurately define 4 vocabulary terms presented in the text.
Assessment Plan *Informal:* Monitor small groups during the reading activity and student discussions while creating posters by assessing the questions students ask each other and asking comprehension questions on the contents of their posters. *Formal:* Students present their posters to the class. Students' posters will be assessed on the completeness and accuracy of the following information (from the Guide to Reading Notes): describe what the geography and climate was like, what jobs were available, and who could participate in government. Emerging English learners are expected to use 4 vocabulary terms correctly during the poster presentation.	

Figure 9.1
(continued)

Formal: Student groups submit their completed Guide to Reading Notes at the end of the unit for a grade.
Instructional Strategies/Student Activities
Into/Through/Closure/Beyond

INTO: Review 13 Colonies—North and South (5 minutes)
Randomly call on students to read the content and language objectives for the day and on other students to restate the objectives in their own words. Reading the objectives will serve as a review of the previous lessons on the thirteen colonies and differences in the North and South.

In prior classes, students were divided into groups that were responsible for learning about and presenting on one of the colonies in a jigsaw activity. During the review, experts from each jigsaw group will share information on each of the colonies while the teacher display graphic organizers groups had previously completed.

THROUGH: Group Reading—History Alive and Supplemental Text (Teachers Curriculum Institute, 2010) (20 minutes)
Present a graphic organizer students will use as a reading guide. The graphic organizer has four columns with the following headings: Why was the colony founded? Describe the geography and climate. What jobs were available? Who could participate in government? Model how groups fill out the organizer by completing it for one colony; students must use complete sentences and use at least 1 new vocabulary term in each of the columns (a minimum of 4 new vocabulary terms). During the modeling activity, each student is completing his or her own graphic organizer on the colony.

Students are divided into groups of four. Each group will read a section of the textbook and the supplemental text on the opportunities of African Americans and women in the North and South in an assigned colony. Small groups will complete their graphic organizers on poster paper and will present their information to other groups during a jigsaw activity (see Chapter 6).

THROUGH: Poster Presentations (10 minutes)
Through a jigsaw activity, groups present their posters to one another. Groups must present information from each column, and each group member must participate in the presentation.

CLOSURE: Class Discussion (15 minutes)
After the jigsaw activity, groups put their posters up in front of the class. Randomly call on students from each group to review the contents of their poster. During the discussion, each student is filling out his or her own graphic organizer for the colonies; these will be used as a study guide for a unit test and then submitted for a grade.

BEYOND: Discussion of Positions of Power (10 minutes)
Students participate in a discussion on the opportunities of African Americans and women. Lead students into talking about who ran the government of the colonies, what roles women played, and what differences marked the lives and opportunities of free African Americans and slaves.

Key Vocabulary
New vocabulary terms identified by students during their reading activity

Materials Needed
History Alive text, supplemental text, overhead projector, chart paper

The second day of this lesson on "North and South: Differing Opportunities for Women and African Americans," presented in Figure 9.2, allows students further opportunities to engage with the topic and practice their English language development skills in activities that focus on listening, speaking, and writing.

Figure 9.2
Sample Social Studies Lesson Plan—North and South (Day Two)

Title of the Lesson North and South: Differing Opportunities for Women and African Americans	**Class (Content Area) & Grade Level** 8th Grade—U.S. History English learners—expanding level
Content Standards *Grade 8—United States History and Geography (California State Content Standards) 8.7: Students analyze the divergent paths of the American people in the South from 1800 to the mid-1800s and the challenges they faced.* #4. Compare the lives of and opportunities for free blacks in the North with those in the South. *CCSS for Literacy in History/Social Studies—Grades 6–8* *Writing: Text Types and Purposes, Standard 2.b* Write informative/explanatory texts, including the narration of historical events, scientific procedures/experiments, or technical processes; develop the topic with relevant, well-chosen facts, definitions, concrete details, quotations, or other information and examples.	**ELD Standards** *Grade 8* *Listening actively* Demonstrate active listening in oral presentation activities by asking and answering detailed questions with minimal prompting and support. (Bridging level) Writing: *Justifying/arguing* Justify opinions or persuade others by providing detailed and relevant textual evidence or relevant background knowledge with light support. (Bridging level)
Content Objectives Students will be able to write a persuasive essay comparing the opportunities of women and African Americans in the North to those in the South supported by relevant facts, details, and quotations.	**Language Objectives** Students will be able to ask at least 2 detailed questions of their partners when discussing the opportunities of women and African Americans in the North and the South. Students will be able to use 3 relevant facts, details, and/or quotes in their persuasive essays.
Assessment Plan *Informal:* Monitor partner discussions on the opportunities of women and African Americans to assess whether each student is asking at least 2 detailed questions. *Formal:* Students' persuasive essays will be graded using a rubric (Table 9.1) covering the comparison of women and African Americans in the North to those in the South using relevant facts, details, and quotes. Expanding-level English learners are expected to use 3 relevant facts, details, and/or quotes in their essays. *Summative*: Information learned during this two-day lesson will be included on the test at the end of the unit.	
Instructional Strategies/Student Activities *Into/Through/Closure/Beyond* *INTO: Tea Party Activity—Review Vocabulary and Content* (20 minutes) Randomly call on students to read the content and language objectives for the day and on other students to restate the objectives in their own words. After reading the objectives, assign students one of six people from their prior readings (multiple students will be each person in the activity). Each student writes two sentences describing the person he or she is assigned using in the description vocabulary terms learned previously. The persons selected for the activity are from the North and South and have varied experiences living in their respective colonies. Students participate in a tea party activity where they introduce themselves and read the description they have written about their person in history.	

Figure 9.2
(continued)

After the tea party activity, ask students to choose two colonies that will serve as the focus of the persuasive essay, one from the North and one from the South. Distribute the rubric that will be used to grade the persuasive essays. Each criterion is discussed and reviewed so students fully understand the expectations of their essays.

Quick writes: For the colonies chosen, students begin to write about the opportunities African Americans and women had. They can create columns, writing on one colony first and then focusing on the second, or integrate their writing. The purpose of this activity is for students to begin to organize their ideas for their persuasive essays.

THROUGH: Partner Discussions (10 minutes)
On the overhead, project the directions for the partner discussions. Students are to actively listen to their partners and ask at least 2 questions about their partner's writing. Students should add and/or clarify their ideas based on their partner's questions. Students turn to their partners and discuss their quick writes.

During the partner discussions, walk around the classroom and monitor the discussions, ensuring that each student is asking at least 2 questions and adding to his or her quick write.

BEYOND: Persuasive Essays (20 minutes)
On the overhead, again project the rubric for the persuasive essays. Students use their quick writes, the posters from the reading activity (Day One), their notes, and the texts to begin writing their persuasive essays. Students are still in their paired groups and are encouraged to continue to use their partners as a resource.

After every 10 minutes of writing, randomly call on students to read a few sentences highlighting a fact, detail, or quotation they are using to support their argument. Walk around the room, asking comprehension questions and answering any questions students may have.

At the end of 30 minutes, students will turn in their essays for a grade. If any student needs more time to complete an essay, arrange for him or her to come in during lunch or after school to complete the work.

CLOSURE: Class Discussion—Connections to the Present (10 minutes)
The teacher leads a discussion on the students' essays and how they connect to the present. Are there still differences in the opportunities of African Americans and women as compared to Anglo Americans (whites) and men? Are women and African Americans in positions of power today? What about opportunities for other groups?

Key Vocabulary
New vocabulary terms identified by students during their reading activity (Day One)

Materials Needed
History Alive text, supplemental text, overhead projector, writing rubric

High School—10th-Grade World History

The 10th-grade world history lesson plans described in this section were originally developed collaboratively with a secondary teacher candidate for a class in a suburban high school in southern California. The lessons were rewritten and modified by the author to include CCSS, ELD standards, and corresponding objectives. As the lessons were designed to be taught in a high school in southern California, California ELD standards have been incorporated into the lesson for English learners; however, note that the process outlined in this book can be used with ELD standards from any state. For the purposes of planning lessons based on what teachers know about their students, the world history class enrolls 15 English learners at the expanding proficiency level, and each class session is 1 hour. The first lesson is presented in Figure 9.3

Figure 9.3
Sample Social Studies Lesson Plan–Southeast Asia and American Imperialism (Day One)

Title of the Lesson Southeast Asia and American Imperialism	**Class (Content Area) & Grade Level** 10th Grade—World History English learners—expanding level
Content Standards *Grade 10—World History, Culture and Geography (California State Content Standards) 10.4.3* Explain imperialism from the perspective of the colonizers and the colonized, and the varied immediate and long-term responses by the people under colonial rule. *CCSS for Literacy in History/Social Studies—Grades 9–10* *Reading: Craft and Structure, Standard 4* Determine the meaning of words and phrases as they are used in a text, including vocabulary describing political, social, or economic aspects of history/social studies.	**ELD Standards** *Grades 9–10* *(Reading): Evaluating language choices* Explain how successfully writers and speakers structure texts and use language to persuade the reader or create other specific effects, with light support. (Bridging level)
Content Objectives After analyzing and discussing political cartoons, students will be able to explain at least two conflicting points of view Americans had about imperialism by creating their own political cartoons. Students will be able to demonstrate they can determine the meaning of vocabulary words in political cartoons by using at least 2 vocabulary terms in the political cartoons they create.	**Language Objectives** After reading the Chinese Exclusion Act, students will be able to understand and describe at least 2 of the claims by the U.S. Congress to persuade Americans that the act was necessary.

Assessment Plan

Informal: Monitor small groups' discussions while they are creating their political cartoons by assessing the questions students ask each other and asking comprehension questions on the contents of their cartoons.

Formal: Students will write a paragraph in their notebooks describing at least 2 of the claims made by the U.S. Congress to persuade Americans that the act was necessary. Students' notebooks are checked and certain activities graded periodically.

Expanding English learners and native-English speakers will be assessed using the same criteria (2 claims represents a level that is accurate bridging-level criteria),

Formal: Students will be graded on the political cartoons they create with the group—each group must use at least 2 vocabulary terms in their presentations of their cartoons.

Summative: Students will be graded on the content of this lesson on a chapter exam at the end of the unit on imperialism.

Instructional Strategies/Student Activities

Into/Through/Closure/Beyond

INTO: Analyzing Political Cartoons (10 minutes)

As students enter the room, a political cartoon is projected on the overhead with these two captions:

1. The Anti-Chinese Wall
2. The American Wall Goes Up as the Chinese Original Comes Down

Figure 9.3
(continued)

The following questions are also printed underneath the cartoon:
What activity is going on in the picture?
What do the two captions tell you about what is going on?
Who is doing the activity?
What is the purpose of the political cartoons?

Ask students to think about the questions before the bell rings. About a minute after the bell rings, students turn to a partner and discuss the questions. Then lead a class discussion on the questions and the cartoons. In the discussion, guide the class to define the vocabulary terms for the lesson: irony and caricature.

Randomly call on students to read the content and language objectives for the day and on other students to restate the objectives in their own words. This will help students understand the expectations of the lesson.

THROUGH: Chinese Exclusion Act (15 minutes)
Present a mini lecture on the Chinese Exclusion Act with a PowerPoint® presentation highlighting the main points and key vocabulary terms. Post directions for the next two activities on the last slide: reading and notebook writing.

With a partner, students read a short passage about the Chinese Exclusion Act and then the act itself. English learners should be paired with native-English speakers. As students are reading, they are taking notes on the claims made by the U.S. Congress for the act. As the partners discuss the readings, walk around the room asking comprehension questions and answering any clarification questions students may have.

When partners have completed their readings, they will write a paragraph in their notebooks describing at least 2 of the claims made by the U.S. Congress to persuade Americans that the act was necessary. If students do not complete their paragraphs, they can finish them as a homework assignment. Notebooks will be checked and the paragraph graded at the end of the unit.

THROUGH: Analyzing Political Cartoons (10 minutes)
Students will be working in small groups of four (English learners paired with native English speakers) to create their own political cartoons. Before students begin creating their own cartoons, use an overhead to project two political cartoons on U.S. imperialism. Give the groups a few minutes to analyze the cartoons by discussing the meaning, purpose, and methods of each one. Randomly call on groups to share one aspect of their analysis (meaning, purpose, or method) with the class.

CLOSURE: Small Group Work—Political Cartoons (15 minutes)
Working in their same small groups of four (English learners paired with native-English speakers), students create their own political cartoons on U.S. imperialism. Instruct groups that they will be graded on the contents of their cartoons—their meaning and purpose and the use of at least 2 vocabulary terms.

As the groups are working on their cartoons, monitor their discussions by assessing the questions students ask each other and ask comprehension questions on the contents of their cartoons.

BEYOND: Sharing Political Cartoons (10 minutes)
Each group presents its political cartoon by describing its meaning and purpose and using at least 2 vocabulary terms in the description.
If time permits, have a broader class discussion on political cartoons and their meanings and purposes.

Key Vocabulary
irony, caricature

Materials Needed
Materials: overhead projector, political cartoons, Chinese Exclusion Act and reading, graphic organizer from Teaching Tolerance website (*www.tolerance.org/activity/editorial-cartoons-historical-example-immigration-debates*)

During the second day of "Southeast Asia and American Imperialism" lesson (Figure 9.4), students make connections between the Chinese Exclusion Act and current immigration policies through listening, speaking, and writing activities. This lesson is taught in a 1-hour period.

Figure 9.4
Sample Social Studies Lesson Plan–Southeast Asia and American Imperialism (Day Two)

Title of the Lesson Southeast Asia and American Imperialism	**Class (Content Area) & Grade Level** 10th Grade—World History English learners—expanding level
Content Standards *Grade 10—World History, Culture and Geography (California State Content Standards) 10.4.3* Explain imperialism from the perspective of the colonizers and the colonized, and the varied immediate and long-term responses by the people under colonial rule. *CCSS for Literacy in History/Social Studies—Grades 9–10* *Writing: Production and Distribution of Writing, Standard 4* Produce clear and coherent writing in which the development, organization, and style are appropriate to the task, purpose, and audience.	**ELD Standards** *Grades 9–10* *Writing: Justifying/Arguing* Justify opinions or persuade others by making connections and distinctions between ideas and texts and articulating sufficient, detailed, and relevant textual evidence or background knowledge using appropriate register. (Bridging level)
Content Objectives Students will be able to write a persuasive letter to the editor of a newspaper requesting a repeal of the Chinese Exclusion Act from the perspective of an immigrant.	**Language Objectives** In their letters to the editor, students will be able to justify their opinions (arguments) by making at least 2 connections to facts and using appropriate language to persuade readers.
Assessment Plan *Informal:* Monitor partners' discussions while they are forming their arguments for their letters to the editor by assessing the questions students ask each other and asking comprehension questions on the contents of their letters. *Formal:* Assess students' persuasive letters to the editor on a 1–4 scale using a rubric (Table 9.2). Expanding-level English learners are expected to perform at a 3 level on the language and content objectives. This level represents a bridging proficiency level and so is an accurate assessment based on their current proficiency level. *Summative:* Students will be graded on the content of this lesson on a chapter exam at the end of the unit on imperialism.	
Instructional Strategies/Student Activities *Into/Through/Closure/Beyond* *INTO: Review Political Cartoons and Chinese Exclusion Act* (15 minutes) Randomly call on students to read the content and language objectives for the day and other students to restate the objectives in their own words. Show students the rubric that will be used to assess the letters to the editor they will write during class. Groups' political cartoons from the previous class are posted around the room. Ask students to think about examples of connections to facts—what contents of the cartoons are connected to facts about U.S. imperialism? After students have a minute or two to think of a connection, they turn to a partner and share their ideas. After another minute or two, the students share their responses in a class discussion (Think-Pair-Share, see Chapter 7). Ask students to open their notebooks to their paragraphs written the day before on the Chinese Exclusion Act. Randomly call on students to share one claim they identified in their paragraphs made by the U.S. Congress to persuade Americans the act was necessary. *THROUGH: Pair Work—Discussion of Letters to the Editor* (10 minutes) Display a letter to the editor on the overhead projector (selected from a local newspaper on a current topic familiar to the students). Ask students to identify the author's argument. Highlight the argument on the letter. Next, ask students to identify a connection to at least one fact the author makes in the letter and then highlight the connection. This letter will serve as a model for the writing activity. Ask students to identify language the author used to persuade the reader. Write these examples on the board as well as other examples of language authors use to persuade readers that students offer.	

Figure 9.4
(continued)

CLOSURE: Writing Letters to the Editor (20 minutes) Give students the rubric that will be used to grade their letters to the editor and review the criteria with the class. Using the rubric, model letter, paragraphs on the Chinese Exclusion Act, and political cartoons as resources, students write a persuasive letter to the editor of a newspaper in favor of repeal of the Chinese Exclusion Act from the perspective of an immigrant. As outlined on the rubric, students must make at least 2 connections to facts in their letters and use appropriate language to persuade readers. After 10 minutes, randomly call on students to read parts of their letters and identify a connection made to facts as well as language they used to persuade readers. Each student uses these responses to review his or her own letter and make any necessary revisions. As students write their letters, walk around the room asking about their letters, the facts they are citing, and the appropriate language they are using to persuade readers. At the end of the activity, randomly select a few students to read their letters aloud. Any student who does not complete the letter during class can complete it as homework. All students will submit their letters during the next class session and are encouraged to edit their letters before the next class. *BEYOND: Class Discussion* (15 minutes) Lead a discussion on the connections between the Chinese Exclusion Act and current immigration policies. How do current policies affect different immigrant groups? Why are some groups affected by policies and others are not? Talk about the context—the political, economic, and social climate then and now.
Key Vocabulary irony, caricature
Materials Needed Overhead projector, political cartoons, Chinese Exclusion Act and reading, graphic organizer from Teaching Tolerance website (*www.tolerance.org/activity/editorial-cartoons-historical-example-immigration-debates*)

The rubric in Table 9.2 is the differentiated assessment for the letter to the editor persuasive writing activity in the second day of the high school lesson example on Southeast Asia and American imperialism. The criteria for the language standard and objective, writing—justifying/arguing, are

Table 9.2 Rubric for Sample Lesson Plan on American Imperialism—Persuasive Compositions (Letter to the Editor)

	1	2	3	4
Language—(ELD) Justifying/arguing—connections to facts and appropriate language	Letter does not make connections to facts and does not establish a controlling idea.	Letter makes 1 connection to facts that supports the argument; establishes a controlling idea.	Letter makes 2 connections to facts that support the argument; structures ideas and arguments in a logical way.	Letter makes 3 connections to facts that support the argument; structures ideas and arguments in a logical way with consistent use of standard grammar.
State Content and CCSS for Literacy in History Persuasive letter on Chinese Exclusion Act	Letter does not present a persuasive argument and is not from the perspective of an immigrant.	Letter uses some persuasive language, but is not from the perspective of an immigrant.	Letter uses some persuasive language and is from the perspective of an immigrant.	Letter uses persuasive language and key vocabulary terms and is from the perspective of an immigrant.

derived from the proficiency levels of the standard. Similarly, the criterion for the content objective is differentiated on the same 1–4 scale as the language objective. Expanding-level English learners are expected to earn a 3 on the rubric for both language and content. English learners have many opportunities to access the content through the strategies and activities designed for the lesson before they are assessed.

Discussion of the Lessons

The social studies lessons described in this chapter present challenging content to all students, using strategies and activities that allow English learners access to the content while developing their English language skills.

Standards, Objectives, and Assessments

Using the backwards mapping principle, content (California State Social Studies Standards and CCSS for Literacy in History/Social Studies, Science, and Technical Subjects) and language (ELD) standards have been chosen for each lesson. Because social studies content can be very language dependent, content and language standards and objectives for each lesson complement one another. Generally, the content standard represents the "what" of the lesson, and the language standards represent the "how"—how English learners will demonstrate mastery of the standard. For example, during the second day of the high school lessons on U.S. imperialism, students write a persuasive letter to the editor, which is aligned to both the content and language standards chosen. The content objective describes the focus of the letters: a persuasive argument on the Chinese Exclusion Act from the perspective of an immigrant (what). The language objective describes the specific elements required of the letter—that the author makes connections to facts that support the argument and structures ideas in a logical way with consistent use of standard grammar—and is differentiated for English learners at various proficiency levels (how).

The next step in the process is to design an assessment plan aligned to the standards and objectives. For all four lessons, informal and formal assessments and a description of the summative assessment for the overall unit are provided. Continuously monitoring students' work during each assigned activity is a type of informal assessment threaded throughout the lessons. In each lesson, the assessment for the language objective has differentiated levels of mastery for English learners targeted at one level above their current proficiency level. In the rubric provided for the persuasive essay on "Differing Opportunities of African Americans and Women in the North and South" during the second day of the middle school lesson (Table 9.1), the criteria written for the levels of the rubric are derived from the ELD standard, ensuring that English learners are accurately assessed on the skill based on their proficiency level. In the rubric used in for the persuasive essay, the criteria for a bridging-level English learner are represented as a 4 on the rubric. As discussed previously, while the column on the rubric is designed to measure mastery of the language standard and objective for English learners, native-English speakers can also be held to the same criteria, using the same rubric for assessment.

Instructional Strategies

In all the lesson examples, a variety of instructional strategies make the content accessible for all students and specifically scaffold instruction for English learners. Lessons include modeling, using multimedia in the forms of visuals and video, vocabulary development, graphic organizers, and strategies that give students time to process the information presented, such as brainstorming and think-pair-shares. These scaffolding strategies are designed to gradually move the lessons from teacher-directed instruction to student-centered activities. For example, during the high school lessons on U.S. imperialism, teacher-directed instruction on the second day includes the teacher reviewing paragraphs students wrote the prior day on the Chinese Exclusion Act, modeling how to write an effective letter, and reviewing elements of the grading rubric. The scaffolds are gradually taken away as students use all these resources to work individually to write a persuasive letter to the editor of a newspaper requesting a repeal of the Chinese Exclusion Act. English learners and many native-English speakers as well can perform tasks (write an essay) independently when they have been provided with a variety of tools to draw from to assist them with the task.

Embedded in many of the instructional strategies presented in these lessons is the concept of repetition. The lessons are models for how the process of repetition and scaffolding instruction helps English learners access the content being taught while practicing their English proficiency skills. Concepts learned during the first day of the lesson or in previous lessons or curricular units are recalled during activities during the *Into* phases of the lesson. During the second day of the middle school lessons on "North and South: Differing Opportunities for Women and African Americans," students begin the class with a quick write activity where they recall the opportunities African Americans and women had in the colonies. Through these quick writes and a class discussion, much of the information learned the previous day is recalled and reviewed, giving English learners the opportunity to build on this knowledge and fully participate in the activities outlined in the day's lesson.

Student Activities

In all the lesson examples, instructional strategies and student activities are aligned to the content and language standards and objectives and to the assessment plan. The activities are student-centered and give English learners the opportunity to practice their listening, speaking, reading, and writing skills and access to the core curriculum being taught. During the jigsaw poster presentation activity of the middle school lesson, students read assigned text, respond to the reading questions on their poster papers, present the information on their assigned colonies to other groups, and listen attentively to the presentations on the remaining colonies. While students specifically are assessed on their presentations (listening and speaking skills) and the contents of their posters (writing), English learners have the opportunity throughout all class activities to practice language skills in all four domains needed to become fully proficient in English. Given the CCSS focus on literacy skill development in the content areas, the incorporation of reading and writing activities into every lesson will help students build and draw on a literacy knowledge base to be successful across all content classes.

Each of the lessons also includes a variety of student grouping activities, including partner work, small groups, and whole class. As English learners work in groups with native-English speakers, they can learn the content presented from their peers as well as from the teacher. In the high school lesson, students read a short passage about the Chinese Exclusion Act and then the act itself with a partner, which gives them the opportunity to hear English spoken by a peer as well as to practice speaking themselves. Giving English learners opportunities to practice language skills multiple times with a partner and/or in a small group also allows them to self-correct their mistakes. The additional time to process information and practice their responses can give some English learners the confidence they need to actively participate in larger class discussions and activities.

Culturally Relevant/Multicultural Resources

The middle and high school lessons include culturally relevant/multicultural resources that teachers have identified as topics students would be interested in based on information they gathered about who their students are. The focus on opportunities for African Americans and women in the middle school lessons is intended to help students make connections between opportunities for different groups of people in the past (in the United States in the 1800s) to current topics on issues of equality and access to positions of power. In the high school lessons, students learn about U.S. immigration policies through topics of imperialism, the Chinese Exclusion Act, and political cartoons. Students are given the opportunity to understand topics from multiple perspectives, including those of their peers. Immigration is a topic that all students in this class have expressed an interest in and have shared their opinions on in past class sessions. By learning about social, political, and economic issues surrounding immigration from a partner or small-group member who comes from a culturally and/or linguistically diverse background, all students can make connections with one another that may not happen otherwise. Promoting an understanding of diversity and choosing materials that are relevant to students' lives increases student engagement and their overall academic achievement.

Summary

As you reflect on how to design social studies lesson plans for your English learner students, keep in mind the main interrelated points of this chapter:

- It is important to fully understand who your English learners are in order to include teaching strategies and student activities in your lessons that build on their strengths and help you address any areas of weakness they have. In addition to their English proficiency levels and learning styles, understanding your English learners' backgrounds, interests, and cultures can help you choose multicultural resources to use in your lessons that are relevant to your students' lives. You should pay particular attention to the prior knowledge your English learners have with social studies content, particularly history. They may not have the same background knowledge of U.S. historical events as other students or may have learned about global historical events from a different perspective than students in U.S. public schools.

- The objectives you write for your lesson should be based on CCSS, social studies content standards, and the ELD standards your state has adopted. The social studies content standard and the CCSS generally represent the "what" of the lesson (what content is being taught), while the language standards represent "how" your English learners will master the content standard chosen at the appropriate proficiency levels for them.
- The assessments and activities you use should be aligned to the content and language objectives you have chosen so that you and your students understand the expectations for each lesson. It is important to use the information you have learned about your English learners in Step 1 of the lesson planning process to differentiate your assessments so they accurately reflect what your students are able to accomplish at the end of the lesson. You should also use the information you have learned about your students to design scaffolded activities that will help them learn the content you are presenting while simultaneously developing their English proficiency.

Applying What You Have Learned

In this chapter, you have learned how to provide equitable instruction for your English learner students by using a four-step lesson planning process. Demonstrate your understanding of the chapter by participating in the following activities and answering the corresponding questions.

STEP 1: Know your English learners

- What difficulties might English learners have with the CCSS for Literacy in History/Social Studies, Science, and Technical Subjects that you can take into account when designing your lessons?
- Explain ways you can obtain information about your English learners so that your lessons are aligned to their English proficiency levels, prior content knowledge, and learning styles.

STEP 2: Choose standards for your lessons

- In the lesson planning process presented in this chapter, you have learned that lessons should focus on CCSS for Literacy in History/Social Studies, Science, and Technical Subjects; social studies content standards; and the ELD standards used in your state. Choose a CCSS for Literacy in History/Social Studies, Science, and Technical Subjects; a corresponding ELD standard; and a social studies content standard. Write measurable and observable content (CCSS and social studies) and language (ELD) objectives based on the standards you have chosen.

STEP 3: Design differentiated assessments and student-centered activities

- You have learned how to differentiate your assessment to accurately assess English learners in your social studies class. You have also learned how to use teaching strategies that can help your English learners access the content you are teaching. Additionally, you have learned specific student activities to use in your class that will promote interactions between English learners and native-English speakers. Using the content and language objectives you wrote previously (in Step 2), design the following components of a lesson plan:
  - Assessments that will allow your students to demonstrate they have met the content and language objectives (Remember to differentiate your assessments based on your English learners' language proficiency levels.)
  - A student activity that is aligned to the objectives you have written and the assessments you have designed
  - An overview of the teaching strategies you will use to ensure that your English learners understand and can complete the activity you have designed

STEP 4: Select culturally relevant/multicultural materials and resources

- List some national, state, and/or local organizations that provide culturally relevant/multicultural resources on their websites that can be incorporated into your social studies lessons.

part 4

Conclusions and Resources

Annie Pickert Fuller/Pearson Education

This final section presents a chapter discussing the importance of differentiation for middle and high school English learners. The chapter also highlights comments from a high school math teacher as she reflects on her experiences using the lesson planning process outlined in this book. The chapter is followed by resources for teachers to use as they begin designing content area lessons for their middle and high school English learners that are both accessible and equitable.

chapter 10

Conclusions

LEARNING OUTCOMES

- Explain why differentiation for English learners is important.
- Discuss what equitable access to the core curriculum looks like for English learners.
- Describe why multicultural curriculum makes content relevant for all students.

The four-step lesson planning process presented in this book outlines an accessible model for teacher candidates and teachers to effectively and equitably teach language, literacy, and content to their middle and high school English learner students. Returning to the literature on secondary teacher preparedness by Gandara, Maxwell-Jolly, and Driscoll (2005), this lesson planning process gives teacher candidates and teachers the necessary tools to effectively teach English learners in their content area classes. This preparedness and the focus on educational equity can provide teachers with a more positive lens to view their English learner students than the negative perceptions presented in the literature (Hudley & Daoud, 2008). Perhaps as a result of feeling more prepared to teach English learners, teacher candidates and teachers will not view meeting their literacy needs or designing assessments as barriers in their lesson planning (Helfrich & Bosh, 2011). After learning about and implementing the lesson planning process, teacher candidates and teachers should view teaching English learners not as a challenge but rather as an opportunity to "make a difference" and to identify and address issues of educational equity for their English learner students.

The strategies and student activities teachers are taught to use in the lesson planning process are rooted in second language acquisition (e.g., Diaz-Rico, 2008; Echevarria, Vogt, & Short, 2010) and culturally responsive and relevant pedagogy (e.g., Gay, 2010; Ladson-Billings, 2001) and are aligned to effective strategies for teaching secondary English learners outlined in the literature (Faltis, Arias, & Ramirez-Marin, 2010). The language skills outlined in the English language development (ELD) standards are crucial for English learners to develop proficiency but are also beneficial skills for many native-English speakers in middle and high school to master. As they recognize the wider applications of the ELD standards, teacher candidates and teachers who have learned this lesson planning process in classes and professional development workshops understand the benefits of incorporating these standards into their lesson plans, particularly in the language domains of reading and writing, to the benefit of all their students.

The Importance of Differentiation for English Learners

In each of the language domains of listening, speaking, reading, and writing, English learners need to master a combination of skills to become proficient in English. The ELD standards outlined in this book are presented as specific language skills divided into five English language proficiency levels. As noted in the language domain chapters (Chapters 3–5), each language skill should be taught in combination with other skills within the context of the content area lesson. The language skills should not be thought of as isolated skills but rather as an integrated part of overall language proficiency. The goal is for English learners to effectively communicate orally and in writing at a level that is needed for academic success across all middle and high school content area classes. The language skills presented in this book will help English learners become proficient in English, learn the core content, and master the literacy skills outlined in the Common Core State Standards (CCSS). Mastering these language skills will help English learners attain academic success in the classroom and communicate in broader contexts within and beyond the classroom.

Given the structure of high schools and to a lesser extent middle schools, English learners need explicit language instruction in all their content area classrooms in order to become fully proficient. Explicitly teaching language development skills in lessons also helps English learners fully understand the core content presented in class. By targeting instruction at a level above an English learner's current proficiency level, teachers provide their students with content that is challenging yet accessible through scaffolded teaching techniques and activities. By teaching the language skill that is one level above a student's current proficiency level (i+1), teachers can better discern between the difficulties English learners have with language and content. If content is presented to English learners at an English proficiency level that is far beyond their current proficiency abilities, they may fail to demonstrate learning because they do not have the level of English proficiency needed to understand content and communicate that understanding through lesson assessments. By using these scaffolded teaching techniques in each content area classroom, teachers of English learners are providing their students with more equitable educational opportunities. English learners can be academically successful in content area classrooms and have access to the core curriculum taught in those classes as they simultaneously become more proficient in English.

Equitable Access to the Core Curriculum

The Common Core State Standards for English Language Arts and Literacy in History/Social Studies, Science, and Technical Subjects can pose challenges for English learners, particularly those at the developing proficiency level or below who are not yet proficient in English. By using the step-by-step lesson planning process outlined in this book, teachers can address these challenges and provide their English learners with equitable instruction. When presented with challenging content through accessible strategies and activities, English learners rise to the occasion. Teachers can design lessons that build English learners' base of knowledge in any content area while also improving their English language proficiency. The lessons described in each of the content chapters (Chapters 6–9) give English learners access to the core curriculum, to interactions with their native-English-speaking peers, and to curriculum that is relevant to their lives and the world in which they live. The lesson examples also demonstrate how teachers can help their English learners access the core curriculum by teaching them academic English as well as building on students' prior knowledge by making connections between what they are studying in the current lesson and what they have learned in prior lessons.

When partner or small-group work is incorporated into lessons, English learners and native-English speakers work together to read texts, participate in discussions, understand information they are learning, and go through the writing process. Having students work with partners or in small groups gives English learners opportunities to practice their language, additional time to process information learned with a partner or a small group of students, and access to knowledge that native-English speakers may have. Whether this knowledge is academic or social, it gives English learners access to school knowledge that can contribute to their overall success in middle and high school. Partner and small-group work also gives native-English speakers the opportunity to interact with students with whom they may not normally converse; in doing so, they learn that they have knowledge to share with other students and they learn from their English learner peers as well.

Multicultural Curriculum for All Students

When teachers include culturally relevant/multicultural resources in their lessons, they are helping all students understand and critically analyze materials from multiple perspectives. For example, literature, stories, poetry, and novels that represent the diverse world in which we live can be incorporated into English language arts classes. Inclusion of such multicultural materials helps students make connections between the content they are learning and the relevance to their own lives. Using culturally relevant/multicultural resources also helps promote a broader understanding of the diversity interwoven into the tapestry of our schools, communities, states, and country. The resources teachers select to use in their lessons will depend on the information they learn about their students, the relevance to the content they are teaching, and a reflection of what they believe students should learn about our diverse world in order to be productive citizens in a democratic society.

As described in the content chapters in this book, culturally relevant/multicultural resources can be found in textbooks, in district and state curriculum materials, and on countless educational websites. Culturally relevant/multicultural resources do not need to be incorporated into every aspect of a lesson for students to make connections between the content and the world in which we live. They can be included in the *Into* phase of a lesson to introduce a topic from another or broader perspective. In the *Through* section of a lesson, culturally relevant/multicultural resources can be incorporated to engage students in a deeper critical analysis of a topic. In the *Beyond* phase of the lesson, the resources can connect content learned to topics that are culturally and socially relevant to students' lives. The lesson planning process outlined in this book encourages teachers to include culturally relevant/multicultural resources in any phase of their lessons that promotes critical thinking and a broader understanding of issues of diversity, equity, and social justice. Using culturally relevant/multicultural resources helps all students better understand the diverse experiences and perspectives of their peers, a first step in promoting increased tolerance among students in middle and high school. Given that the CCSS require students to identify, analyze, and evaluate multiple sources of information, teachers have increased opportunities to include culturally relevant/multicultural resources in their lessons.

Reflections from a Classroom Teacher

What follows are the reflections of a high school algebra teacher whose lessons are presented and analyzed in Chapter 7. After the unit was taught, the algebra teacher completed a questionnaire asking for her feedback on the process we followed to modify her unit and on the resulting student outcomes. Concerning the process outlined in this book to include ELD standards and multicultural content into her lessons, the teacher responded:

> The process is very easy to follow. It almost becomes as easy as doing a routine activity like walking or driving. The process is not hard at all if you plan well. In fact, it makes lessons more structured, easy to follow, and more effective.
>
> You must plan while having the standards and the objectives in mind. The standards don't just help teaching become effective for EL [English learner] students. These standards make teaching overall much more effective since English speakers also benefit a great deal from ELD standards.

The teacher also was asked to rate how her students performed on this unit as compared to prior units she had taught. The first question focused on student engagement. She was asked to rate whether she felt students were more engaged or less engaged or if there was no change in student engagement in comparison to other lessons. The teacher responded that her students were more engaged than in the past. Next, the teacher stated that peer interactions had increased as a result of the activities she designed for this unit, again as compared to past units taught. Finally, she rated student performance as "better" than it had been in prior units. The teacher's comments on each of these specific areas follow.

When asked about student engagement, the teacher noted that her Algebra II students were "more engaged than in other lessons I have taught." In her commentary, she specifically discusses the *Into* activity and the impact she felt it had on student engagement in the lesson. She also discusses how even the quiet students were attentive and participated in their group discussions and activities.

> First of all, I had the students' attention from the start. They did not know what was coming up. The *Into* activity just asked students to find a pattern, which seemed like one of those brain-teaser games to them. Immediately most were engaged. Once they found a pattern, I told them this is what we would be learning today—patterns and sequences. Thus they started with a positive mindset, "This is going to be easy."
>
> They participated, and were not hesitant to volunteer or even be volunteered. In previous lessons I would ask a student to come up to the board and she would say "I don't want to because I don't get it." The students know they are accountable and if they are given a problem to work on they will do it. The *Into* activity usually serves as my best ally since it is what gets the students warmed up to the lesson. If this activity has a tie to something they know from before [or in life] they can automatically make a connection.
>
> Students were more attentive from the start. What struck me the most is that the quiet students were active amongst their tables. This was a treat to watch.

On the questionnaire, the teacher stated that student performance was better than that for past units she had taught. The teacher provided the following comments on her students' outcomes in her Algebra II class:

> The students were successful. The success is mainly measured by me asking students questions, and their willingness to respond in accurate, correct ways. If a student can answer a teacher's questions (and they are meaningful questions), then we can determine success.
>
> I gave daily quizzes, and I don't usually have high passing rates. I ran an assignment analysis and the results are pleasing (higher than normal).

As middle and high school teachers implement the CCSS into their content area classes, they must take into consideration the educational impact on their English learner students. The accessible, step-by-step lesson planning process outlined in this book gives teachers the tools they need to provide equitable instruction for secondary English learners. Freire (1990) stresses the importance of teaching students, including English learners, how to read the word and the world. In middle and high school content area classes with a mix of English learners and native-English speakers, students are able to learn from one another and together learn about the world they live in from multiple perspectives. The CCSS present an opportunity for middle and high school teachers to revise their pedagogy and help their English learner students master the skills outlined in the standards for college and career readiness.

Summary

As you reflect on the conclusions drawn from using the four-step lesson planning process outlined in this book, keep in mind the main points of this chapter:

- English learners at the secondary level are still developing their listening, speaking, reading, and writing skills so they can become fully proficient in English. Therefore, it is imperative that middle and high school teachers across all content areas learn who their English learner students are by first identifying their proficiency levels in all four language areas. By doing so, teachers can include differentiated teaching strategies and assessments in their lessons that are scaffolded just beyond their English learners' current proficiency levels.
- The lessons presented in this book include teaching strategies and student activities that make challenging content accessible to middle and high school English learners, thus providing them with more equitable educational opportunities. By following the lesson planning process in this book, teachers can help their English learner students access the core curriculum and give them opportunities to interact with and learn from their native-English-speaking peers. Additionally, when teachers incorporate culturally relevant/multicultural resources in their lessons, they are helping all their students understand the diverse experiences and perspectives that are represented in their class and in the world in which we live.
- The reflections of a high school algebra teacher who has used this lesson planning process help illuminate the benefits she felt were inherent in the process. She noted that the process is easy to follow, that students were more engaged in the lesson, that peer interactions had increased, and that overall student performance had improved for all her students, including her English learners, as compared to the previous lessons she had taught while not following the four-step lesson planning process.

Applying What You Have Learned

In this chapter, you have reviewed the lesson planning process presented in this book and learned about the reasons why the process is an effective and equitable method for teaching middle and high school English learners. Demonstrate your understanding of the chapter by responding to the following statements:

- Explain why differentiation for English learners is important.
- Discuss what equitable access to the core curriculum looks like for English learners.
- Describe reasons why multicultural curriculum makes content relevant for all students.

appendix A

Language Skills Aligned to the Common Core State Standards

Grades 6–8 and Grades 9–12

LISTENING AND SPEAKING SKILLS—Middle School (Grade7)
CCSS Aligned to California ELD Standards at the Expanding and Bridging Levels

	Expanding	**Bridging**
CCSS—Listening/ Speaking: Comprehension and Collaboration		
ELD Standard/Skill **Exchanging Information/Ideas** (CCSS 1)	Contribute to class, group, and partner discussions by following turn-taking rules, asking relevant questions, affirming others, adding relevant information, and paraphrasing key ideas	Contribute to class, group, and partner discussions by following turn-taking rules, asking relevant questions, affirming others, adding relevant information and evidence, paraphrasing key ideas, building on responses, and providing useful feedback
ELD Standard/Skill **Listening Actively** (CCSS 2) (CCSS 3)	Demonstrate active listening in oral presentation activities by asking and answering detailed questions with occasional prompting and moderate support	Demonstrate active listening in oral presentation activities by asking and answering detailed questions with minimal prompting and support
CCSS—Presentation of Knowledge & Ideas		
ELD Standard/Skill **Supporting Opinions and Persuading Others** (CCSS 4)	Negotiate with or persuade others in conversation using learned phrases and open responses	Negotiate with or persuade others in conversation using an appropriate register, a variety of learned phrases, indirect reported speech, and open responses
ELD Standard/Skill **Adapting Language Choices** (CCSS 6)	Adjust language choices according to purpose (e.g., explaining, persuading), task, and audience	Adjust language choices according to purpose (e.g., facilitating a science experiment), task, and audience

(*continued*)

	Expanding	Bridging
ELD Standard/Skill **Presenting** (CCSS 4) (CCSS 5 in all)	Plan and deliver longer oral presentations on a variety of topics using details and evidence to support ideas	Plan and deliver longer oral presentations on a variety of topics in a variety of disciplines, using reasoning and evidence as well as a growing understanding of register

READING SKILLS—Middle School (Grade 7)

CCSS Aligned to California ELD Standards at the Expanding and Bridging Levels

	Expanding	Bridging
CCSS—Key Ideas and Details		
ELD Standard/Skill **Reading/viewing Closely:** explain ideas, processes, and relationships (CCSS 1 & 2)	Explain ideas, phenomena, processes, and text relationships based on close reading of grade-level texts and viewing of multimedia with moderate support	Explain ideas, phenomena, processes, and text relationships based on close reading of a variety of grade-level texts and viewing of multimedia with light support
ELD Standard/Skill **Reading/viewing Closely:** explain inferences and conclusions (CCSS 3)	Express inferences and conclusions drawn based on close reading of grade-appropriate texts and viewing of multimedia using a variety of verbs	Express inferences and conclusions drawn based on close reading of grade-level texts and viewing of multimedia using a variety of precise academic verbs
CCSS—Craft and Structure		
ELD Standard/Skill **Analyzing Language Choices** (CCSS 4)	Explain how phrasing, different words with similar meanings, or figurative language can produce shades of meaning and different effects on the audience	Explain how phrasing, different words with similar meanings, or figurative language can produce shades of meaning, nuances, and different effects on the audience
ELD Standard/Skill **Reading/viewing Closely: Knowledge of Morphology** (CCSS 4)	Use knowledge of morphology, context, reference materials, and visual cues to determine the meanings of unknown and multiple-meaning words on familiar and new topics	Use knowledge of morphology, context, reference materials, and visual cues to determine the meanings, including figurative and connotative meanings, of unknown and multiple-meaning words on a variety of new topics
ELD Standard/Skill **Evaluating Language Choices** (CCSS 5 & 6)	Explain how well writers and speakers use specific language to support arguments and provide detailed evidence when provided with moderate support	Explain how well writers and speakers use language resources to present ideas or support arguments and provide detailed evidence when provided with light support

	Expanding	Bridging
CCSS—Integration of Knowledge and Ideas		
ELD Standard/Skill **Reading/Viewing Closely:** explain inferences and conclusions (CCSS 7)	Express inferences and conclusions drawn based on close reading of grade-appropriate texts and viewing of multimedia using a variety of verbs	Express inferences and conclusions drawn based on close reading of grade-level texts and viewing of multimedia using a variety of precise academic verbs
ELD Standard/Skill **Evaluating Language Choices** (CCSS 8)	Explain how well writers and speakers use specific language to present ideas or support arguments, and provide detailed evidence when provided with moderate support	Explain how well writers and speakers use language resources to present ideas or support arguments, and provide detailed when provided with light support
CCSS—Range of Reading and Level of Text Complexity		
ELD Standard/Skill **Understanding Cohesion:** structuring texts (CCSS 9) (CCSS 10 in all)	Apply growing understanding of how ideas, events, or reasons are linked throughout a text using a variety of connecting words or phrases to comprehending texts and writing texts with increasing cohesion	Apply increasing understanding of how ideas, events, or reasons are linked throughout a text using an increasing variety of academic connecting and transitional words or phrases to comprehending texts and writing texts with increasing cohesion

WRITING SKILLS—Middle School (Grade 7)

CCSS Aligned to California ELD Standards at the Expanding and Bridging Levels

	Expanding	Bridging
CCSS—Text Types and Purposes		
ELD Standard/Skill **Justifying/Arguing:** express opinions (CCSS 1)	Express attitudes and opinions or temper statements with a variety of familiar modal expressions	Express attitudes and opinions or temper statements with nuanced modal expressions
ELD Standard/Skill **Justifying/Arguing:** justify opinions and positions (CCSS 1)	Justify opinions or persuade others by providing relevant textual evidence or relevant background knowledge with moderate support	Justify opinions or persuade others by providing detailed and relevant textual evidence or relevant background knowledge with light support
ELD Standard/Skill **Understanding Cohesion:** apply knowledge of resources (CCSS 1)	Apply knowledge of familiar language resources for referring to make texts more cohesive, and to comprehending and writing texts with increasing cohesion	Apply knowledge of familiar language resources for referring to make texts more cohesive, and to comprehending and writing cohesive texts

(*continued*)

	Expanding	Bridging
ELD Standard/Skill **Selecting Language Resources:** use a variety of words (CCSS 2)	Use a growing set of academic words, domain-specific words, synonyms, and antonyms to create precision and shades of meaning when speaking and writing	Use an expanding set of general academic words, domain-specific words, synonyms, antonyms, and figurative language to create precision and shades of meaning when speaking and writing
ELD Standard/Skill **Understanding Text Structure** (CCSS 2)	Apply understanding of organizational features of different text types to comprehending texts and to writing texts with increasingly clear and coherent arguments, informative/explanatory texts, and narratives	Apply understanding of organizational features of different text types to comprehending texts and to writing clear and cohesive arguments, informative/explanatory texts, and narratives
ELD Standard/Skill **Writing:** literary and informational texts (CCSS 2)	Write longer literary and informational texts collaboratively and independently using appropriate text organization	Write longer and more detailed literary and informational texts collaboratively and independently using appropriate text organization, and a growing understanding of register
CCSS—Production and Distribution of Writing *ELD Standard/Skill* **Writing:** summaries (CCSS 4)	Write increasingly concise summaries of texts and experiences using complete sentences and key words	Write clear and coherent summaries of texts and experiences using complete and concise sentences and key words
ELD Standard/Skill **Interacting via written English** (CCSS 5)	Engage in longer written exchanges with peers and collaborate on more detailed written texts on a variety of topics, using technology when appropriate	Engage in extended written exchanges with peers and collaborate on complex written texts on a variety of topics, using technology when appropriate
CCSS—Research to Build and Present Knowledge *ELD Standard/Skill* **Selecting Language Resources:** use a variety of words (CCSS 7 & 8)	Use a growing set of academic words, domain-specific words, synonyms, and antonyms to create precision and shades of meaning when speaking and writing	Use an expanding set of general academic words, domain-specific words, synonyms, antonyms, and figurative language to create precision and shades of meaning when speaking and writing
ELD Standard/Skill **Selecting Language Resources:** use knowledge of morphology (CCSS 7 & 8)	Use knowledge of morphology to appropriately select affixes in a growing number of ways to manipulate language	Use knowledge of morphology to appropriately select affixes in a variety of ways to manipulate language

	Expanding	Bridging
ELD Standard/Skill **Understanding Cohesion:** apply knowledge of resources (CCSS 9)	Apply knowledge of familiar language resources for referring to make texts more cohesive, and to comprehending and writing texts with increasing cohesion	Apply knowledge of familiar language resources for referring to make texts more cohesive, and to comprehending and writing cohesive texts
CCSS—Range of Writing		
ELD Standard/Skill **Connecting Ideas** (CCSS 10)	Combine clauses in an increasing variety of ways to make connections between and join ideas, for example, to express a reason or to make a concession	Combine clauses in a wide variety of ways to make connections and join ideas, for example, to show the relationship between multiple events or ideas or to evaluate an argument
ELD Standard/Skill **Condensing Ideas** (CCSS 10) (CCSS 6 in all)	Condense ideas in an increasing variety of ways to create precise and detailed sentences	Condense clauses in a variety of ways to create precise and detailed sentences

Source: California Department of Education (2012b); Common Core State Standards (2010).

LISTENING AND SPEAKING SKILLS—High School (Grades 9–10)
CCSS Aligned to California ELD Standards at the Expanding and Bridging Levels

	Expanding	Bridging
CCSS—Listening/ Speaking: Comprehension and Collaboration		
ELD Standard/Skill **Exchanging Information/Ideas** (CCSS 1)	Contribute to class, group, and partner discussions, sustaining conversations on a variety of grade- and age-appropriate topics by following turn-taking rules, asking and answering relevant and on-topic questions, affirming others, providing additional relevant information, and paraphrasing key ideas	Contribute to class, group, and partner discussions, sustaining conversations on a variety of grade- and age-appropriate topics by following turn-taking rules, asking and answering relevant and on-topic questions, affirming others, and providing coherent and well-articulated comments and additional information
ELD Standard/Skill **Listening Actively** (CCSS 2) (CCSS 3)	Demonstrate comprehension of oral presentations and discussions on a variety of social and academic topics by asking and answering questions that show thoughtful consideration of ideas or arguments with moderate support	Demonstrate comprehension of oral presentations and discussions on a variety of social and academic topics by asking and answering detailed and complex questions that show thoughtful consideration of ideas or arguments with light support

(*continued*)

	Expanding	Bridging
CCSS—Presentation of Knowledge and Ideas		
ELD Standard/Skill **Supporting Opinions and Persuading Others** (CCSS 4)	Negotiate with or persuade others in conversations using a growing number of learned phrases and open responses to express and defend nuanced opinions	Negotiate with or persuade others in conversations in appropriate registers using a variety of learned phrases, indirect reported speech, and open responses to express and defend nuanced opinions
ELD Standard/Skill **Adapting Language Choices** (CCSS 6)	Adjust language choices according to context, purpose, task, and audience	Adjust language choices according to task (e.g., group presentation of a research project), context, purpose, and audience
ELD Standard/Skill **Presenting** (CCSS 4) (CCSS 5 in all)	Plan and deliver a variety of oral presentations and reports on grade-appropriate topics that present evidence and facts to support ideas using growing understanding of register	Plan and deliver a variety of oral presentations and reports on grade-appropriate topics that express complex and abstract ideas, are well supported by evidence and reasoning, and are delivered using an appropriate level of formality and understanding of register

READING SKILLS–High School (Grades 9–10)
CCSS Aligned to California ELD Standards at the Expanding and Bridging Levels

	Expanding	Bridging
CCSS—Key Ideas and Details		
ELD Standard/Skill **Reading/viewing Closely:** explain ideas, processes, and relationships (CCSS 1 & 2)	Explain ideas, phenomena, processes, and relationships within and across texts based on close reading of a variety of grade-appropriate texts presented in various print and multimedia formats, using increasingly complex sentences and an increasing variety of general academic and domain-specific words	Explain ideas, phenomena, processes, and relationships within and across texts based on close reading of a variety of grade-level texts presented in various print and multimedia formats, using a variety of detailed sentences and a range of general academic and domain-specific words
ELD Standard/Skill **Reading/Viewing Closely:** explain inferences and conclusions (CCSS 3)	Explain inferences and conclusions drawn based on close reading of a variety of grade-appropriate texts and viewing of multimedia using a variety of verbs and adverbs	Explain inferences and conclusions drawn based on close reading of grade-level texts and viewing of multimedia using a variety of verbs and adverbs

	Expanding	Bridging
CCSS—Craft and Structure		
ELD Standard/Skill **Analyzing Language Choices** (CCSS 4)	Explain how a writer's or speaker's choice of phrasing or specific words produces nuances and different effects on the audience	Explain how a writer's or speaker's choice of a variety of different types of phrasing or words produces nuances and different effects on the audience
ELD Standard/Skill **Evaluating Language Choices** (CCSS 5 & 6)	Evaluate how successfully writers and speakers structure texts and use language to persuade the reader or create other specific effects, with moderate support	Evaluate how successfully writers and speakers structure texts and use language to persuade the reader or create other specific effects, with light support
CCSS—Integration of Knowledge and Ideas		
ELD Standard/Skill **Reading/Viewing Closely:** explain inferences and conclusions (CCSS 7)	Explain inferences and conclusions drawn based on close reading of a variety of grade-appropriate texts and viewing of multimedia using a variety of verbs and adverbs	Explain inferences and conclusions drawn based on close reading of grade-level texts and viewing of multimedia using a variety of verbs and adverbs
ELD Standard/Skill **Evaluating Language Choices** (CCSS 8)	Evaluate how successfully writers and speakers structure texts and use language to persuade the reader or create other specific effects, with moderate support	Evaluate how successfully writers and speakers structure texts and use language to persuade the reader or create other specific effects, with light support
CCSS—Range of Reading and Level of Text Complexity		
ELD Standard/Skill **Understanding Cohesion**: structuring texts (CCSS 9) (CCSS 10 in all)	Apply knowledge of familiar language resources for linking ideas, events, or reasons throughout a text to comprehending texts and to writing increasingly more cohesive texts for specific purposes and audiences	Apply knowledge of familiar language resources for linking ideas, events, or reasons throughout a text to comprehending grade-level texts and to writing clear and cohesive grade-level texts for specific purposes and audiences

WRITING SKILLS—High School (Grades 9–10)

CCSS Aligned to California ELD Standards at the Expanding and Bridging Levels

	Expanding	Bridging
CCSS—Text Types and Purposes		
ELD Standard/Skill **Justifying/Arguing:** express opinions (CCSS 1)	Express attitudes and opinions or temper statements with a variety of familiar modal expressions	Express attitudes and opinions or temper statements with nuanced modal expressions
ELD Standard/Skill **Justifying/Arguing:** justify opinions and positions (CCSS 1)	Justify opinions and positions or persuade others by making connections between ideas and articulating relevant textual evidence or background knowledge	Justify opinions and positions or persuade others by making connections and distinctions between ideas and texts and articulating sufficient, detailed, and relevant textual evidence or background knowledge using appropriate register
ELD Standard/Skill **Understanding Cohesion:** apply knowledge of resources (CCSS 1)	Apply knowledge of a growing number of language resources for referring to make texts more cohesive, and to comprehending and writing increasingly cohesive texts for specific purposes and audiences	Apply knowledge of a variety of language resources for referring to make texts more cohesive, and to comprehending grade-level texts and to writing clear and cohesive grade-level texts for specific purposes and audiences
ELD Standard/Skill **Selecting language Resources:** use a variety of words (CCSS 2)	Use an increasing variety of grade-appropriate general academic words and domain-specific academic words accurately and appropriately when producing increasingly complex spoken and written texts	Use a variety of grade-appropriate and domain-specific academic words and phrases, including persuasive language, accurately and appropriately when producing complex spoken and written texts
ELD Standard/Skill **Understanding text Structure** (CCSS 2)	Apply analysis of the organizational structure of different text types to comprehending and writing increasingly clear and cohesive arguments, informative/explanatory texts, and narratives	Apply analysis of the organizational structure of different text types to comprehending texts and to writing clear and cohesive arguments, informative/explanatory texts, and narratives
ELD Standard/Skill **Writing:** literary and informational texts (CCSS 2)	Write longer literary and informational texts collaboratively and independently using appropriate text organization and a growing understanding of register	Write longer and more detailed literary and informational texts collaboratively and independently using appropriate text organization and register
CCSS—Production and Distribution of Writing		
ELD Standard/Skill **Writing:** summaries (CCSS 4)	Write increasingly concise summaries of texts and experiences using complete sentences and key words	Write clear and coherent summaries of texts using complete and concise sentences and key words

	Expanding	Bridging
ELD Standard/Skill **Interacting via written English** (CCSS 5)	Collaborate with peers to engage in increasingly complex grade-appropriate written exchanges and writing projects, using technology as appropriate	Collaborate with peers to engage in a variety of extended written exchanges and complex grade-appropriate writing projects, using technology as appropriate
CCSS—Research to Build and Present Knowledge *ELD Standard/Skill* **Selecting Language Resources:** use a variety of words (CCSS 7 & 8)	Use an increasing variety of grade-appropriate general academic words and domain-specific academic words accurately and appropriately when producing increasingly complex spoken and written texts	Use a variety of grade-appropriate and domain-specific academic words and phrases, including persuasive language, accurately and appropriately when producing complex spoken and written texts
ELD Standard/Skill **Selecting Language Resources:** use knowledge of morphology (CCSS 7 & 8)	Use knowledge of morphology to appropriately select affixes in a growing number of ways to manipulate language	Use knowledge of morphology to appropriately select affixes in a variety of ways to manipulate language
ELD Standard/Skill **Understanding Cohesion:** apply knowledge of resources (CCSS 9)	Apply knowledge of a growing number of language resources for referring to make texts more cohesive, and to comprehending and writing increasingly cohesive texts for specific purposes and audiences	Apply knowledge of a variety of language resources for referring to make texts more cohesive, and to comprehending grade-level texts and to writing clear and cohesive grade-level texts for specific purposes and audiences
CCSS—Range of Writing *ELD Standard/Skill* **Connecting Ideas** (CCSS 10)	Combine clauses in a growing number of ways to create compound and complex sentences that make connections between and link concrete and abstract ideas, for example, to express a reason or to make a concession	Combine clauses in a variety of ways to create compound and complex sentences that make connections between and link concrete and abstract ideas, for example, to make a concession or to establish cause
ELD Standard/Skill **Condensing Ideas** (CCSS 10) (CCSS 6 in all)	Condense ideas in a growing number of ways to create precise and detailed simple, compound, and complex sentences	Condense ideas in a variety of ways to create precise simple, compound, and complex sentences that condense concrete and abstract ideas

Source: California Department of Education (2012b); Common Core State Standards (2010).

ELD Skills to Use Throughout the Year CHECKLIST: Grades 6–8

Listening/Speaking

Date(s) Covered

_____ _____ _____ _____ Exchanging Information/Ideas
_____ _____ _____ _____ Supporting Opinions and Persuading Others
_____ _____ _____ _____ Listening Attentively
_____ _____ _____ _____ Adapting Language Choices
_____ _____ _____ _____ Presenting

Reading

Date(s) Covered

_____ _____ _____ _____ Reading/Viewing Closely: explain ideas, processes, and relationships
_____ _____ _____ _____ Reading/Viewing Closely: explain inferences and conclusions
_____ _____ _____ _____ Reading/Viewing Closely: knowledge of morphology
_____ _____ _____ _____ Evaluating Language Choices
_____ _____ _____ _____ Analyzing Language Choices
_____ _____ _____ _____ Understanding Cohesion: structuring texts

Writing

Date(s) Covered

_____ _____ _____ _____ Writing: summaries
_____ _____ _____ _____ Writing: literary and informational texts
_____ _____ _____ _____ Justifying/Arguing: express opinions
_____ _____ _____ _____ Justifying/Arguing: justify opinions and positions
_____ _____ _____ _____ Selecting Language Resources: use a variety of words
_____ _____ _____ _____ Selecting Language Resources: use knowledge of morphology
_____ _____ _____ _____ Understanding Cohesion: apply knowledge of resources
_____ _____ _____ _____ Understanding Text Structure
_____ _____ _____ _____ Interacting with Written English

_____ _____ _____ _____ Connecting Ideas

_____ _____ _____ _____ Condensing Ideas

ELD Skills to Use Throughout the Year CHECKLIST: Grades 9–12

Listening/Speaking

Date(s) Covered

_____ _____ _____ _____ Exchanging Information/Ideas

_____ _____ _____ _____ Supporting Opinions and Persuading Others

_____ _____ _____ _____ Listening Attentively

_____ _____ _____ _____ Adapting Language Choices

_____ _____ _____ _____ Presenting

Reading

Date(s) Covered

_____ _____ _____ _____ Reading/Viewing Closely: explain ideas, processes, and relationships

_____ _____ _____ _____ Reading/Viewing Closely: explain inferences and conclusions

_____ _____ _____ _____ Evaluating Language Choices

_____ _____ _____ _____ Analyzing Language Choices

_____ _____ _____ _____ Understanding Cohesion: structuring texts

Writing

Date(s) Covered

_____ _____ _____ _____ Writing: summaries

_____ _____ _____ _____ Writing: literary and informational texts

_____ _____ _____ _____ Justifying/Arguing: express opinions

_____ _____ _____ _____ Justifying/Arguing: justify opinions and positions

_____ _____ _____ _____ Selecting Language Resources: use a variety of words

_____ _____ _____ _____ Selecting Language Resources: use knowledge of morphology

_____ _____ _____ _____ Understanding Cohesion: apply knowledge of resources

_____ _____ _____ _____ Understanding Text Structure

_____ _____ _____ _____ Interacting with Written English

_____ _____ _____ _____ Connecting Ideas

_____ _____ _____ _____ Condensing Ideas

appendix C

Sample Lesson Plan Format

Title of the Lesson	Class (Content Area) & Grade Level
Content Standard(s)	ELD Standard(s)
Content Objective(s)	Language Objective(s)
Assessment Plan	
Instructional Strategies/Student Activities *Into/Through/Closure/Beyond* INTO: THROUGH: CLOSURE: BEYOND:	
Key Vocabulary	
Materials Needed	

appendix D

Description of Student Activities Used in Content Area Lesson Plan Examples

Jigsaw Activity

A jigsaw activity is a cooperative learning technique in which students are given the opportunity to become "experts" on a piece of knowledge and then share their expertise with other students in the class (Aronson, 1978). In a class that enrolls English learners, a jigsaw activity is often used when a significant amount of text or difficult text has been assigned. Students are divided into small groups (usually four per group), and each group is given a section of the text. Group members review the text and are assigned one of several reading tasks, such as:

- Answering questions about their section of the text
- Summarizing their section of the text
- Writing comprehension questions about their section

Whatever task is chosen for the jigsaw activity, the goal is for each group member to understand what he or she has read and to become an expert on that section of text. When each group has completed its "expert" task, those students teach the content of their section to the other groups. This can be done as group presentations to the whole class or with each group sharing its expert knowledge with one another by partnering two groups at a time. Teachers can also ask one member of each group to form a new group that will now consist of an expert on each topic that groups were asked to learn about. Each expert then shares his or her knowledge with the others in the new group. However teachers design their jigsaws, the activity allows English learners an opportunity to develop their English proficiency in all four language domains: listening, speaking, reading, and writing. Additionally, during a jigsaw activity, English learners can learn from and with their native-English-speaking peers.

"Mix and Mingle" Party Activity

A "mix and mingle" party (sometimes referred to as a "tea party") is an activity in which English learners can practice listening, speaking, reading, and writing skills as they interact with their native-English-speaking peers. The activity described here has been adapted from one presented by Kylene Beers in her book *When Kids Can't Read* (2003).

The description of the activity provided here is based on an activity designed for an 11th-grade history class at the end of a unit on the civil rights movement. The activity serves as an assessment of what students learned about key individuals of the movement as well as a review for an upcoming unit test.

- Students are seated in groups of four or five (depending on class size). Each group is assigned an individual they have learned about during the civil rights movement unit.
- Students in the small group are given note cards and instructed to write a description and a quote for their individual. Each note card must have the same information on it, so students must agree what to include on their note cards before writing on them.
- Students are told that they will be participating in a "party" where they are required to meet and learn about the perspectives of all individuals at the party. They are given the following directions:
  - As you "work the room," introduce yourself to someone by describing who you are and then reading your quote and description to that person.
  - After you have finished, the other person should do the same.
  - Find someone else, and introduce yourself to him or her. Continue to work the room until you have met all the people at the party.
  - Return to your seat. Describe and sum up each person's perspective and contribution to the civil rights movement by writing a complete sentence for each person.
- As students are participating in the activity, the names of all the civil rights leaders should be projected on the overhead. NOTE: Multiple students from each small group will be reading the quote and description of one civil rights leader. Students should be instructed that if they meet a repeat civil rights individual, they do not need to hear the quote and description a second time. However, some English learners may need to hear the quote and description multiple times for full comprehension.
- Once students have returned to their seats and have written their sentences describing each civil rights leader, the teacher leads a small-group discussion on what they have learned about each individual. The teacher can ask students which individuals from the civil rights movement were not invited to the mix and mingle party (the activity focuses on key figures only).

A mix and mingle party activity can be used in any content area in lessons where multiple perspectives, outcomes, situations, or definitions are presented. For example, students can engage in a mix and mingle party activity in a math class where each group of students is assigned an equation. Group members write explanations of how they solved equations on their note cards and then share their work with students from other groups. In an English language arts class, students can be assigned characters in a book, play, or other piece of literature and asked to write a quote and/or description of their characters on note cards. However teachers use a mix and mingle party activity in class, English learners have multiple opportunities to develop their English proficiency across all the language domains. For English learners at lower proficiency levels, teachers can assign them to be a character and write a description with less complex language so they can participate in all aspects of the activity. Purposely partnering English learners with native-English speakers can also create opportunities for English learners to interact with their peers so they can hear them speak English and to create a community of learners in the classroom.

Quick Write Activity

A quick write is an activity in which students begin to express their ideas on topics they are learning in class that can lead to a more structured writing assignment (Graves & Kittle, 2005). Students can complete a quick write activity during any phase of the lesson. As an *Into* activity, a quick write can be used as a review of information students have previously learned. Teachers can use the quick write to assess the amount and type of information students recall on the subject. Quick writes can also be used as a brainstorming tool to gauge how much students know about a topic that will be the focus of an upcoming lesson. As a *Through* activity, quick writes can serve as a foundation for a variety of writing activities, presentations, and discussions. As a *Beyond* activity, they can be used as an assessment tool in many ways, such as students responding to a question about the lesson content, using vocabulary learned in the lesson, and recapping key concepts.

- Present students with a topic, question, and/or statement and give them a minute or two to think about the topic.
- Ask students to write everything that comes to mind on the topic during a specified amount of time, generally two to five minutes depending on the complexity of the topic.
- Ask students to share their quick writes. Depending on the proficiency levels of English learners in the class and the amount of practice they need with their speaking skills, teachers can ask students to share their quick writes with a partner, then a small group, and finally the whole class to give students multiple opportunities to share their work.
- During the discussions, suggest that students can add to and/or edit their quick writes so they have a complete description or response.

Students can use their quick writes as a foundation for a variety of activities, such as a more structured writing assignment or notes on a topic to be covered in an upcoming lesson.

Reciprocal Teaching Activity

Reciprocal teaching is a group reading activity in which each student is assigned a role based on the reading and is responsible to complete a task assigned to that role (Palinscar & Brown, 1984). In this activity, students are placed in groups of four. As is the case with other student activities described in this book, it is beneficial to group English learners with native-English speakers. The teacher then distributes a note card to each member of the group identifying each person's unique role: summarizer, questioner, clarifier, and predictor. Students read the assigned text or a few paragraphs of the text if it is a long passage. Encourage students to use note-taking strategies such as selective underlining or sticky notes to help them better prepare for their role in the upcoming group discussion.

- At a given stopping point, the *summarizer* begins the activity by highlighting the key ideas up to this point in the reading.
- The *questioner* will then pose questions about the selection: unclear parts, puzzling information, connections to other concepts already learned, etc.
- The *clarifier* addresses confusing parts of the text and attempts to answer the questions that were just posed by other group members.
- The *predictor* can offer guesses about what the author will tell the group next or, if it is a literary selection, what the next events in the story will be.

The roles in the group then switch one person to the right, and the next selection is read. Students repeat the process using their new roles (e.g., the summarizer is now the questioner). If the text consists of only one selection, group members should switch roles the next time the activity is used in class. Teachers can purposefully assign roles to their English learner students based on the information they know about their language and content abilities. For example, an English learner at the expanding level may have the necessary English proficiency to be the summarizer or questioner but may not be proficient enough in reading to be the clarifier or predictor. However, as other students in the group discuss these aspects of the reading, English learners will benefit from a reciprocal teaching activity.

SQP2RS Reading Activity

SQP2RS, or Survey, Question, Predict, Read, Respond, and Summarize, is a reading activity that can be used during assigned readings of any type of text, such as textbooks, articles, research reports, and novels (Vogt, 2000). Students can participate in a SQP2RS (or "Squeepers") activity individually, with a partner, in small groups, or as a whole class. The activity gives English learners the opportunity to learn how to engage with the text so they can read with a purpose. Teaching English learners SQP2RS or any other reading activity gives them a valuable academic tool they can use to read text across all content area classes, first with the aid of a teacher (scaffolded instruction) and eventually as an independent reading activity.

To begin a SQP2RS activity, a teacher can give students a handout (or show it on an overhead projector) with the following information down the left-hand column, leaving space next to each step for students to respond:

- Survey: (Before you read) Think about or discuss what this reading assignment will be about. Look at titles, headers, pictures, etc., for clues.
- Question: (Before you read) Write 1–3 questions you believe you will be able to answer from the reading.
- Predict: (Before you read) Can you predict 1–3 things we will learn?
- Read: (You don't need to write anything in this space.)
- Respond: (After you read) Try to answer your questions. Modify, add, or drop questions you wrote above.
- Summarize: (After you read) Write a 4-sentence summary. Sentence 1: Identify the main idea of what you read. Sentences 2–4: State details, reasons, examples, and facts from the text to support the main idea.

Like many other reading activities, SQP2RS can help English learners read with a purpose. Reading activities can also help English learners focus on the main ideas in the text while understanding that supporting details are important but often not as critical.

Think-Pair-Share Activity

Think-Pair-Share is an excellent and quick activity that teachers can use to allow English learners time to process information they are asked to learn before participating in a class discussion (McTighe & Lyman, 1988). It can be used in any phase of the lesson. In the *Into* phase, this activity can help gauge the background knowledge students have of the content that will be presented in the lesson. In the *Through* phase, the strategy is a useful assessment tool to monitor if students have fully understood the content or if material needs to be reinforced or retaught. In the *Beyond* or *Closure* phase of the lesson, a Think-Pair-Share activity allows students to share what they have learned in the lesson (again, this is an assessment tool).

- Pose a question or present a concept to the students.
- Give students a few minutes to individually think of and/or write an answer or form a statement about the concept. (Think)
- Pair the students and give them a few minutes to share their responses with one another. The partners should be instructed to discuss any similarities or differences in their responses. (Pair)
- Ask students to share their responses in a class discussion. (Share)

English learners need time to process information learned and to form grammatically correct sentences to answer the question posed or think about the concept presented. With a Think-Pair-Share activity, English learners have multiple opportunities to practice their responses and hear other students' responses to ensure they comprehend the question posed or fully understand the concept. Purposely partnering English learners with native-English speakers can also create opportunities for English learners to interact with their peers to hear them speak English and create a community of learners in the classroom.

Vocabulary Four Square Activity

Vocabulary Four Square is a vocabulary development activity that students can use across all content area classes. It gives English learners the opportunity to engage with vocabulary in ways that enhance their ability not just to learn new vocabulary terms but also to use the vocabulary in the context presented. Once students complete this activity, they will have a vocabulary bank they can continue to add to during the course of the academic year. The following steps describe the activity as a pen-and-paper activity. Vocabulary Four Square, like many vocabulary development activities, can also be done electronically through a variety of software programs.

- Students divide a piece of paper into four squares.
- In the upper left-hand corner or square, students write the vocabulary term.
- In the upper right-hand corner or square, students write the definition of the vocabulary term. You can provide a definition for the term or develop one as a class. The key to this step is that you and your students write the same definition in this square.
- In the lower left-hand corner or square, students write their own original sentence using the vocabulary term in the specified context. For example, if the vocabulary term is *table* and students are in a science class, their sentences should refer to a scientific table or a table used to present data rather than a dining room table.
- In the lower right-hand corner or square, students can draw a picture of the vocabulary term or any other visual or mnemonic device that helps them remember it.

In any content area class, students need to learn a multitude of vocabulary terms, so it may be unrealistic to use this vocabulary activity with every term you present in class. Instead, this activity should be used for vocabulary terms that represent the main ideas of the lesson and those that are necessary for students to bridge concepts from one lesson or unit to the next. By doing so, English learners will understand which vocabulary terms to focus on.

references

Aronson, E. (1978). *The jigsaw classroom.* Los Angeles, CA: Sage.

Banks, J. (2003). Teaching literacy for social justice and global citizenship. *Language Arts, 81*(1), 18–19.

Barron, R., & Sanchez, F. (2007). Fulfilling the commitment: Excellence for all students. *Leadership, 36*(3), 8–10.

Beers, K. (2003). *When kids can't read: What teachers can do. A guide for teachers 6–12.* Portsmouth, NH: Heinemann.

Bowers, E., Fitts, S., Quirk, M., & Woo, J. (2010). Effective strategies for developing Academic English: Professional development and teacher practices. *Bilingual Research Journal, 33,* 95–110.

Bromley, K., Irwin-DeVitis, L., & Modlo, M. (1995). *Graphic organizers.* New York, NY: Scholastic.

California Department of Education. (2012a). Educational demographics unit. Retrieved from http://dq.cde.ca.gov/dataquest/

California Department of Education. (2012b). Specialized programs: English learners. Retrieved from http://www.cde.ca.gov/sp/el/er/eldstandards.asp.

California State University. (2009). *Composite results for distinct credential programs.* Long Beach, CA: CSU Chancellor's Office.

Callahan, R. (2005). Tracking and high school English learners: Limiting opportunities to learn. *American Educational Research Journal, 42*(2), 305–328.

Chamot, A., & O'Malley, J. (1994). *The CALLA handbook: Implementing the cognitive academic language learning approach.* Reading, MA: Addison-Wesley.

Chubbuck, S. (2010). Individual and structural orientations in socially just teaching: Conceptualization, implementation, and collaborative effort. *Journal of Teacher Education, 61*(3), 197–210.

Cochran-Smith, M., Shakman, K., Jong, C., Terrell, D., Barnatt, J., & McQuillan, P. (2009). Good and just teaching: The case for social justice in teacher education. *American Journal of Education, 115*(3), 347–377.

Collier, V. (1995). *Acquiring a second language for school.* Washington, DC: National Clearinghouse for Bilingual Education.

Crawford, J. (2007, June 6). A diminished vision of civil rights. *Education Week.* Retrieved from http://www.edweek.org/ew/articles/2007/06/06/39crawford.h26.html

Daoud, A. (2003). "The ESL kids are over there": Opportunities for social interactions between immigrant Latino and white high school students. *Journal of Hispanic Higher Education, 2*(3), 292–314.

Daoud, A. (2011). Providing equitable instruction for high school English learners: How teacher candidates define and enact social justice. *International Journal of Humanities and Social Science, 1*(7),14–22.

Darling-Hammond, L., French, J., & Garcia-Lopez, S. (2002). *Learning to teach for social justice.* New York, NY: Teachers College Press.

De Jong, E., & Harper, C. (2005, Spring). Preparing mainstream teachers for English-language learners: Is being a good teacher good enough? *Teacher Education Quarterly,* 101–124.

Diaz-Rico, L. (2008). *Strategies for teaching English learners* (2nd ed.). Boston, MA: Pearson.

Diaz-Rico, L. (2013). *Strategies for teaching English learners* (3rd ed.). Boston, MA: Pearson.

Dutro, S., & Kinsella, K. (2010). English language development: Issues and implementation at grades six through twelve. In *Improving education for English learners: Research-based approaches.* Sacramento, CA: California Department of Education Press.

Echevarria, J., Vogt, M., & Short, D. (2010). *Making content comprehensible for secondary English learners: The SIOP model.* Boston, MA: Pearson/Allyn & Bacon.

Faltis, C., Arias, M. B., & Ramirez-Marin, F. (2010). Identifying relevant competencies for secondary teachers of English learners. *Bilingual Research Journal, 33,* 307–328.

Freedman, D., Bullock, P., & Duque, G. (2005). Teacher educators' reflections on moments in a secondary teacher education course: Thinking forward by challenging our teaching practices. *Teachers and Teaching: Theory and Practice, 11*(6), 591–602.

Freire, P. (1990). *Pedagogy of the oppressed.* New York, NY: Continuum.

Gandara, P.; Maxwell-Jolly, J., & Driscoll, A. (2005). *Listening to teachers of English language learners.* Sacramento, CA: The Center for the Future of Teaching and Learning.

Gay, G. (2010). *Culturally responsive teaching: Theory, research, & practice* (2nd ed.). New York, NY: Teachers College Press.

Graves, D., & Kittle, P. (2005). *My quick writes: For inside writing.* Portsmouth, NH: Heinemann.

Helfrich, S., & Bosh, A. (2011). Teaching English language learners: Strategies for overcoming barriers. *The Educational Forum, 75*(3), 260–270.

Herrell, A., & Jordan, M. (2012). *50 strategies for teaching English language learners* (4th ed.). Boston, MA: Pearson.

Holt, R. & Holt, W. (2009). Literature and language arts, California: Teacher edition, grade 11. Chicago, IL: Houghton Mifflin Harcourt Publishing.

Hudley, C., & Daoud, A. (2008). Cultures in contrast: Understanding the influence of student culture on student engagement. In *Academic Motivation and the Culture of Schooling.* New York, NY: Oxford University Press.

Ladson-Billings, G. (1994). The dreamkeepers: Successful teachers of African American children. San Francisco, CA: Jossey-Bass.

Ladson-Billings, G. (2001). *Crossing over to Canaan: The journey of new teachers in diverse classrooms.* San Francisco, CA: Jossey-Bass.

McDonald, M. (2005). The integration of social justice in teacher education: Dimensions of prospective teachers' opportunities to learn. *Journal of Teacher Education, 56*(5), 418–435.

McTighe, J., & Lyman, F. (1988). Cueing thinking in the classroom: The promise of theory-embedded tools. *Educational Leadership, 45,* 18–24.

National Governors Association Center for Best Practices, Council of Chief State School Officers. (2010). *Common Core State Standards.* Washington, DC: National Governors Association Center for Best Practices, Council of Chief State School Officers.

Nieto, S., & Bode, P. (2008). *Affirming diversity: The sociopolitical context of multicultural education* (5th ed.). Boston, MA: Pearson.

Olson, L. (2010). *Reparable harm: Fulfilling the promise of educational opportunity for California's long-term English learners.* Long Beach, CA: Californians Together Press.

Palinscar, A., & Brown, A. (1984). Reciprocal teaching of comprehension-fostering and comprehension-monitoring activities. *Cognition and Instruction, 1,* 117–175.

Rumberger, R., & Gandara, P. (2004). Seeking equity in the education of California's English learners. *Teachers College Record, 106*(10), 2032–2056.

Sleeter, C. (2005). *Un-standardizing curriculum: Multicultural teaching in the standards-based classroom.* New York, NY: Teachers College Press.

Teachers Curriculum Institute. (2010). *History alive! The United States through modern times.* Middle school programs. Rancho Cordova, CA: TCI.

Thomas, W., & Collier, V. (2002). *A national study of school effectiveness for language minority students' long-term academic achievement.* Santa Cruz, CA: Center for Research on Education, Diversity, and Excellence (CREDE). Retrieved from http://repositories.cdlib.org/crede/finalrpts/1_1_final

Vogt, M. (2000). Content learning for students needing modifications: An issue of access. In M. McLaughlin & M. Vogt (Eds.), *Creativity and innovation in content area teaching: A resource for intermediate, middle, and high school teachers.* Norwood, MA: Christopher Gordon.

index